Beyond
Self-Interest

Krzysztof Pelc

Beyond Self-Interest

Why the
Market
Rewards
Those
Who
Reject It

BLOOMSBURY PUBLISHING

LONDON · OXFORD · NEW YORK · NEW DELHI · SYDNEY

BLOOMSBURY PUBLISHING
Bloomsbury Publishing Plc
50 Bedford Square, London, WC1B 3DP, UK
29 Earlsfort Terrace, Dublin 2, Ireland

BLOOMSBURY, BLOOMSBURY PUBLISHING and the Diana logo are trademarks of
Bloomsbury Publishing Plc

First published in Great Britain 2022

A catalogue record for this book is available from the British Library

ISBN: HB: 978-1-5266-4813-6; TPB: 978-1-5266-4814-3; EBOOK: 978-1-5266-4812-9;
EPDF: 978-1-5266-4811-2

2 4 6 8 10 9 7 5 3 1

Typeset by Newgen KnowledgeWorks Pvt. Ltd., Chennai, India
Printed and bound in Great Britain by CPI Group (UK) Ltd, Croydon CR0 4YY

To find out more about our authors and books visit www.bloomsbury.com
and sign up for our newsletters

CONTENTS

Introduction

Success in Circuit lies.
— *Emily Dickinson*

T he pursuit of self-interest makes the world go round. This is
the standard story we tell ourselves, most often with a sigh of
resignation. Self-interest has brought about a society of greed and
naked ambition. Faced with an increasingly competitive economy,
we have no choice but to vie for an edge at our neighbour's expense.
The causes are structural, technological, and outside our control: foreign competition, rising automation, looming uncertainty.
We feel this pressure as individuals, too: in this cut-throat marketplace, we must curate our personal brand, polish our résumés, and
prepare our children to do the same. We bemoan how instrumental
our attitude has become — how everything we do, we do to get
ahead, rather than for its own sake. We blame the internet, the
rise of social media, the devices in our pockets, all of which have
hijacked our self-interested reflexes to purposes not our own.

That same story was once told triumphantly. As eighteenth-century Enlightenment thinkers saw it, the pursuit of self-interest was the magic social glue that led strangers to serve one another's needs. It was the essential building block of civilisation. If we could count on getting our daily bread, it was because a self-interested farmer sold wheat to a self-interested miller, who delivered flour to the self-interested baker who made us our sourdough.

These seemingly opposite accounts share a basic premise, namely that self-interest is the undisputed driver of human behaviour in modern market societies. Those who want to do well are advised to toe the line: to set their goals, arm themselves with strong will, and work relentlessly towards reaching them. According to which of the two accounts we choose to believe, the effects of self-interest are either socially beneficial or socially destructive. But neither story departs from the shared belief that markets reward individually rational, self-seeking actions. It is this unquestionable premise that I want to question in this book.

I want to suggest instead that the true idols of our market-driven age are its most committed dissidents. That the market actually celebrates those who openly flout market rules: the producers who pooh-pooh productivity; the makers who disdain efficiency and economies of scale; the workers who shun work and profess instead to be pursuing their *passion*. Those who opt out, those who give up on the rat race, those who downsize rather than expand – to follow their whim, their calling, their true nature. In a world given over to interest, the disinterested passionates are the ones we can trust.

Actions that appear disinterested often bear more fruit than those that come across as self-interested. Unintended effects are often more potent by virtue of being unintended. As a result, the most compelling force driving today's affluent market societies is not the pursuit of self-interest, but its opposite. Increasingly, those who prosper do so by spurning prosperity. Or better yet, by convincing others that they are pursuing purpose, passion, love of craft – anything, in fact, but their own self-advancement. There are limits to the returns of calculation, planning, and resolve, and in a growing number of instances, these limits have been reached. Increasingly, in the age of self-interest, the world belongs to the *credibly disinterested*.

Consider what strange sounds we hear market actors making above the apparently dominant din of self-interest. Hear the company founders who vow, 'We don't do [it] for money. We get the biggest investors emailing us every day, but we say no. A guy in a tie tells you what to do... the business becomes like a machine.' Or the investors who claim to be more interested in 'passionate founders' than in balance sheets. Or look at the polls that tell us millennials choosing careers are looking for 'meaning, not money' and that they value 'purpose over paycheck'. Or consider the consumers who swear that what they really want is to feel a 'connection' to the people who made their chair, designed their dress, baked their bread. They want chairs, dresses, and bread made with passion, and they're willing to pay premium for it.

Doesn't this sound like market heresy? Shouldn't CEOs be in it precisely for the money? Shouldn't they be single-mindedly focused on expanding their business, for their shareholders' sake and their own? And shouldn't workers provide their labour only on the condition of getting paid as high wages as possible? What about consumers: shouldn't they seek the highest-quality goods at the lowest price, and to hell with their makers' intentions?

One might think that a capitalist society would rush to condemn anyone who questions its iron logic. That those who dare flout its rules would swiftly fall by the wayside, ground up by the steady advance of economic progress. Yet these market dissidents never quite manage to become outcasts. Somehow, just the opposite happens: the dissidents are embraced by the very market they claim to be shunning. Pitching their passion against ruthless market forces is flattering to the passionates, who can portray themselves as fighting nobly against an unbending capitalist machine. But the truth is more complicated – and far more interesting.

Declaring passion over profit has become a profitable move. The company founder above, sneering at money and investors, was being quoted in the *Financial Times*, in an article that concluded: 'The way to build a globally successful [brand], it seems, is to not really try to build one at all.' The same esteemed publication informs its readers that today's consumers 'want committed brands with authentic products ... and if possible small, as small as you can.' As the consulting firm McKinsey advised the world's corporate giants in a recent report, while the conventional wisdom has always been that 'in the long run Goliaths beat Davids', the times have changed: 'These days [scale] does not in itself guarantee consumer appeal – so Goliaths need to find their inner David.' What the McKinsey report omitted to say is how fraught this exercise is: the Goliaths' impersonations had better be convincing, because the market swiftly punishes any hint of misrepresentation.

The story of passion over profit is not new. It is merely the latest iteration of a longstanding fascination with disinterested behaviour that lies at the very heart of capitalism. As I show in this book, markets have long put their greatest trust in those who do not subscribe to market values. And since credibility is the most precious asset in any market-based system, these market dissenters have often thrived, quite in spite of themselves.

The original American capitalists, the descendants of seventeenth-century Puritans, were above all *reluctant* capitalists. They were pursuing not profits, but a divinely ordained calling. They prospered in spite of their best intentions. This is also how a handful of nineteenth-century utopian communes, and their 1960s hippy successors, all equally committed to a rejection of bourgeois capitalism, turned themselves into flourishing commercial enterprises, in seeming contradiction with their founding visions. They prospered commercially because those they dealt with trusted that commercial prosperity was the last thing on their minds. Today, the world's most forward-thinking and fastest-growing firms are applying these lessons, styling themselves after passionate, disinterested utopians: they are 'changing the world', 'building global communities', 'doing what they love' – anything, in fact, but seeking profit. And in so doing, they're making a killing.

None of this is to say that passion is any guarantee of success. There are countless obsessive entrepreneurs, artists, scholars and saints toiling away on their projects, oblivious to any outside recognition, who never come out of obscurity. In fact, part of the implication of this book's central story is that we should expect the number of such passionates to grow. Being disinterested in market returns is thus not a sufficient condition for market success – but increasingly, it may be a necessary one. In advanced economies premised on self-interest, successful market actors can no longer afford to be merely self-interested.

There are market settings where shunning market principles has long been expected. In October 2018, the British street artist Banksy, who has staked his career on disdaining the art market, pulled off an inspired stunt. Having managed to secretly encase a shredder in the frame of one of his paintings, he had the piece self-destruct moments after it was sold at Sotheby's auction house for \$1.4 million. So evidently marketable was this apparent assault on market forces that observers suspected Sotheby's executives of being in on the coup. The market value of the half-shredded painting is now considerably higher than it was prior to the stunt, enhanced as it is by this spectacular expression of scorn against market principles. Its value would have risen even more, in fact, were it not for the enduring suspicion of Sotheby's involvement in the affair: the faint whiff of commercial calculation is the one thing that has put a cap on the dividend from disinterest. Had Banksy's intention been to maximise the value of his work, he could not have acted any more shrewdly; but had value maximisation actually been his declared intent, it would have failed entirely.

Which gives rise to a bit of a conundrum: being seen to try is the surest way to fail. As it turns out, British street artists trying to outsmart the art market are not the only ones facing this paradox, which is increasingly cropping up across a wide range of market settings. Much like the artist who grows popular by being seen to shun popularity, the very strength of our intentions seems to thwart their object. The greater and more evident our resolve, the less fruitful it becomes. But if the greatest rewards go to disinterested behaviour, what are the self-interested to do?

A Recurrent Paradox

The spectacle of market actors professing 'passion over profits' is merely one instance of a broader phenomenon. Many of the things we value most highly are becoming less attainable through instrumental means. And this shift is in every way expected. It is, in fact, an unavoidable part of the economic development of any advanced society.

The examples run from the prosaic to the profound. Those who are most eager to make a favourable impression become most likely to fail; the transparency of the effort does them in. That is why the nouveaux riches are always being unmasked by the old money, who fault them for trying too hard. It's also why gifts can sway minds and elevate the giver's status, but only if swaying and elevating are not too obviously their intent.

The best toasts are those that sound convincingly impromptu. Politicians who seem too eager for power become less likely to attain it; Plato himself argued that the best rulers were those who did not want to rule and who had to be forced into taking office. The game of seduction in its various guises usually consists of concealing, rather than revealing the effort. What I show in the coming chapters is that these various settings share a common explanation: namely, a concern for credibility. The main reason why these valuable goals elude wilful effort is because we have all evolved well-honed social sonars to scrutinise one another's intent. In these circumstances, the only ones to be trusted are those who seem blind to their own interests – driven by other, higher concerns, or more base ones.

This paradox of intention is only becoming more prevalent. As societies grow more affluent, they naturally shift their sights away from objects that can be obtained through wilful exertion, like physical security and material comfort, and towards things that resist an instrumental, goal-oriented approach, like status, esteem, influence, creative flow, and self-actualisation. Increasingly, the things that individuals care for most can no longer be planned for, grasped at, or captured; they can only be stumbled upon, fallen into, or obtained in passing. Which poses a problem, because while advanced societies have got very good at planning and grasping, they are not so good at stumbling upon.

An instrumental attitude is the modal approach to life in advanced societies. As I argue throughout this book, we live in a consequentialist world bequeathed to us by the eighteenth-century Enlightenment, refracted through a particular nineteenth-century Utilitarian worldview, buffeted by the assumptions of twentieth-century neoclassical economics, and made digestible by a twenty-first-century combination of pop-managerial insights and New Age tenets. We champion will, determination, effort. We set our goals and we work to reach them. We keep our eyes on the prize.

This intellectual tradition has served us well. It has contributed not only to tremendous economic growth, but it has also provided a powerful set of arguments for expanding individual freedoms. Even in the wake of a devastating once-in-a-century pandemic, ours remains the wealthiest, healthiest, and safest society that has ever roamed the earth. Then how is it that we are here, coming up short? At once conscious of our good fortune, and oddly bereft? Asking ourselves, if we are so lucky as to live in a world of plenty, if our consumption is bounded only by our appetites – which keep duly expanding – if we can instantly satisfy our curiosity by looking up anything we want on a device in our pocket, why does it not seem like quite enough?

Why is the number of working hours in advanced economies increasing, as the amount and quality of leisure continues to decline? Why does this appear to be especially true for the luckiest segments of our lucky societies, those whom we might think most able to enjoy their leisure? Why are rates of anxiety increasing across the wealth spectrum, and why are these trends most pronounced among young people, in the generation of my undergraduate students? The fact that the people who have been maximised – overeducated, overfed, and overconsuming – are nonetheless beset by doubts over what to aspire to, and how to achieve it, should give us pause.

The same approach that has served us so well until now begins to fall short when it is deployed towards goals that elude wilful effort. The original theorists of commercial society sensed this: they never envisioned capitalism as an end in itself, but only ever as a splendid means to furthering higher human aims. Commercial society can still accomplish this, if only we treat it once more as the tool it was conceived as. Prosperity is hugely desirable, but only insofar as it increases human agency, and through it, allows for individual flourishing.

This is not to say that the current outlook for economic prosperity is especially rosy. We continue to weather the aftershocks of a once-in-a-century pandemic, the uneven impact of which has only highlighted existing inequities. The recovery will be an extended one, and it will have to contend with the necessity of reducing global emissions.

The success of that recovery will be measured against where we stood prior to the pandemic; but that was a world already saddled with a long list of socio-economic concerns. The labour force participation rate in the US was at its lowest in half a century, with concerns that it may continue to fall in all advanced economies due to automation, a trend the pandemic has only accelerated. Inequality has become a salient issue, and the study of past economic crises suggests it will only increase in the coming years before it decreases. Recent mass demonstrations have underscored how such inequality intersects with racial and social cleavages in ways that perpetuate historical inequities, which means that opportunities continue to be unevenly distributed.

All this might be seen as a reason to focus on the emergencies at home and direct all our attention on these most pressing, near-term concerns. Adding jobs. Boosting growth. Building resilience. Yet one recurrent theme of this book is how often thinkers and writers have taken to questioning social goals precisely as these have seemed suddenly out of reach.

It was in 1930, as the world was sliding into the Great Depression, that the economist John Maynard Keynes wondered about whether we were up to the challenge that would come when the economic problem of scarcity would be permanently resolved, and we would have to confront 'our real problems – the problems of life and of human relations, of creation and behaviour and religion'. Two years later, with the Depression reaching its nadir as global unemployment peaked, the philosopher Bertrand Russell found the space to question the instrumental mindset he saw all about him, observing how 'the modern man thinks that everything ought to be done for the sake of something else, and never for its own sake'. And it was in the wake of another global crisis, as Europe was recovering from its material and moral devastation following the Second World War, that the philosopher Josef Pieper warned against the 'restlessness of a self-destructive work-fanaticism'. As he sought to remind himself and his readers, 'Work is the means of life; leisure the end.'

We find ourselves once more in such a moment of flux, calling into question long-held assumptions. And it is precisely in this moment of reconstruction and uncertainty, as we come out of our respective cells of self-isolation, that a reassessment of long-term social goals may be most timely. Moments of economic distress often coincide with a calling into question of collective values. As we think of the optimal means of addressing the demands that need urgent attention, it is also worth considering anew the nature of our highest aspirations: what we understand 'the real values of life' to be, and whether our current efforts are best suited to achieving them.

We are relying on means developed during the industrial nineteenth century to attain twenty-first-century post-industrial aspirations. In so doing, we are coming up against the limits of what a single-minded pursuit of self-interest can achieve. In a growing number of settings, advancing our interest demands that we suspend our default self-interested approach. This calls for a fundamental adjustment of how we set about achieving our aims.

The shift in mindset is a task for every one of us, but it isn't only up to individuals. It relies on an appropriate set of social institutions. Moving away from a strictly instrumental outlook is inherently risky, and governments have a concrete role to play in response, by providing social insurance policies that can cover downside risk. Humdrum public policies, from healthcare to wage insurance, may be a key requirement for individual epiphanies. Self-reform depends on social reform, and social reform depends on people pushing for it. That shift in mindset is ultimately a political project.

Increasingly, we find ourselves in the shoes of British street artists jockeying with the art market's conflicting incentives: to get ahead, we must convince others that merely getting ahead is not our prime objective. This is no easy trick. It is, in fact, so difficult, that maybe only the truly disinterested are able to pull it off. To persuade others, it might be necessary to persuade ourselves.

This book tells the story of that paradox. From its unlikely emergence among a group of thinkers in the early nineteenth century, to its development over the subsequent two centuries, as it is successively picked up by philosophers, theologians, psychologists, novelists, economists, and political scientists. All of them arriving at a common realisation: disinterest pays – but only for those who appear truly disinterested. Which leaves the self-interested in a pickle. This book is about that pickle.

I

Crisis and Conversion

Autumn in London is a dreary time of year. In the 1820s, it was drearier still: newly built factories coughed up sulphurous smoke into the sky and pumped their waste into the Thames. The burning of cheap coal covered the city with soot. London's pea-soup fog was at its worst in November, when the season trapped the city's emissions under a blanket of cold air. The first half of the nineteenth century was also a moment of great social and political flux for England. The industrial revolution was nearing its peak; London was about to become the world's largest city. Mounting social movements were questioning the twin pillars of received power, the aristocracy and the Church. Doubts were emerging over the British Empire's relations to its colonies. Cheap imports from India were threatening domestic manufactures, and English workers were calling for bans on all foreign goods.

In the midst of all the fog and flux, a home-schooled British twenty-year-old – call him John – was having a mental breakdown. It was a crisis that would mark John for the rest of his life. He still vividly remembered it half a century later when, looking back on it as an older man, he described its beginnings as 'a dull state of nerves' of the kind anyone might occasionally fall into. 'One of those moods in which what is pleasure at other times, becomes insipid and indifferent.'

John tried to reason himself out of this impasse. He had an unusually sharp mind, and reasoning through problems was what he'd been taught to do from a young age. But in this case, introspection seemed only to aggravate the problem: 'The more I dwelt upon it, the more hopeless it appeared,' he later wrote. Autumn turned into winter, and by the start of 1827, John was still in the grips of the malady. He lost all drive for life. Dark thoughts came over him. Looking ahead, he wondered how long he could last in this state: 'I did not think I could possibly bear it beyond a year.'

Had the circumstances been different, John might have turned to his father, to whom he was close. But his father was actually part of the problem, making him 'the last person to whom ... I looked for help.' In fact, as John saw it, his inner despair was itself proof that his father's grand plan had failed in an 'irremediable' way.

Had this twenty-year-old been living today, it would have made for a quick diagnosis. Say, Xanax for the anxiety, Zoloft for the depression, and Ambien for the sleeplessness. But in the 1820s, with the invention of the telegraph still two decades away, no such remedy was on offer. This didn't keep John from wishing for one: he kept returning to a line from Shakespeare, where Macbeth complains of doctors' uselessness in dealing with existential gloom. In vain, Macbeth pleads with his own doctor for some 'antidote':

Canst thou not minister to a mind diseased ...
And with some sweet oblivious antidote
Cleanse the stuff 'd bosom of that perilous stuff
Which weighs upon the heart?

John knew the doctor's reply, and now it fell on him like a dark verdict: 'Therein the patient / Must minister to himself.' But his inner resources, tremendous though they were when faced with problems of calculus, logic, or metaphysics, now came up short.

John had been a child prodigy. Kept away from regular schooling, he was imbibing Greek and Latin classics at an age when most boys are concerned with playing with toy trucks. By age eight, he was reading Plato's dialogues, the plays of Sophocles, and the histories of Thucydides, in the original Greek. By age thirteen, he had mastered Newton's theories, and the latest advances in the burgeoning field of economics. As a sixteen-year-old, he was expounding on his policy ideas in British newspapers. By his twentieth year, he had taken up a covetable position in government, founded two thriving debating societies, was entrusted with editing the writings of major philosophers of his day, and had taken up, as a sideline, the study of German. All told, by the time of his breakdown, he was in all likelihood the best-read twenty-year-old in Britain. That was part of the trouble. Fed on a steady diet of reason, logic, and analysis, he now felt bereft when overcome by a dark mental fog that lacked an identifiable cause.

Since books were all he knew, it is to books that he turned in search of a cure – though these were very different from the treatises his father had plied him with. What finally offered John solace were the writings of a group of contemporary Romantic poets. The Romantics gave him a language through which to understand his state of dejection.[1] He read William Wordsworth, the nature poet, one of the founders of the

English Romantic movement, and it proved to be 'the precise thing for my mental wants at that particular time'. In part, it was Wordsworth's depiction of outward beauty, in particular his veneration of mountains, which John had developed a love for in his teens, while hiking through the Pyrenees. But mostly, it was Wordsworth's recognition of the legitimacy of *feeling*. To a youth brought up on reason and analysis, this came as a small revelation. Wordsworth's verse presented to him a wholly new set of aspirations. 'I seemed to learn from them what would be the perennial sources of happiness when all the greater evils of life should be removed.' John had grown up surrounded by people whose only concern had been the alleviation of these evils through carefully designed social policy. Now he sensed there had to be greater, more elusive ends beyond the removal of life's material obstacles, and reading Wordsworth confirmed this inkling.

Eventually, the 'Wordsworthian medicine', as John called it, started to kick in. He found in it 'a source of inward joy'. The clouds began to lift, and little by little, he was able to return to his projects, to exert himself 'for my opinions and for the public good'. Eventually, he succeeded in fulfilling his destiny, surpassing even his father's expectations, by becoming the greatest British philosopher of the nineteenth century.

I may have given him away just now. The John in question is John Stuart Mill. But there is a reason to first consider John the twenty-year-old, lost in the haze of clinical depression amidst the London fog, before revealing J. S. Mill, the famous philosopher. Because that Mill comes prepackaged with a ready set of associations. He has been, like many thinkers in the Enlightenment tradition, treated unfairly by history. Just as Adam Smith is distorted as an exponent of greed, reduced to the trope of the invisible hand (a relatively minor and misrepresented bit of his thought), Mill is depicted as ever calculating and ever rational.

He is the dispassionate exponent of Utilitarianism – the theory according to which all our actions can be assigned positive or negative values, thanks to which we can maximise total human happiness to the greatest possible extent.

But Mill was anything but dispassionate. Here is a twenty-year-old prodigy who was put through the Utilitarian wringer, who precociously saw its limitations, and who felt them on his own skin. His childhood had consisted of one long experiment in utility maximisation, and as became clear to him in the autumn of 1826, the experiment had not gone as planned. Rather than an unsentimental policy wonk, J. S. Mill turns out to be a down-right subversive figure, in ways that prove uniquely relevant to our own time.

We who live in an advanced market society are experiencing a malaise that bears an odd likeness to the crisis that J. S. Mill endured as the failed subject of that Utilitarian experiment. That the sources of the malady are so closely related is no coincidence: in more ways than one, the nineteenth-century Utilitarians' project has become our own. The discipline of economics has adopted its key tenets, and as economics has gone from the 'dismal science' to the dominant lens through which we examine social problems,[2] we have come to internalise those Utilitarian tenets as individuals, and we now apply them in our daily lives. When we seek 'peak experiences' or invest in 'self-care'; when we beseech ourselves to spurn negative emotions and 'think positively'; when we count our steps and take our vitamins to stay fit and healthy, when we search, in short, for keys to the happiness that is our birthright, we continue to live out the vision of a nineteenth-century offshoot of the European Enlightenment that J. S. Mill happens to have been born into.

In many ways, Western society has delivered on the promise of Utilitarianism's principles, by adopting a scientific approach to policy based on maximising growth and social betterment.

A Utilitarian view of the world deserves credit for leading us to discard scores of social prejudices. It has provided a powerful set of arguments for abandoning sticky and outdated dogma, for expanding liberties – from women's enfranchisement to more recent advances like same-sex marriage. Each of these has been an exercise in weighing the historical inequity imposed on some groups against the blind upholding of old ways of doing in the name of vague moralities. The same approach has also been a force for choosing economic policies that favour aggregate welfare against pressures from small, concentrated interests, in issues ranging from international trade to redistributive taxation.

The result is the freest and most affluent society in history. Yet a malaise persists. Despite all this maximisation, we are faced with a prevalent feeling that we are falling short. Yes, we may have delivered on the promise of a Utilitarian approach to social and economic reform. But we have yet to deliver on Mill's own insights about the limits of that Utilitarian approach.

The insights that followed his mental breakdown remained with J. S. Mill for the rest of his life. Most of that life was not given over to contemplation and introspection; it was spent arguing in exhaustive detail about concrete policy issues. Inheritance taxes, free trade, government regulation, economic redistribution, social equality, public education, women's rights, environmental destruction, colonialism. For a nineteenth-century thinker, J. S. Mill proved to be on the right side of history remarkably often. As the writer Adam Gopnik once put it, as he surveyed the range of social questions Mill had taken position on, 'It is a hard thing, being right about everything all the time.'

Keep in mind the hardships and inequities that accompanied British industrialisation of that time. Dickensian urban conditions were yet to come. Consider that in 1842, just as Mill was reaching his prime, it was a significant victory for social reformists that a law was passed against the employment of girls, and boys under the age of ten, in underground coal mines.[3] When children are toiling in coal mines, musing over what constitutes the highest aspirations of society and individual citizens might seem quaint, at best.

Yet across all the policy debates that J. S. Mill waded into during his lifetime, this concern with ultimate social ends, a lasting imprint of the crisis of his youth, remained. From his writings on economic redistribution to his work on public education, he kept asking himself whether the means of addressing the pressing issues of the day would eventually come to conflict with the fundamental reasons for which these issues were being addressed.

Today, challenges like economic uncertainty and rising inequality appear so complex and overwhelming that resolving them seems like an end in itself. Let's worry about the rest later, we might reasonably say, and let's focus on the immediate problem. Yet it is worth reminding ourselves that insofar as we value a more prosperous or more equal world, it is as means to some other aim – it is because we believe that economic prosperity and equality are best suited for bringing about a set of human ends worth pursuing for their own sake. What are these? J. S. Mill's own answer originated in the 'Wordsworthian medicine' that eventually alleviated his period of 'dejection'. He came to see the ultimate goal of social institutions as that of maximising each person's ability to cultivate their human potential. He came to believe that self-reform was the goal, but that social reform was its prerequisite. It is no exaggeration to say that Mill's elevation of the idea of self-development, his own and that of others, underlies the Western liberal project. Today, we ought to pose the question anew: what is it that we actually care to maximise, and are our current means still best adapted to doing so?

Much like the young Mill, we find ourselves seeking some 'antidote' for our own malaise. And just as Macbeth's doctor admitted, there is no simple remedy on offer: we must, instead, minister to ourselves. Twenty-year-old Mill, before he became his country's most celebrated thinker, may have done more than anyone before him to distil the problem that all advanced societies eventually come to face. Mill identified, though never fully resolved, a tricky paradox that stayed with him to the end of his life: an inherent clash between the goal of maximal social utility, and the best means of achieving it. A recognition that our most cherished goals might be best attained by not directly seeking to attain them. This book is an attempt to take up this paradox anew. Doing so holds some unexpected lessons for how we might go about reforming not only our social institutions, but also our own selves.

The Origins of Crisis

With the benefit of hindsight, J. S. Mill's mental breakdown seems bound to have happened. As one of his biographers put it after listing the scarcely conceivable list of his accomplishments for that year, 'retribution inevitably followed'.[4] And although it occurred almost two centuries ago, it strikes me as being very much a twenty-first-century crisis. A product of high parental expectations, social pressure to perform, and existential disorientation? I see some of my best students similarly afflicted after one too many all-nighters. In an age of overwork, rising anxiety and self-doubt, how could we not relate to the young Mill's despair?

As a child, John had been revved at full force. It was a daily regimen that would make today's most wound-up helicopter parents green with envy. All efforts were directed towards the development of his mind. Insofar as attention was paid to physical pursuits, it was in the classical tradition: a means of keeping the body sufficiently fit to allow further investments in the intellect.

As Mill described in a report to his father at age fourteen, on a typical day, he got up at 5 a.m., starting with a morning swim, then it was on to French lessons until breakfast, then music theory, and then back to French. This was followed by Greek, Latin, mathematics, logic, and political economy. Music lessons came later in the afternoon, then horseback riding until 6 p.m., fencing until 7 p.m., and dancing lessons until 8.30 p.m. The evening was his time to work on personal projects. On the day John happened to be sending this account to his father, it had consisted of working on an ode to the economies of scale featured in oligopolistic competition: 'a dialogue on benefit of large estates to commerce'.

The master planner of this educational regimen was John's father, James Mill, himself an accomplished philosopher, if not the prodigious thinker his son would eventually become. At a time when Britain was going through a maelstrom of social upheavals and dissent, the Mill family was at the very centre of this ferment of new social ideas. James Mill was part of a loose band called the Philosophical Radicals, who rejected the Anglican Church and aristocratic agrarianism, and called for sweeping social reforms.

It is often said that we are all children of the Enlightenment. But no one can lay more literal a claim to the title than the young Mill. He was taught the classics, botany, and zoology by eminent experts in each field. Yet it was his exposure to the nascent field of economics that was most singular.[5] James Mill's close friend was David Ricardo, the man behind the theory of comparative advantage, and undoubtedly the greatest economist of his time – a time when economics was not yet a self-contained field taught in universities. At the age of thirteen, Mill took up the close study of Ricardo's great treatise, *On the Principles of Political Economy and Taxation*. The book had been published only two years earlier, and there existed as yet no popularised version or digest for students, so James Mill worked through its ideas during daily walks with his son, and made John summarise these peripatetic lectures in writing the next day. John was then made to rework those summaries relentlessly, and these became the basis for James Mill's own master treatise, *Elements of Political Economy*.

In the 1820s, the economic issues that Ricardo was dealing with were high on everyone's minds. England was facing new doubts over the results of the global economic openness it had been instrumental in bringing about. As one contemporary writer put it, it was a time when the issue of free trade was, 'next to the Reformation, next to the question of free religion, the most momentous that has ever been submitted to human decision'.[6] The issue went far beyond trade barriers; it would prove decisive for the social status of the landed gentry, which favoured protectionism, and the rising consumer class in England, who sought access to foreign goods. The basic questions of how a society ought to be run were being asked anew, through the prism of economics. Two decades later, economists would for the first time in British history make their mark on national policy: the Corn Laws were repealed, tariffs on foreign goods were lifted, and Britain decisively took up its position at the centre of the global economy, a position it would keep until the First World War. Mill, more than anyone else in the country, had a leg-up on these debates. To him alone, the nascent language of economics was a native tongue.

Yet by far the greatest intellectual influence over J. S. Mill's childhood was Jeremy Bentham, the founder of Utilitarianism. James Mill, who was twenty-five years younger than Bentham, proudly considered himself his chief disciple. He introduced his son to Bentham when John was three years old. Bentham himself had also been a child prodigy, mastering the Greek and Latin classics by the time he turned six. He took an immediate interest in the young boy. Later, at James Mill's request following a bout of illness, Bentham took on the role of a godfather – in a secular mode, naturally – committing to taking over John's education in the event that anything happened to his father.

The Utilitarians were openly hostile to the received dogma of religion, but by the age of twenty, Mill began realising just how dogmatic their own ideas were. As a young Benthamite, he had been brought up in a high-pressure intellectual echo chamber: 'more exclusively under the influence of a peculiar kind of impressions than any other person ever was', as he later wrote.

The high pressure and the narrowness were both by design. J. S. Mill's father embodied not only the ideas, but also the very temperament of Utilitarianism.* As James Mill saw it, John's development was his greatest intellectual creation. And as is sometimes the case with ambitious parents, he sought to remedy his own shortcomings through his gifted son's accomplishments. Having failed to gain a seat in parliament, he hoped to steer his son's political career as a means of projecting his own influence.

---

* A contemporary observer described James Mill as 'the prototype of the Utilitarian character, almost to the point of caricature: self-made, manly, independent, rationally controlled (especially in the areas of sex and work), not giving way to feelings of any kind (especially of love)'. Another described him as 'stern, harsh, and sceptical'. And although James Mill's work was directed at alleviating the suffering of the masses, this does not seem to have come from a love of his fellow man. As Bentham himself put it, 'He rather hated the ruling few, than loved the suffering many.' See: Fox, Caroline 1882, *Memories of Old Friends, Being Extracts from the Journals and Letters of Caroline Fox*, H. N. Pym, Vol. I, p. 113.

James Mill had strong ideas about how best to achieve this. His beliefs on pedagogy, based on Locke's epistemology, were published in the *Encyclopedia Britannica* of the day. In his view, childhood education could be optimised, much like the output of the factories that were springing up across the country. Children started out as empty vessels, and those vessels ought to be filled with reason and fact and argument. How much could they contain? The young John would be the test of it. Hence the Greek, Latin, metaphysics, and political economy. John's readings were as carefully curated as were his playmates. Little wonder that the vessel, filled to the brim, eventually burst.

If there is a defence of James Mill, it's that he was a true believer. He offered his eldest up for the greater good of society, shaping him into his vision of a great thinker and reformer. In the Benthamite mindset, the value of individual actions was measured by their contribution to overall social utility. An optimised child would make an optimal contribution to society. An increase in overall happiness would result.

James Mill had drunk the Kool-Aid of Utilitarianism, and John was bottle-fed those ideas from a young age. This is why, as a twenty-year-old, he chose to lead a 'double life', fearing that his bout of depression represented, in itself, an affront to his father's understanding of the world.[7] But how could the strict application of Utilitarianism, an ideology premised on the standard of the 'greatest happiness', result in such misery? What exactly was in that Kool-Aid?

The Utilitarian Kool-Aid

Utilitarianism is highly seductive. It is geared towards outcomes and interested in results: if a given action has desirable consequences, then that action is desirable. And all that is desirable – happiness, pleasure, satisfaction – is subsumed under a single category: utility. I remember an Australian economics professor who once referred to this overarching concept of utility in a lecture as *jollies*, which he pronounced with a strong Aussie accent. We all want more jollies, and you get to define jollies in whatever way you wish. The catch-all quality of its central concept is the spark of genius at the core of Utilitarianism.

As Jeremy Bentham put it, 'By utility is meant that property in any object, whereby it tends to produce benefit, advantage, pleasure, good, or happiness (all this in the present case comes to the same thing).' And all the good and the bad can be placed on the same scale: we want more of the good, less of the bad. So the avoidance of 'mischief, pain, evil, or unhappiness … comes again to the same thing'. At the end of the day, we add up everyone's jollies, and that is the common good. Our social mission is to maximise the social good. The legislator's role, and the subject of much of Bentham's writing, is how to ensure that everyone's actions, motivated by their own seeking of greater jollies, amount to a net increase in the jollies of society.

The Benthamites were suspicious of moral reasoning. Actions were not intrinsically good or bad, only instrumentally so: they had either good or bad effects. Morality was the product of prejudice and received ideas. Bentham's own views on homosexuality are illustrative. Some people, he recognised, were put off by the idea of homosexual acts; but since they themselves were not the ones directly concerned, their feelings had no bearing on the matter: 'The act is to the highest degree odious and disgusting, that is, not to the man who does it, for he does it only because it gives him pleasure, but to one who thinks of it. Be it so, *but what is that to him?*'[8]

Quite at odds with the England of 1785, Bentham thus advocated decriminalising homosexuality, arguing that its outlawing was prone to false prosecutions and incidents of extortion. Similar reasoning through the prism of social utility led the

Benthamites to argue for greater separation of Church and state, to take a stand against both corporal punishment and the death penalty, and campaign for expanded women's rights.* They were instrumental in the passage of some of the first labour laws in Britain, aimed at regulating child labour, especially.[9] It also meant the Benthamites were perpetual reformers: no law could be taken as permanent, since the consequences of laws changed continually, requiring their constant re-evaluation.

The simplicity, logical rigour and all-encompassing nature of utility seduced the young Mill. As he put it, Benthamism provided him with a set of ideas sufficiently potent to devote one's life to. It offered him 'opinions, a creed, a doctrine, a philosophy; in one (and the best) sense of the word, a religion'. He was a quick study, and an early proselytiser. At age sixteen, Mill founded the Utilitarian Society: it is credited with introducing the term 'Utilitarianism' into common parlance.

Today, the discipline of economics largely retains the young Mill's infatuation with utility as the 'keystone' which holds the whole edifice together.[10] Insofar as economics has 'a creed, a doctrine, a philosophy', it is highly similar to the one that Mill first took as his guiding principle.† The strength of Benthamite utility, and what largely accounts for its having been embraced by economics, is that it does not dictate the content of people's desires. But therein may also lie its weakness.

I must admit I am not immune to the charm of utility. Until recently, when a student would ask me in class, as they often do,

* Of course, the Utilitarians' policy positions were only as good as their predictions of their effects. Cue Bentham's much-derided idea for an all-seeing prison ('a sort of invisible omnipresence'). The panopticon was nonetheless designed to foster inmates' self-regulation. (Bentham, Jeremy, *Panopticon, or The Inspection House*, 1791, published by Thomas Byrne.)

† One notable shift from Benthamite utility to its treatment by neoclassical economics was the collapsing of the *property* of any object to produce benefit, and the

whether there might not be other goals for individuals to pursue than the maximisation of utility, I was quick to offer the conventional response: that the beauty of utility is precisely that it can accommodate whatever desirable end one finds worthy of pursuit: McMansions, gold watches, and fast cars, but also leisure for creative pursuits, the cultivation of friendships, or time spent with family. And with only a small tweak, the concept of utility can also accommodate altruistic motives, whereby others' utility functions become a component of one's own.[11] The beauty of the concept, I would insist, lies in its capaciousness. Nothing escapes it, so long as it is something someone finds desirable. All that is individually and socially desirable can thus be subsumed under one shared notion, and inserted into the same maximisation equation. Over time, however, and owing in no small part to J. S. Mill's thinking on the matter, I have come to think this capacious concept may suffer from its capaciousness more than is commonly acknowledged.

A New 'Theory of Life': Happiness 'by the way'

At the core of Mill's breakdown was a crisis of faith – *faith* being the apt term. Although he never strayed from the atheism of the Philosophical Radicals, Mill also repeatedly referred to this period of his life using religious language. He saw that

---

benefit itself. In common current usage in economics, individual utility refers to the individual's good, or their happiness, rather than that individual's tendency to produce good, or happiness. J. S. Mill himself started letting these two meanings bleed into one another in *Utilitarianism*. Today, even philosophy has growingly taken up economics' treatment of utility, a tendency opposed by some philosophers on the grounds that utility in the sense used within economics is too broad and ambiguous. See Broome, John, 1991, 'Utility', *Economics and Philosophy*, 7(1–12), 5: 'The ambiguity is intolerable.'

Benthamism required a suspension of disbelief, and he no longer had it in him. He likened this change to the kind of 'conviction of sin' that is said to occur in Methodist circles when a new convert stands up and yells in pain before dropping down to the floor, as if dead, only to rise and proclaim their newfound faith. That, in Mill's case, was a new belief in the usefulness of cultivating within oneself a space of unreason, a zone lacking in forethought or intent.

Religious conversions are often said to be triggered by visions or voices from heaven; knowing what we know about Mill, it should come as no surprise that his conversion was triggered instead by a logical conundrum. Amid his crisis of faith, Mill asked himself a question that should gnaw at any Utilitarian. It was a version of the one posed by the eighteenth-century German philosopher Gotthold Lessing: 'What is the use of use?'[12] Mill wondered what would happen if the sought-out objective was attained, if one's utility function was duly maximised. Would this produce happiness?* He had an immediate answer to his own question: 'No!' If all these ends were achieved, Mill sensed that the reasons for individual striving would not suddenly disappear. If anything, 'the pleasures of life, being no longer kept up by struggle and privation, would cease to be pleasures'. Mill found this difficult to account for: how was it that the end somehow rested on the means of attaining it, and what did this say about what constituted the correct end to strive towards?

* As Mill later wrote: 'Suppose that all your objects in life were realised; that all the changes in institutions and opinions which you are looking forward to, could be completely effected at this very instant: would this be a great joy and happiness to you?' And if society reached a similar state of plenty, 'if the reformers of society and government could succeed in their objects, and every person in the community were free and in a state of physical comfort', could we finally rest? No again. (1981, *The Collected Works of John Stuart Mill, Volume I – Autobiography and Literary Essays*, University of Toronto Press.)

We see Mill repeatedly drawing a parallel between the experiment of his own life and the grand social experiment the Benthamites were calling for. He linked his own state of plenty to the eventual state of plenitude that he and those around him were striving towards in their efforts at social reform. If happiness was the point, how could the maximisation of those things that led to happiness produce anything less than full contentment? The vessel had been filled, yet what he felt was an acute lack. He held in himself, in his inexplicable sorrow, evidence that the system was faulty: 'I felt that the flaw in my life, must be a flaw in life itself.'

But what was the flaw? Where did a system designed to maximise human happiness fall short? How *could* it fall short? In response, Mill didn't dismiss the concept of utility. Its logic appeared to him as incontrovertible as before: 'I never, indeed, wavered in the conviction that happiness is the test of all rules of conduct, and the end of life.' No, the problem lay elsewhere, in the way of going about it. The problem lay in the belief that maximising utility was the best means of maximising utility.

J. S. Mill described this as a new 'theory of life, very unlike that on which I had before acted', and this new theory led him to a staggering conclusion. He came to think that utility could not be maximised wilfully; utility could only be maximised *incidentally*. Or as the Francophile Mill put it, it had to be acquired *en passant*: by the way. The sought-after end could not be the product of reason or intent: 'to know that a feeling would make me happy if I had it, did not give me the feeling'.

Insofar as some lucky individuals achieved the happiness the Utilitarians spoke of, they did not do it by making that their goal, as the Utilitarians did. Rather, they stumbled upon it unknowingly, busy with other ends: 'aiming thus at something else, they find happiness by the way'. Mill's insight, in other words, was that the maximisation of utility was a byproduct of actions taken for other ends – ends that had nothing to do with the maximisation of utility. He was explicit about the paradox this presented: 'I now thought that this end was only to be attained by not making it the direct end.'

This is the first time in Western thought that this devastating idea was stated so clearly. It remained little more than the expression of an intuition. Mill stops short of fully unfurling its implications. What is it about the Utilitarian *summum bonum*, the highest good, that makes it impervious to intent? What other desirable objects are of this form? And what other ends might be best pursued to attain this one – what was the 'something else' that should be aimed at? J. S. Mill leaves all these questions unanswered. Yet his hunch that some goals eluded planning gave voice to an idea that had long been floating in the post-Enlightenment air, but that only began to crystallise at the start of the nineteenth century, and would take on a more defined form in the decades that followed.

It is perhaps no surprise that the first elaboration of this idea should have come just then, and from just this person. It took someone reared on the notion of utility, in a system of thought premised on rational means directed at rational ends, to appreciate its devastating implications. It took the Utilitarians' young *dauphin* to wonder whether the most effective Utilitarian might be a non-Utilitarian.

But from that moment on, observations of this paradox would start appearing in different places and guises, like disparate sightings of a newly identified sea creature: in the writings of social thinkers, behavioural scientists, philosophers, and novelists. It would bear many names. The hedonist paradox; the paradox of choice; the paradox of teleology. William James, the father of psychology, would refer to it as 'an invisible law, as strong as gravitation'. The philosopher Josef Pieper would describe it as the inescapable paradox of leisure. The political scientist Jon Elster would refer to the 'fallacy of by-products'. The classical historian Paul Veyne discerned it in the practice of wealthy Ancient Roman elites who 'selflessly' bestowed lavish gifts on the masses, and gained in doing so. The literary scholar Ruth Bernard Yeazell observed it in nineteenth-century codes of courtship, according to which women won men over by their 'modesty', seducing them by affecting an innocent ignorance of the very possibility of seduction.

All these thinkers provide us with clues to a modern-day version of that same paradox, one that can be seen in the cap-italist marketplace. This might seem an especially unlikely setting in which to observe the limitations of self-interest, since the market is usually held up as a ruthless Darwinian arena that opposes everyone's interest against everyone else's; where participants must either bend to market rationality, or be chewed up in the market's gears. But as we will see, even the modern market increasingly celebrates those who appear to spurn their self-interest.

There have been just as many attempts to resolve this paradox in its different guises as there have been formulations of it. Careful plans to cultivate spontaneity. Clever stratagems for self-deception. Self-interested efforts at appearing disin-terested at all costs. Perhaps it is unavoidable that the market is drawn in: market actors, sensing fresh opportunity where all other opportunities have been duly exploited, try and tap this unexpected source of value – because what could be better than reaping benefits without planning to? But it always comes down to the apparent contradiction that the young J. S. Mill butted up against: his inkling that there existed a class of desirables that could only be obtained by not aiming to obtain them.

Insofar as Mill's new 'theory of life' has been examined as anything more than a side note by scholars of his work, the tendency has been to reduce it to the idea that happiness lies in its pursuit.[13] But this has the effect of bringing Mill's insight down to the commonplace observation that 'it's about the journey, not the destination', which was as humdrum an idea in Mill's time as it is in ours.

Mill's point is at once more subtle and more troubling: the destination you set out for will shift around by dint of your setting out for it. The intent and the outcome do not correspond. And if the destination is shifting, so too must the journey be different from the one planned out. If you set out for Rome, you aren't likely ever to get there. You ought to walk the dog around the neighbourhood instead, pack the car and drive out west; only in such a circuitous way might you find yourself, somewhat unexpectedly, in Rome. And this was coming from someone who had, as it were, grown up in a travel agency; someone whose presumptive task had been to guide people to their appointed destinations in the most efficient way possible.

It is hard to overstate what an affront to Utilitarian thinking Mill's new 'theory of life' represented. For a philosophy built on rationally pursuing the optimal means of attaining a rational social end, the suggestion that the two were fundamentally disconnected was a devastating claim. It had all seemed so simple, so unassailable. The greatest happiness for the greatest number. Maximise individual utilities, and in doing so maximise total social utility. But suddenly the basic premise was disrupted, and by none other than the teenage founder of the Utilitarian Society. If the attainment of utility required suspending utility as the ultimate goal, what was left of the Utilitarian approach? It comes as no surprise to learn that the same year Mill struck upon this insight, he dissolved the Utilitarian Society.[14]

There has been no shortage of attacks on Utilitarianism over time. Most often, these have consisted of pointing out that being happy is not the same as being good. We can look to Kant for the classic version: 'Such incentives merely teach one to become better at calculation, while the specific difference between virtue and vice is entirely obliterated.'[15] Yet I find Mill's own a far more potent and insidious critique of classical Utilitarianism, because it is served from within: Mill retains happiness as the catch-all concept to hold up and aspire to,[16] but he implies that to attain it fully would require doing so unknowingly. And of course, accident has no place in the systematic Utilitarian logic. Today, Mill's paradox remains as confounding to a rationality-based approach to human behaviour as it did in his own time.

Yet Mill held fast to his new insight. 'This theory now became the basis of my philosophy of life.' Looking back half a century later, this conviction had not left him: 'And I still hold to it as the best theory for all those who have but a moderate degree of sensibility and of capacity for enjoyment, that is, for the great majority of mankind.'

The remainder of this chapter gives chase to this idea. It traces its origins before Mill gave it voice, and follows the range of forms it then went on to take. It shows how this idea remains an overlooked challenge not only to nineteenth-century Utilitarianism, but to our modern market-driven worldview, premised as it is on those Utilitarian principles. To this day, the notion that many of the objects we most desire are in fact *byproducts* – ends that elude any wilful effort to grasp them – remains one of the greatest challenges to our shared Enlightenment values.

Romantic Origins

John Stuart Mill could smell his own heresy. It's why he was reluctant to speak of his growing doubts with those around him. But where did these doubts originate from in the first place? How was it that the young Mill was pushing back against everything he had learned, while all the others about him, who had drunk of the same Utilitarian Kool-Aid, kept on preaching the gospel? Where did Mill draw the insight from to distance himself from his own father's views, and from those of the Benthamites?

At one point, Mill himself seems to tell us. We know a great deal about Mill's inner life during this period, because he later wrote a remarkable account of the evolution of his ideas, an autobiography that ranks among the greatest of intellectual memoirs. And in it, Mill points us to the precise origin of his conversion. In recounting how he came to realise that the ultimate ends that individuals seek can only be attained incidentally, rather than wilfully, Mill tells us that this conclusion drew on Thomas Carlyle's 'theory of anti-self-consciousness'.[17]

So here we have it! All that remains to do is examine what this theory proposes, and how it provides the key to unlocking the existential crisis of the greatest philosopher of the nineteenth century. Here's the bad news: there is no such thing as the 'theory of anti-self-consciousness' in all of Carlyle. Thomas Carlyle himself, a Scottish prose poet and essayist who had been highly critical of the Philosophical Radicals to which the Mills belonged, never even used the term; it is an invention of Mill's. It is, in fact, very Mill-like in tone: a little laborious, a tad overly spelt-out. As for Carlyle, too much the poet by far, he would have scoffed at being identified with anything resembling a 'theory'. But then these were the roles the two men, who became close friends despite their considerable differences, came to play for one another. Carlyle was the poet and the mystic; Mill was his keen interpreter.

Mill himself only mentions the 'theory of anti-self-consciousness' in this single instance, when describing his change of faith. But let's take Mill at his word: here is the source that led him to question his intellectual heritage and adopt a new worldview, which he would reaffirm looking back on it half a century later. So what did Mill have in mind when he referred to Carlyle's 'theory'?

The writings of the English Romantics, to whom Carlyle belonged, bring to mind misty mountaintops and hypochondria. Yet underneath their odes to butterflies in the wind, there lay a powerful set of transgressive ideas. Poetry today rarely draws directly from philosophy. But until the twentieth century, artistic movements were often nested within a given school of thought. The demarcation between art, philosophy and politics was also more fluid than in our own highly specialised age. The Romantics had a habit of dying young – by suicide, in foolish exploits, or else as victims of the various lung diseases that decimated the nineteenth century. But those who lived into their thirties invariably turned from poets into public intellectuals who opined on current social questions, from education to international trade.[18]

The school of thought that lay under Romantic art and literature was centred around serious and sombre, and mostly German thinkers: figures like Hegel, von Schelling, and Goethe. It is amidst these ideas – which had been bumbling since the start of the century on the continent before the English Romantics began drawing on them – that we pick up the trail of Carlyle's 'theory of anti-self-consciousness', and the insight that so troubled Mill: namely that too much self-awareness might be self-defeating, and that the intellectual tradition into which he was born might be inherently limited.

Romanticism is born of backlash. Steeped in an age of reason, the Philosophical Romantics and the Romantic poets shared in a common humanistic polemic, a conviction that the Enlightenment's devotion to the intellect had come at a steep cost. They were rising up against an age of restraint, prudence, and good governance. What they recognised as marks of social progress were also inextricably linked, in their view, with an impoverishment of the individual. Reason had triumphed, yes, but it was a sad, pedestrian victory, a victory for calculation and analysis, one that demanded the sacrifice of the human spirit. The Romantics preferred stormy seas to calm waters.[19] To the clarity of science, they preferred the opacity of mysticism.* Their deepest commitments were aesthetic; they identified the moral with the beautiful.

They were especially suspicious of the premise that the human spirit could be studied in the same way one studied earthworms and planetary orbits. Once applied to the self, the scientific reflex of the Enlightenment turned into self-doubt and hesitation. Scepticism could be liberating when aimed at social institutions, but when directed on the individual, it produced a loss of spontaneity. It came at the cost of intuition; it proved crippling. Despite his cerebral temperament, J. S. Mill was sensitive to this criticism, as when bemoaning that his upbringing had resulted in a mind that was 'now irretrievably analytic'.[20]

In a recurrent trope, the Romantics compared the Enlightenment's triumph of reason over passion to the story of Adam and Eve being booted out of Paradise. In their telling, the Fall from Grace was the birth of self-consciousness. Adam and Eve are seduced by the serpent into eating from the tree of knowledge, and for the first time, they step outside themselves.

---

* In particular, the Romantics scorned the sceptical empiricist's habit of dividing the world into parts for the purpose of studying each one as separate from the others. As Wordsworth warned in 'The Tables Turned':

Our meddling intellect
Mis-shapes the beauteous forms of things:
We murder to dissect.

They realise they are naked, feel shame, and run for cover. From that moment on, they are self-aware. No longer merely the subject of their story, looking out at the world and acting within it, they now also become an object for their own scrutiny. In this transformation, they begin second-guessing themselves.

Warring Views of the Self

The Romantics' suspicion of self-awareness turned on its head a key tenet of the Enlightenment, which Utilitarianism grew out of. Thinkers like David Hume and Adam Smith had touted self-awareness as the very capacity that made social life livable. They talked up our capacity for what they called 'sympathy', an ability closer to what we might today call empathy. Sympathy was the uniquely human ability to put ourselves in others' shoes, and to feel what they felt. The pro-social value of sympathy came from the way it could inform our judgements of ourselves: as we inhabited the minds of others, as we momentarily felt their joys and their griefs, we also grew able to imagine how they might view us in turn. An 'impartial spectator', as Adam Smith called it, was born of that act of imagination.[21] That inner arbiter checked our most craven passions, our worst instincts. Sympathy, through its reflection back on ourselves, made us into better social beings. The Enlightenment thinkers did not deny the division of the self that occurred in the Fall; they celebrated it.

In fact, they would have found the Romantics' retelling of the story of Genesis mostly spot on; only they would have drawn the opposite conclusion. Adam and Eve's prudery comes from the realisation that they can be seen. The revelation of their own nudity is humanity's first social reflex: lacking mirrors, but seeing the other naked, Adam and Eve realise themselves to be naked, too, and they grab for a fig leaf. And along with the emergence of prudery would come reflexes like attentiveness, accommodation, leniency: all traits resulting from the appearance of that internal spectator. A newly divided self, trained on the spectacle of others' behaviour, and judging its own actions by the same token. Had it not been for the internal spectator, Adam and Eve would not only have gone on gallivanting about naked, they would also have thought little of thwacking one another in a moment of anger. With prudery also came self-restraint, and restraint made way for society: as Adam Smith put it, sympathy means that we view ourselves 'not in the light in which our own selfish passions are apt to place us, but in the light in which any other citizen of the world would view us'.[22]

The Romantics rebranded the internal spectator into a tyrant. The Age of Reason, in their view, turned us all into spectators of ourselves. Rather than acting, doing, and living, we now spend our time wondering how those actions might be perceived. We get lost in recursive mental loops, second-guessing our actions based on what we think they might reveal about us. Our self-awareness has been allowed to run amok; the internal spectator has usurped all power.

In the Romantics' telling, the self-awareness that grew from knowledge could prove downright fatal. In an 1810 story by the German writer Heinrich von Kleist, a young man blessed with 'an astounding beauty', but not yet afflicted by vanity, is at the baths. As he dries his foot with a towel, he inadvertently reproduces the pose of a famous sculpture of a boy removing a thorn from his foot. His friends notice the resemblance, and applaud it. Charmed by the accident, they call on him to repeat the gesture. He tries, to please them, but 'as one might well have predicted, the attempt failed. Befuddled, he raised his foot a third and fourth time, indeed he raised it ten more times: but for naught!' The attempt to reproduce the spontaneous act proves his undoing:

> from that moment on, the young man underwent an incomprehensible transformation. He began to stand for days at a time in front of the mirror; and he lost one charm after another. An invisible and inconceivable force, like an iron net, seemed to settle over and impinge upon the free play of movements, and after a year had gone by, not a trace could be found of the charming allure that had once entranced all those whose eyes fell upon him.[23]

Doesn't some of this cut uncomfortably close? Think of all those people curating their selfies for social media. Retaking pictures of themselves in better light, choosing the optimal filter, pondering an appropriately witty caption? Unable simply to experience the world, they are condemned to looking upon themselves experiencing the world. They do their best to gauge how others will look upon them so as to optimize their self-presentation. They are the objects of their own critical glance at least as much as they are the subjects of their lives.

As the writer Jia Tolentino put it in a recent essay on the millennial generation: 'It is a constantly self-conscious sensibility, that of someone who is always performing, always watching themselves be watched: maybe that was once primarily the condition of women, but it seems increasingly to apply to us all.'[24] Their experience of the world is always mediated by how they imagine it will be received by others. The contemporary critique carries more than a distant echo of the Romantics.

We know what happens when this mediation of experience turns excessive: we start walking around with the secret conviction that a moment didn't happen unless it was captured on our phone. A meal at a food stall in a market in Hanoi gains in reality by virtue of being snapped and posted and liked by others. If the battery on your device dies at the wrong moment, so does the substance of the experience. We post ourselves – our honeymoons, our trips to the museum, our children's birthday parties, the deaths of our parents – to ratify their occurrence, and to add to the materiality of our lives.

Self-awareness now proves fatal in ways Kleist could hardly have foreseen. A new term, the selficide, has had to be coined. Every year, the Darwin Awards, a meme-ready prize, is given out to 'commemorate those who improve our gene pool by removing themselves from it in the most spectacular way possible'. The top prize is now regularly won by some unfortunate soul who paid the ultimate price for their attempt at presenting themselves in a striking pose or setting – in front of injured bears, irate wild elephants, or on the edge of mountain lookouts.

What the Romantics were pining after was a time before selfies. It follows that we may now be as far as we have ever been from returning to the unified self that the Romantics so bemoaned the loss of. It's no surprise that the Romantics' ideas have lost none of their appeal, and that we have been instinctively returning to them; not always recognising their origins, but tacitly sensing their value.

When we're now told to disconnect and 'just be', to 'let go', and to 'lose ourselves in the moment', those commonplace New Age commands are channelling a group of German thinkers writing around 1800, whose ideas were brought to Britain, where they quickly took root in the very birthplace of the Enlightenment, and were expressed in new forms by the likes of Coleridge and Wordsworth and Carlyle. That's when Mill first encountered them, in breathless verse about jagged mountain peaks, as a confused twenty-year-old beset by doubts over what ends were worth pursuing, and what means were best designed to achieve them.

In the rapidly industrialising nineteenth century, these ideas caught on and kept spreading, eventually making their way across the Atlantic, and finding voice through the likes of Ralph Waldo Emerson and Henry David Thoreau and their fellow Transcendentalists.[25] It has been difficult to escape the recent return to fashion of Thoreau, especially. The pond, and the cabin, are sold on blogs, printed onto mugs and T-shirts and fridge magnets. We are all instructed to 'find our Walden'. In 1852, Thoreau wrote in his journal: 'There probably has been no more conscious age than the present,' and he did not mean it as a good thing. If he only knew.

The Romantics were questioning modernity before modernity ever came into being. In doing so, they cast a long shadow.[26] Later thinkers might have regarded the Romantic project of vying for some lost unity through the redemptive quality of art as naive, but they all started from the original Romantic insight of the inner split of the self.[27] In this original denouncement, the Romantics remain exquisitely current.

From the Romantics' misgivings about self-awareness, it was a small step to the paradox that so confounded J. S. Mill. After all, if self-awareness was the trouble, then let us simply be rid of it. 'Just be spontaneous; just act natural.' The problem is immediately apparent: how does one will an absence of will? Suddenly, the desirable objects that elude our grasp as we reach out for them seem to multiply.

That there might be value to be gained in conveying a lack of intent is a longstanding notion. The maxim *ars est celare artum*, 'the art consists in concealing the art', is usually (and apocryphally) attributed to Ovid, the ancient Roman poet.[28] But the fascination with producing effects that eluded direct effort took on unprecedented prominence in the aspirational nineteenth century, amid the rise of the middle class and the dance of collusion between the bourgeois and the bohemian – a term that took on its current meaning in the early 1840s. Even writers outside the Romantic movement grew obsessed with attaining qualities that became unattainable once they were made the explicit goal. The young Stendhal, writing in his journal in 1813, instructed himself thus: 'Exercise restraint in conversation, do not try to shine ... to come across well, I simply cannot be seen to want it.'[29]

The Romantic project stands and falls on this paradox: how to escape self-awareness, once we are stricken with it?* Much like Kleist's doomed adolescent, the Romantics were trying in vain to reproduce a spontaneous gesture. They sought a way of returning to that prior state of innocence, the mind's muscle memory. Hence their turn to nature, which they valued not only for its dramatic aspects – misty mountains and raging rivers – but also for its unthinking character. As they saw it, Nature was all passion and no intellect. Thus we get the idealisation of the New World's indigenous people going back to Rousseau, who portrayed those 'noble savages' as living a blessed, prelapsarian existence. Later, this same instinct would give us Gauguin's vivid paintings of nineteenth-century Tahiti,

---

* The paradox appears in Hegel's broodings, in his own retelling of the Fall: 'The principle of restoration [of the sense of Grace] is found in thought, and thought only: the hand that inflicts the wound is also the hand that heals it ... the same history repeats itself in every son of Adam.' And it reappears in von Kleist's story of the doomed youth: 'Paradise is bolted shut ... we are obliged to circle the globe and go around to the other side to see if perhaps there's a back way in.' And once we're in? Kleist's response: 'We then have to eat of the fruit of the tree of knowledge again to fall back into the state of innocence.'

unselfconsciously undressed *bons sauvages* basking in an undiscovered, eroticised Eden.

Which Way Back to Eden?

While Mill sensed the Romantics were on to something, he also realised they were bad at expressing any of it clearly.[30] He was convinced that 'they possessed much truth', but that this truth was obscured by 'the transcendental and mystical phraseology in which they were accustomed to shut it up'. The impenetrable prose, of course, was an intrinsic part of the package. The Romantics put their money on intuition, rather than the Enlightenment virtues of clarity. This is why they wrote not theories and tracts, but poetry, novellas, and plays. Their art was always ahead of their thought, which was just how they would have had it. Coherence simply wasn't what they were after.[31]

J. S. Mill thus became an interpreter between two worlds: an ambassador of reason among the poets, and a peddler of poetry among the political economists. He was characteristically explicit about this goal: 'If I have any vocation, I think it is exactly this, to translate the mysticism of others into the language of Argument.'*

As such, Mill proves an ideal guide to charting the border between the zones of reason and passion, examining what drives individuals to go from one to the other, and what obstacles they might encounter as they attempt the crossing.

Conversions often prove socially costly, and J. S. Mill's was no exception. His former friends from the Utilitarian Society could not understand what had got into him. The Benthamite

---

* Similarly: 'I did not despair of separating the truth from the error and expressing it in terms which would be intelligible and not repulsive to those on my own side in philosophy.'

old guard spurned him. One of them described him as 'a rene-
gade from philosophy', complaining that Mill was once 'most
emphatically a philosopher, but then he read Wordsworth and
that muddled him, and he has been in a strange confusion ever
since, endeavouring to unite poetry and philosophy.'[32]

In 1830, at the tail end of J. S. Mill's period of gloom, just
as he was wrestling with the conflicting impulses of poetry
and philosophy, he met a woman who embodied both, and
who would eventually become his wife. Harriet Taylor was a
married woman when Mill first met her, and their relationship
initially proceeded under the pall of scandal. Yet their meeting
came at just the right moment. She was at once a fierce intellect with grand plans for social reform, including the advancement of women's rights, and what Mill himself later described
as a uniquely 'poetic nature'. It was she who inspired Mill's first
attempt at reconciling the ideas of the Romantics with the ideas
he had been brought up with.[33]

The Romantics had an intuition of the fundamental problem
of modernity: the inner spectator was a tyrant. And they had a
sense of the solution: self-forgetfulness, a pining for renewed
authenticity. J. S. Mill's own bit of genius was to apply these
sometime mystical insights to the questions that preoccupied him and the social reformers around him. In doing so,
he ran up against the same paradox that the Romantics had
confronted in devising a return to Edenic innocence. What
J. S. Mill also gleaned, however, was that there was value in
the process. His own crisis had nearly cost him his life, but
the conversion it produced would prove decisive for the
remainder of his career.

Indeed, had it not been for his moment of conversion,
Mill might never have come to believe in the very possibility of intellectual conversions. He might never have gained
an appreciation for the human ability to programme and

reprogramme itself, if offered the chance. And that, perhaps more than anything, remains the central insight that guided the rest of his life's work. It is what fuelled his renewed conviction in social reform, as a means for providing the space for individuals to consummate their own conversions. The Romantics had claimed that the reform of the self had to precede social reform; yet what Mill the structuralist, Mill the institutionalist, Mill the social justice advocate understood is that social reform is also a necessary prerequisite for reforms of the self. This insight animated his work on social equality: he was working to create the social conditions for individual emancipations.

Mill's Legacy

Scarcity is not the only burden that came with the Fall from Eden. The Romantics were on to something: self-awareness may be the foundation of civilised society, but it has a price, one that is growingly apparent in our exceedingly self-conscious age. We see it manifested in the elusive quality of some of the things we most yearn for. As I argue in the following chapters, a growing number of the things we aspire to – the esteem and consideration of others, influence, even creative inspiration – are of the form J. S. Mill believed Utilitarian happiness to be. They are not attainable instrumentally, through efforts of will, but only incidentally, en passant. Most interestingly, the capitalist market itself, which was meant to discipline us all into conforming, rational, self-interested agents, has come to embody the same paradox: increasingly, the market rewards those who shun its logic. Because of the premium that wary market actors put on credibility, and because of the difficulty of attaining such credibility, commercial success increasingly requires pursuing goals other than market success.

The Enlightenment celebrated the splitting of the self. The ability to look at oneself from a remove, and thus to anticipate how others would view one's own actions, was an essential stepping-stone to life in society. It not only produced 'sympathy' for one's fellow human, but it also led to the emergence of an internal 'impartial spectator' who could move the individual to self-restraint. With the Romantics, that same splitting of the self amounted to a crippling loss of spontaneity, grace, and virtue, all of which eluded the social animal cursed with self-awareness.

These two warring views of the self – as civilising impulse, and as fundamental impediment – are with us still. J. S. Mill was among the first Western thinkers to consider the implications of this conflict. To his dying day, he never fully let go of Bentham's ideas. Happiness, or maximal social utility, remained the goal and the standard by which to take the measure of human action. But a deeper recognition of human nature, starting with his own, suggested that convenient though utility was as a metric, it was an end best attained by setting out for different ends. J. S. Mill's conversion led him to try and kindle further conversions in others. He envisioned a social and political system that would allow individual changes of heart. The result was the elevation of the concept of individual freedom, which gave us modern liberalism. It is the water we swim in today.

This provides a corrective to the common view of liberalism as a middle path of political restraint, prizing stability above all, a meek compromise between the excessive impulses of the Left and Right. Because insofar as liberalism does value stability, insofar as it proceeds through piecemeal reforms, it does so in the service of countless individual uprisings. It is always the technocrats and the centrists who claim Mill for their own, portraying him as the even-tempered representative of restraint, the all-time winner of the Marshmallow Test. Yet J. S. Mill also fervently believed in inserting zones of passion, and excess, into regions of analysis. After that twentieth year, his writing was always one part Wordsworth.

That crisis was J. S. Mill's turning point; and I believe we are now reaching our own. What's more, both of these crises are born of a similar frustration. And that is because the ideas of the nineteenth-century Utilitarians continue to suffuse our thinking. Like the young Mill, raised among the Benthamites, we think in instrumental terms: we do things for a reason; we are devoted to outcome; we seek self-improvement, and we go about it in the same consequentialist manner as the Utilitarians did. And like Mill, we are coming up against the limitations of a strictly instrumental approach. The moment feels ripe for a social conversion of our own.

A Conversion of My Own

J. S. Mill's story has always stuck with me. I was neither a child prodigy nor an intellectual goose stuffed by overly ambitious parents. But my belief in instrumental rationality – as both the most useful baseline assumption about human nature, and a state to strive for – was overdetermined in its own way. Born in a Soviet-controlled country and coming to North America as a toddler, I grew up being told that we had no safety net or family network to count on. My mother would regularly trot out the same line: 'Remember, you have no uncle with a factory,' she would say. For that matter, neither did any of my friends, but her point was clear: with no connections to count on, we had to make it on our own.

The result was a pragmatic attitude that I suspect many immigrants can relate to: a single-minded pursuit of economic security and social respectability. Doing things for their own sake seemed like an idle frivolity. Free time was best spent on productive endeavours, with an eye to their future rewards. My choice of majors at university was ruled by risk aversity. I was drawn to the humanities and the arts, but the notion of studying literature never occurred to me; that was a luxury reserved for people who had uncles with factories.

It is a sign of the current times that what I think of as a bias borne of immigrants' economic uncertainty seems to now be shared by students across the economic spectrum, who are eschewing liberal arts en masse in favour of STEM majors that promise to equip them with job-market-ready skills. The intellectual legacy of precarity, whether the result of immigration or structural economic conditions, is a pragmatism that has a deep affinity with the Utilitarian approach. It is instrumentalism borne of perceived necessity.

Later, my choice of academic field of research was similarly overdetermined. I found a familiar system of thought in the study of political economy, one premised on individual rational behaviour. It is almost a motto of political economy that those who stray from rational means to rational ends invariably 'fall by the wayside'. My mother couldn't have said it better. The market inexorably weeds out those who fail to learn its lessons and behave according to its rules. Sure, mistakes are made, and flights of fancy take place, but as the political scientist Stephen Krasner once put it, 'stupidity is not an interesting analytical category'. That is, rational actors have an incentive to learn from their own mistakes and those of others, which means that stupidity rarely lasts. Irrationality occasionally crops up – an entire field at the juncture of economics and psychology has emerged to document systematic biases of human behaviour – but most of our theories still assume such quirks of irrationality will be corrected when the stakes grow sufficiently high; the individual pursuit of self-interest remains the most useful approximation of behaviour.

These days, I am no longer certain that a focus on the rational pursuit of self-interest is either the most analytically useful approach to the study of human behaviour, or indeed what we ourselves should aspire to in our own lives. I have come to side with J. S. Mill on this: come a certain point of development, the way to further maximise individual and social utility may require us to let go of maximisation as our default approach. What's more, my sense is that this paradox looms ever larger as time passes and as our advanced society grows more advanced. And we have yet to reckon with the implications.

In this way, this book also charts a conversion of my own – from someone who used to look to self-interest as an elegant, all-encompassing category, flawless in its internal coherence, to someone who now thinks that if we do in fact want to make the most of our time down here, we must harbour within ourselves reserves of whimsy, zones free of instrumental purpose. If we are to be consistent utility maximisers, we must, at some point, abandon maximisation as our method. In a market-driven society such as ours, taking our eyes off the prize may be the required means of capturing it. As J. S. Mill intuited, this turns out to have implications for how we choose to lead our own lives, and how we think about social reform.

2

The Byproduct Society

From Products to Byproducts

It used to be easy. It used to be that one could gain the esteem and consideration of friends and strangers the way one bought a pound of potatoes. Or perhaps an expensive watch. Possessing and displaying such a watch was in itself proof of one's status; it was sufficient to command respect, honour, admiration.

For that was always the goal. Sure, some part of wealth was devoted to necessities, like potatoes. Or securing food, shelter, a degree of material comfort. But it was always the case that as soon as these basic necessities were attained, wealth began serving an altogether different, *social* function. And as average wealth grew across Western countries, the share of wealth devoted to this social function began to overwhelm the share allocated to necessities. More objects of consumption looked like the expensive watch than the pound of potatoes.

This is what we mean when we say that we live in a consumer society. The label starts to apply once the greater part of consumption is directed not at procuring the basics of life, but at fulfilling a wider range of social and relational needs. The esteem and consideration of others, a sense of belonging, a favourable public image, a glowing reputation. Books are bought to be displayed on the coffee table more than to be read. Bottles of Bordeaux are brought out not so much for their full-bodied boldness, but for the impression they produce at a dinner party. Even the organic watercress bought at farmers' markets serves as signal more than salad. Brand names, limited editions, one-of-a-kind knick-knacks: these aspirational goods telegraph our belonging to a knowing, well-off elite.

Lest we think any of this is new, Adam Smith, the presumptive father of the 'greed is good' mindset – a misconception there is yet time to dispel – was already making fun of the consumerist urges of his time, and their hidden social functions, in 1759: 'For to what purpose is all the toil and bustle of this world? What is the end of avarice and ambition, of the pursuit of wealth, of power, and preheminence? Is it to supply the necessities of nature?' No, Smith answers, 'The wages of the meanest labourer can supply them … It is the vanity, not the ease, or the pleasure, which interests us.' This vanity was at the bottom of everything; it was all there was. 'Nature, when she formed man for society, endowed him with an original desire to please.'

Note that Adam Smith believed that the necessities of life could already be met with the eighteenth-century wages 'of the meanest labourer', which is worth keeping in mind when thinking of the changing meaning of 'necessities'. But the greater point is that Smith was clear on how the aim of the greatest part of the 'toil and bustle in the world', all the producing and all the consuming, was symbolic, rather than material. There lay the engine of growth. The economy ran not so much on greed, as on the underlying desire to please, and to be approved of. The 'great purpose of human life which we call bettering our condition' is simply 'to be observed, to be attended to, to be taken notice of with sympathy, complacency, and approbation'.

Once this is clear, the contortions people went through to make the right impression on one another quickly reveal themselves to be silly. If we weren't all on the inside, we would find it risible. Adam Smith made unrelenting fun of the consumption habits of his day, belying the popular view that has him singing the praises of personal ambition. He quipped that people were devising new, unheard-of pockets in their clothing, to carry around more trinkets, all this to impress those around them, who saw themselves forced to do the same.

What Smith realised was that eighteenth-century Britain had become a consumer society: the true purpose of most goods was only distantly related to their immediate use.[1] A tin spoon could accomplish its food-bearing mission as well as a silver spoon. But they had different social functions; the silver spoon sent a social signal which the tin spoon could not. If one found oneself on a desert island, Smith concluded, most of the modern functions of wealth would promptly lose all meaning.[2]

Of course, the opportunity to signal one's status to the world by flaunting one's possessions was not given to everyone. In fact, scarcity was a necessary premise: it was *because* not everyone could afford to wear a flashy watch that it became useful as a social signalling device. Still, for those who could afford it, the game in Adam Smith's time was simple enough to play. By surrounding themselves with beautiful things, by filling their specially designed pockets with useless baubles, the well-to-do gained one another's esteem as discerning members of a common elite. They grew content. For the rich in the eighteenth century, consumption as a mechanism of social distinction *worked*.

This began to change with the advent of the industrial revolution. Productivity increased, wages rose, a new merchant class emerged. Factories began to churn out mass-produced goods. Foreign trade boomed. Previously exotic goods were now regularly supplied from the colonies: tea, sugar, spices, printed cotton calico from India. What Adam Smith had derided as 'trinkets of frivolous utility' were no longer the singular preserve of the wealthy. More and more people could now afford nice watches, both because the ranks of the middle class were swelling, and because clocks and watches could now be cheaply assembled at scale.[3]

The well-to-do were suddenly in a bind. It was now more difficult to signal to one another their distinction from the *arrivistes* of the merchant class. Small enterprising businessmen who worked hard could, with a bit of luck thrown in, afford the same outward tokens of luxury that until recently only the wealthy had had access to. But for those wealthy individuals who could previously rely on flashy consumption to convey their social rank, the implications were serious: consumer goods became less good at accomplishing their social function. How to distinguish themselves from the masses, now that the masses all went about in imported clothing and fancy watches of their own?

The well-to-do grew inventive. They resorted to increasingly rarefied means of signalling status and maintaining the esteem of their peers. If the emerging merchant class could aspire to join their ranks through increased productivity, the well-to-do could hit back by courting the opposite: *non-productivity*. Idle leisure, and its public display, increasingly became the distinctive trait of the elite. Here was a far more effective means of displaying wealth than mere consumption. Progressively, the true mark of higher status became not so much the ability to afford the finer things in life through hard work, but the ability to do so in a purposefully wasteful fashion, without ever having to stoop to anything like labour or industry. Among the upper ranks of the social hierarchy, mere trinkets were thus devalued. Leisure took their place.

This is the phenomenon that the American economist Thorstein Veblen famously describes in his *Theory of the Leisure Class*, published in 1899. Veblen offered the world the handy concept of 'conspicuous consumption' to designate an accumulation of material goods that primarily serves as evidence of status. It is telling that the phrase has been in continuous rotation ever since. He also demonstrated that the same impulse led to the emergence of a class that actively championed waste. If the aspiring merchant class had to be productive, then the elites would squander.

Veblen was intent on showing that the privileged classes across different times and cultures had enacted similar rituals to similar ends. In Veblen's stylised view of history, as soon as people were able to produce more than they strictly needed to get by, the accumulation of goods became a means of telling apart the powerful from the weak. Modern societies retained the aggressive urges of pre-industrial feudal societies; these urges merely took on different forms. The mighty replaced the active exercise of power with the accumulation of property, and then with non-productive leisure. The most convenient shorthand for distinction was now a taboo on labour. By elevating non-productivity as an agreed-upon signal of one's standing in the social hierarchy, the American elites of his day were mimicking the chiefs of small Polynesian bands. The gentlemen of leisure who spent their afternoons smoking cigars at the club were thus enacting rituals which warrior tribes and pre-industrial societies had played out for centuries before them.

Veblen's tone tends to the playfully cynical, and the mode of *The Theory of the Leisure Class* is never far from satire, which may explain why so many turn-of-the-century novelists plundered it for material. Yet Veblen also recognised that the stakes were real. In a consumer society, where the possession of property takes on a social function, it also becomes the main basis for self-worth. It is by looking over his lands, and comparing them to his neighbour's, that the wealthy landowner consummates his identity as landowner.

Replace land with lawn, and you approximate modern suburbia. The money expended on the upkeep of American lawns is greater than the entire US foreign aid budget.[4] These lawns are not made to walk on, but to signal the consumption capacity and competence of their owners. An enviably trim and well-maintained lawn of the correct hue means its owners either have the spare time to fertilise, water, and mow a rectangle of non-functional, non-native vegetal species, or they have the means of employing others to do it for them.

Non-productivity, in this sense, was the most efficient solution to a social problem. The point of leisure, Veblen claimed, was not its inherent enjoyability, but the aggressive display of indolence. It became popular to loudly complain of boredom, or *ennui*, the chic affectation of the late nineteenth century. The mood of the day demanded to be seen as having fallen victim to a languid idleness. But this boredom served an economic function. It accomplished what economists call a 'separating equilibrium': it successfully distinguished types of people in a situation where everyone aspired to the same type. Separation into 'types' occurs even as everyone does their best to be seen to belong. And those too busy earning their keep clearly did not belong. Which meant that the truly well-to-do could sleep soundly, safe in the knowledge that the aspiring classes could not easily pass for their equal through mere mimicry.

So the well-to-do, like the characters in a Henry James novel – who was among the writers who drew heavily from Veblen, in works like *The American Scene* – engaged in playing games, breeding dogs, racing horses, and cultivating capricious orchids. Anything to pass the time in a way that did not inadvertently generate something of use. The social function of idleness even extended to the people employed by the well-to-do. In ancient times, power had traditionally been asserted through the ownership of slaves, who laboured so that their masters could devote themselves to higher contemplative pursuits, like philosophy. Instead, the turn-of-the-century wealthy class now employed large staffs of servants whose main task was to 'wait on' their employers, according to strict rules of decorum,[5] which themselves required considerable time and training to acquire. That these servants did not produce anything of value was intentional.[6] The same went for women of the elite. Veblen saw the wives of upper-crust society as performing a similar function, reduced to agents for wasteful spending and leisure, which resulted, among other things, in the perverse decoration and redecoration of homes according to rapidly changing fashions.

Fashion was another site of waste as spectacle. Veblen's proto-feminism – which he was able to reconcile with a tendency to court his female students and the wives of his colleagues – led to a fanatical campaign against corsets, a subject Veblen repeatedly returns to in his writings. Corsets, along with high heels, decorative canes, and other similar sartorial affectations, were manifestations of the cult of nonproductivity seeping into fashion. From an economic standpoint, these were wilful mutilations, 'undergone for the purpose of lowering the subject's vitality and rendering her permanently and obviously unfit for work'. By wearing impractical implements that rendered them unfit for physical exertion, the well-to-do proved beyond doubt that work was beneath them. When corsets began falling out of fashion, Veblen observed, the taste for them endured in economically emerging American backwaters, in 'those American cities ... which have recently and rapidly risen into opulence'.

If we were to look for a contemporary equivalent of the corset in 1900 – an otherwise incongruous item of clothing to send the appropriate social signal – we might find no better than athleisure pants. Favoured by the corresponding class to the one Veblen was studying, these now proclaim the wearer's devotion to utility. They are the quintessential uniform of self-betterment, suggesting one might at any moment drop into an asana, or join a Pilates class. That these garments happen to be exact opposites, the latter enabling, the former disabling, underscores the fluidity with which the desired social signal can change, while the underlying goal of distinguishing oneself remains the same.

Ritual Analogues

Just as Veblen was describing how the practices of American elites were the continuation of pre-industrial social rituals, North American governments were banning similar rituals among Indigenous groups.

The ceremony of the potlatch has been much written about by anthropologists, to the point where it has become the object of an almost prurient popular interest. This fascination, which began with Marcel Mauss's 1925 study in *The Gift*, one of the foundational texts of anthropology, is likely due to how foreign the incentives underlying the potlatch are from the standpoint of modern market-based societies. Veblen's point was that the same incentives were driving his urban gentleman of means. Tellingly, the government response proved rather different in each case.

The term *potlatch* comes from the word for 'gift' in the Chinook language. It usually designated a feast thrown by a wealthy member of the band with the (never explicitly spelt-out) expectation that their social standing would rise as a result.

It included shared consumption, craft-making, and gift giving, but also the ritualistic destruction of property. Such destruction, where precious objects might be thrown into the sea, and which often took on a competitive element, acted as an extension of consumption. It was its logical next step. As Mauss put it, 'destruction in the strict sense seems to constitute a superior form of expenditure'.[7]

The potlatch originated among Indigenous nations living in the Pacific Northwest, and reached its most elaborate form in the Kwakiutl nation, which was made up of tribes living on Vancouver Island in the mid-nineteenth century. The Kwakiutl were highly hierarchical, with the equivalent of an aristocratic ruling class, and especially prosperous. As a result, they produced a great amount of artefacts and texts that are now available for study, which largely accounts for why they have been a frequent focus of scholarly attention.

For a time, during the initial stages of their integration into a larger market economy through the Canadian state, the prosperous Kwakiutl grew even more prosperous. Those at the bottom of the social hierarchy began accumulating wealth in ways that threatened the status of those at the top. The result was at once a great flourishing of non-productive activities, in the realms of art and craft, and what the anthropologist David Graeber describes, in his consideration of Mauss's work, as an 'enormous inflation of potlatches'.[8] During these increasingly elaborate ceremonies, the aristocracy gave away tremendous amounts of its wealth in a bid to retain its elevated status, and outcompete others doing the same. But as Graeber puts it, it proved to be 'a losing struggle – an effort of an elite to redefine its privilege in the face of equalizing forces'.[9]

Yet the formal end of the traditional potlatch was imposed by outside forces. The giving and open destruction of wealth so unnerved Western observers, who viewed it as a sure sign of decadence, that it led to the 1884 Potlach Ban in Canada. Spurred on principally by Christian missionaries, the Canadian government banned the practice on the grounds that it ran against the 'Christian capitalist society'.[10]

The irony, of course, is that turn-of-the-century capitalism had generated, in Veblen's telling, similar customs with similar social functions at the heart of the most elite Western circles. The historical evidence suggests that the potlatch ritual actually did much to fuel a capitalist spirit among Indigenous peoples. The principal motivation behind members of Indigenous groups seeking paid labour in canneries, sawmills, mines, and other colonial industries appears to have been to earn enough money to be able to give it all away during potlatch ceremonies.[11] Once potlatches were banned, Indigenous peoples seem to have become less interested in wage labour. Nonetheless, Canada's Potlach Ban remained in place until 1951.

The Demise of Idleness

No ban was imposed on the wasteful leisure of Veblen's high-society elite. And for a while, leisure *did* provide the wealthy a measure of protection against the encroaching masses. Just as consumption had once worked as a tool of distinction, the projection of idleness now achieved the same. In fact, the chief worry of Veblen's well-to-do was the vexing question of how to continue communicating their higher status when no one was watching. As Veblen laid out, tongue firmly in cheek:

> For some part of the time his life is perforce withdrawn from the public eye, and of this portion which is spent in private the gentleman of leisure should, for the sake of his good name, be able to give a convincing account. He

58

should find some means of putting in evidence the leisure that is not spent in the sight of the spectators.

If a well-bred gentleman fanned himself while reclining in a chaise in his garden, but no one was there to see it, had the well-bred gentleman truly been fanning himself? We have now devised modern solutions to such problems. Today, the gentleman of leisure, or anyone similarly eager to distinguish themselves, can signal their status to all those around them on a continual basis. Social media seems purposefully designed to broadcast one's ease for all to see. While there may still be no one to witness your state of leisurely repose on a beach chair, you can now post a selfie of yourself drinking out of a coconut for all the world to see.

But before the advent of social media, the solution the gentlemen of leisure converged on was to bring back tangible evidence of all the leisure performed with no one to witness it. They collected trophies: golden cups awarded in sporting events, or the antlers of animals killed during hunting expeditions. Objects were thus imbued with a social function once more. Yet they now no longer signalled status through their high cost, which could be derided as vulgar showmanship. Instead, they provided the material evidence of their possessor's ability to invest inordinate amounts of time in sports, games, hunting, travel. Evidence of past leisure could also come from the acquisition of skills and refined forms of non-remunerative knowledge: being conversant in dead languages, taking up rarefied hobbies, starting collections of all sorts, accumulation of arcane erudition – all these were occupations which Veblen claimed served a principally social function. These things were done not for their own sake, but to convince others of one's standing.

What is again remarkable is that for a short while, these contortions appear to have been truly effective. For all of

Veblen's skewering the turn-of-the-century well-to-do, they seem rather content. Through waste and frivolity, and the collecting of various trophies to serve as evidence of it, they come into their own. Just as consumption achieved its social function in Adam Smith's time, so does the pursuit of non-productivity attain its end in Veblen's time. For a span, leisure *worked*.

Until, of course, it no longer did. Where Thorstein Veblen failed was in his inability to see what lay ahead for his gentleman of means. He did not realise that the turn-of-the-century leisure class he had roasted was an endangered species, and for the very reasons he had identified. For just as fancy trinkets and baubles had begun to lose their social currency once they entered mass production, so too would the social power of leisure soon begin to erode. After all, Veblenian idleness was just another form of consumption, harder to achieve only because it required prior wealth. Leisure could not be a permanent solution to the social problem of distinction. It could never remain respectable.

Veblen's leisure class was thus doomed from the start. By the post-war period, the social signal sent by leisure had changed once more. As the economist John Kenneth Galbraith noted in *The Affluent Society*, published in the 1950s, 'Nearly all societies at nearly all times have had a leisure class.' Yet, he went on, 'in the United States, the leisure class, at least as an easily identifiable phenomenon, has disappeared. To be idle is no longer considered rewarding or even entirely respectable.' Corsets have given way to athleisure pants. Galbraith's observation was correct, and it has only become more so in the meantime, with what many are decrying as a cult of productivity. In less than a century, productivity went from virtuous to vulgar, to virtuous once more. Is it any surprise that the pendulum is preparing to swing again?

The Veblen Treadmill

The process by which material goods and then leisure lose their social function might be called the Veblen Treadmill. The idea behind the Veblen Treadmill is that no matter how fast you run, the treadmill keeps speeding up, precisely *because* of how fast you're running. It is insofar as the well-to-do wear expensive watches in order to distinguish themselves that these eventually become ineffective at their task of social signalling. And it is because they engage in leisure as a means of distinction that leisure eventually loses its social significance. What proves disqualifying is the *intent* to distinguish oneself. Which is problematic, because as both Adam Smith and Veblen correctly observed, distinguishing oneself is always the intent. Our natural and unvarying longing is to gain the esteem and consideration of our peers: 'to be observed, to be attended to, to be taken notice of with sympathy, complacency, and approbation'. That was the goal all along.

Veblen had a good sense of how this progressive erosion occurred with regard to the accumulation and the parading of luxury items. He noted how 'loud dress' and overly fussy clothing was disqualifying of status, because it 'evince[d] an undue desire to reach and impress'.[12] But he failed to see that leisure as a mark of status would become equally obsolete by the very same logic. Because there too, as he kept pointing out, there lay an 'undue desire to reach and impress' the audience. And that audience would soon clue in.[13] Once it did, those eager to impress would be picked apart and sneered at.

The flaw of conspicuous consumption of any sort, whether of material goods or of leisure, lies precisely in their conspicuousness, in the transparency of the intent. The desire to impress is the surest way to fail in doing so. We know this to be the undoing of the nouveaux riches of every era, including our own. A fancy watch might telegraph the status of its wearer, unless it is so ostentatious that its intent to impress becomes too apparent. A watch that, as the writer Gary Shteyngart once put it, 'looks like a Russian oligarch just curled up around your wrist and died' sends the opposite signal to the one intended. It makes plain the desperation to impress. The undoing of the newly rich lies in trying too hard. Having nothing but their finances to lean on, they lean on them too heavily. In their eagerness to awe, they come across as upstarts, posers, blowhards. The fashionable set immediately marks them out as fashion victims.

What is no longer distinguishing becomes *vulgar*. That is invariably the term that is reached for, and for good reason.[14] Its origin is in the Latin *vulgaris*, which comes from the *vulgus*, or common people. Vulgarity is attached not to the object, but to the intent behind it. Because we know from Adam Smith that the wish to please is Nature-given. What can be less distinctive?

The Contortions of the Wealthy

The wealthy are the serial victims of the Veblen Treadmill. In trying to police entry into their high-status group, they make it progressively harder to show evidence of their own belonging. They must resort to ever more sophisticated means of signalling their 'type', until no material object, no matter how subtle its conspicuousness, and how reliant on in-group knowledge its possession, accomplishes its social function.

The Veblen Treadmill turns products into byproducts; what could previously be grasped directly can then only be had by working towards some other aim. At the outset, the esteem of one's peers is akin to a flashy watch: a product that one can go out and purchase. Then, the inner spectator clears his throat.

Suddenly people know better, and the flashy watch grows vulgar. The way to respectability shifts to alternatives, like conspicuous leisure. But soon, the pose of languor becomes affected, and it, too, is seen as questionable. Instead of spending their money on watches or on frivolous games, the wealthy might thus try and give it away. The leisure class graduates, it becomes the philanthropic class.

Much of the social interaction of today's wealthy American elites – various galas, fundraisers, and charity events – consists of watching one another give their money away. But this, too, is unlikely to last in its present form. The benefactors' motives are increasingly probed. To put one's name in big letters on the new symphony orchestra becomes gauche. Soon, all conspicuously large gifts meet with suspicion, and their social function among the elite is jeopardised. The growing criticism that decries philanthropy as an instrumental exercise, a means of reifying the elite's elite position, only speeds up the treadmill.[15] Montaigne's observation on spectacular good deeds begins to ring true: 'The more glittering the deed, the more I subtract from its moral worth, because of the suspicion aroused in me that it was exposed more for glitter than for goodness.' Until the only respectable way of giving is to give anonymously – but how will the wealthy collect their social dividend then? Once this last stage is reached, once the only remaining avenue is secrecy, esteem has gone from a product to a byproduct; it can now only be obtained by those who appear convincingly uninterested in obtaining it – which leaves the interested in a pickle.

The culture of philanthropy is often described as peculiarly American, a reaction to a small-government approach where private citizens are expected to step up and provide public goods. But it was already present in Ancient Rome, where it was prone to the same paradox. The French historian Paul Veyne, in the beautiful book *Bread and Circuses*, describes the practices by which wealthy Romans would offer large gifts to the masses. Festivals, games, banquets, monuments, public works. In return, they could expect their social standing to rise – but only if the intent behind their show of generosity was not evident. If these seemed overly calculated moves, the effort failed. The wealthy patrons had to be persuasively uninterested in the effect of their gifts. 'The ruling power obtained additional prestige from the very irrationality of its expressions, which spoke for themselves and were proudly indifferent to their audience.'[16]

The Veblen Treadmill was at work in Ancient Rome, too. Over time, the quid pro quo nature of the elites' largesse became increasingly ambiguous. While they had initially 'paid in order to rule', public figures were increasingly made to look upon their entire lives as a liturgy, until 'ruling and giving were one and the same'.[17] Through these growingly elaborate rituals, an equilibrium was reached that allowed both the plebs to accept the gift, and the rulers to collect their dividend of respectability. The social incentives of the rich forced them to conceal the intent behind their gifts, in ways that eventually affected their true motivations. The elites would commit to great gifts, and then deliver more than they promised. They were made to perform their rule as an act of self-sacrifice. Insofar as instrumental giving today is just another form of instrumental consumption, we should expect similarly inventive reworkings of our modern philanthropic practices.

It bears asking, why should we concern ourselves with the efforts of the wealthy at gaining one another's esteem, either in Veblen's day or in our own? At a time when the problem of scarcity remains far from resolved for the greater part of humanity, and just as our sights are turned towards resolving urgent problems from inequality to social injustice, what do the strenuous contortions of the rich philanthropic class have to do with the rest of us?

Examining those on top is valuable if it offers us a preview of what may lie ahead. It pushes us to ask J. S. Mill's question: assuming that our social objectives were attained – that the problem of scarcity, for instance, were in fact resolved – what then? Would we be content? Well, let's consider the wealthy. As John Maynard Keynes pointed out, they are 'our advance guard – those who are spying out the promised land for the rest of us'. What we wish for ourselves and for our children is to have similarly unlimited financial means, so that we may finally focus on the 'real business of life'.[18] And yet, as Keynes observed in 1930, the early reports sent back by these scouts are not favourable; the rich, he concluded then, have 'failed disastrously'. Just as with Veblen's nineteenth-century leisure class, the value of consumption among elites invariably extinguishes itself; its social potency becomes debased. What self-worth they can derive through their material ease is progressively eroded by their inner 'impartial spectator' who, in detecting the intentions of others, comes to second-guess their own. The point is not to pity the rich. It is, rather, to understand that the social benefits that come from joining their ranks are eroded just as our ability to do so increases. Social functions that were previously achievable through efforts of will – saving, anticipating, purchasing, and rejoicing – increasingly elude us. The more ardent our will and the clearer our intention, the less likely we are to make the impression we want to make.

The takeaway is that in those few pockets where affluence has been attained, not only has full contentment not followed, but the means of affluence have been getting in the way of that contentment. The wealthy thus represent a particularly good case study for how products turn into byproducts. Yet the Veblen Treadmill affects us all.

You will be relieved to hear that the rich have not given in. The Veblen Treadmill keeps running, and the wealthy huff and puff to keep up. Under Adam Smith, they sewed additional pockets to hold more goods to show off to one another. Under Veblen, they embraced waste. Today, they are reversing course. Aspiring instead to an outward image of thriftiness, today's most discerning elites have turned to acquiring goods that have the credible pretence of utility. Effective means of doing this include investing in private healthcare, childcare, and higher education. In the United States, especially, higher education has become – in ways that conveniently serve its social signalling purposes – exorbitantly expensive. Crucially, however, in paying $70,000 a year for the education of each of their children, a well-off family can plausibly claim that they are not doing so to impress anyone, but because they value the education of their children for its own sake.

The success of this strategy of distinction rests on the ambiguity of the parents' intent. It is precisely *because* it can be seen to serve an inherent purpose ('in today's competitive economy, a good education is more important than ever') that a degree from a prestigious school achieves its social function. The same goes for spending on healthcare and its self-care offshoots.

As the professor of public policy Elizabeth Currid-Halkett has noted, this shift towards non-ostentatious, functional goods has real social consequences.[19] By not actively flaunting their advantage, it becomes easier for the wealthy to deny its existence, which may end up having more pernicious effects on inequality than the open displays of ease by Veblen's well-to-do.

The nineteenth-century leisure class made for an easier target for popular economic grievances and the political leaders that emerged to represent them. By comparison, the well-off family living in a Brooklyn walk-up and spending their money on expensive dental care, tutors, and Ivy League educations is a less obvious object of scorn. But the functional nature of these goods may end up perpetuating class divides, in ways that expensive watches and yachts merely made more apparent. The ownership of a yacht did not pay its own dividend; it did not make the gap deeper. By contrast, fancy educations not only serve an effective social signalling function by camouflaging the underlying intent, but they may also be the most effective means of passing one's higher status on to the next generation. Similarly, private healthcare spending (especially if it displaces public sector investments) contributes to a widening gap in life expectancy between rich and poor.

By this shift towards functional goods, the well-to-do thus achieve the goal of social distinction once more. Yet this too will invariably change. The Veblen Treadmill keeps running, and the effectiveness of any good at signalling status rarely endures.

Training the Impartial Spectator

What keeps the treadmill running is a process of social learning we have seen in a different context in the previous chapter. In this case, Adam Smith's 'impartial spectator' is not calling for restraint from violent human passions, but whispering into one's ear: 'too gaudy, a little too obvious'. As Smith advocated, 'we must become the impartial spectators of our own character and conduct. We must endeavour to view them with the eyes of other people, or as other people are likely to view them.' Smith had in mind benevolent behaviour towards others, but the same learning allows us to predict whether peaked lapels will come off as rakish or rash. In both Veblen and Smith, we are dealing with a type of social learning that happens through a feedback loop between our perceptions of others and what we reckon to be their perceptions of us. In judging others, we calibrate our judgement of ourselves.

What underlies that learning is the incentive to distinguish those who truly belong to the in-group, or the inner circle within that in-group, from those who are merely pretending. All social groups rely on the ability to police boundaries, and each of us hones this ability relentlessly. Our verdicts are instantaneous, and merciless. 'Why does he put on such airs?' 'She's trying too hard.' 'That actor is overacting.' 'That pose is affected.' 'Wasn't that movie a little on the nose?' In all these ways, we judge others' gestures by guessing at the intention behind them.

Walking down the street, you might turn your head to admire a yellow convertible gliding by, until you catch the driver's eager look and detect their hope of catching your admiring glance. You roll your eyes and smirk. 'Show-off,' you mutter. If the driver has any sense, they will know they've been unmasked. You cast them out of the society of people of taste (to which you naturally belong), and into the eighth circle of hell that is home to braggarts and blowhards. It's in the pinging back and forth between the driver's glance and your own that the learning happens. You tell yourself: if ever I come into money, I won't be caught dead driving a yellow convertible. And thus the Veblen Treadmill speeds along; social expectations of propriety evolve.

Fortified with such lessons, people adjust their behaviours. They still wish to make a favourable impression on others. But they face a recurrent challenge: namely to persuade anyone watching that if they *did* find themselves on Adam Smith's desert island, they would behave in just the same way as they do now, in the presence of an audience. The social standing of Veblen's well-to-do thus rests on convincing one another that even without any witnesses, they would still wear uncomfortable corsets, learn Latin, cultivate finicky orchids, and raise exotic dog breeds. Their parade of idleness must be but a daily walk in the park: to accomplish the purpose of the parade, it has to credibly come across as an innocent stroll. The social effect of their affectations is only achieved on condition of appearing non-social. They must be meant not for others, but for themselves.

And so we arrive at another instance of our central paradox. If there are gains to be had in adopting an unconscious posture, what are the conscious among us to do? And though the stakes in this instance consist of people trying to impress one another, the challenge is of the same logical form as the one J. S. Mill came up against in the Utilitarians' striving for happiness. In both cases, we are dealing with states that can only be obtained without being intentionally pursued. Just as with the maximisation of individual utility according to J. S. Mill, the esteem of others is attained 'en passant' – in passing rather than in striving.

There is another parallel between the challenge faced by Veblen's well-to-do and J. S. Mill's Utilitarian. To preview an idea that later proves important, what gives rise to the paradox in both cases is the existence of multiple selves. In the first instance, the social learning that speeds up the Veblen Treadmill comes from the interaction between the self and the self's projected perceptions of the other; between the driver at the wheel of the yellow convertible and the onlooker. In the case of J. S. Mill's Utilitarian, the two selves are contained with the individual. Self-awareness splits the self, giving rise to the Romantics' 'daemon of self-consciousness'.[20] As Nietzsche had it, we act as a *dividuum* rather than an *individuum*. It is that 'other' – be it the internal 'impartial spectator', or the projection of our peers' judgements – that denounces the self's true intent, and in so doing pushes the desired object just out of our reach. For the gentleman of means as much as the Utilitarian, the resulting challenge is the same: to somehow do by not intending to.

The Paradox of Consumption

Where do we stand today? The Veblen Treadmill has kept turning, as the result can be seen in the changing attitudes towards material goods of the younger consumer cohort in affluent societies. As the philosopher and bioethicist Peter Singer has said, 'This could be the last generation that flaunts their wealth.'[21] Luxury goods purveyors have, in fact, begun to despair over how millennials seem less taken in by conspicuous branded luxury than prior generations. The marketing professor and brand consultant Gina M. Eckhardt has described the bewilderment of these firms: 'Their reaction is, "What are we going to do? Our entire strategy is based on people buying products to signal their social status to others." That's what they learned in their MBA programs.'[22] Survey data support the occurrence of a shift: the millennial generation appears less likely than those that preceded to use material goods as a means of social distinction.[23]

The same arc of change can be observed across whole societies, as they pass through different stages of economic development. Today, emerging economies can be seen reprising the changing modes of Veblen's turn-of-the-century elites. When a new wealthy class emerges, as it did in post-communist countries after the fall of the Berlin Wall, it begins by embracing conspicuous consumption, until it opts for more ambiguous modes of distinction, leaving conspicuousness to the rising middle class. Accordingly, the growth markets for luxury brands are currently all found in emerging economies like China, India, and Brazil. Young Chinese consumers, for instance, claim to value 'having the latest products' twice as highly as their Italian, American, or British peers.

This shift in attitudes, across generations in affluent societies, and across societies along the development spectrum, reflects a process that is hardwired into consumption patterns.

The paradox of consumption is that the more things there are to buy – flashy material objects, leisure, or philanthropy – and the greater the material means people have to acquire them, the fewer things of actual value can be bought. Consumer goods do less and less for us, precisely as their availability increases – and this, *because* their availability increases.

To claim that consumer society is on its last legs, that it has reached a stage of 'decadence', as the commentator Ross Douthat suggests in his recent book, *The Decadent Society*, is common enough.[24] Even some economists have viewed consumer society as doomed from the start. Fred Hirsch's classic *Social Limits to Growth* may be the high point of this line of argument, claiming that there are limits to how much economic growth can improve overall well-being, given how much of individual well-being is tied to social comparison and a concern for keeping up with the Joneses. Hirsch coined the term 'positional goods' to denote goods whose main value comes from signalling status through their intrinsic scarcity. In recent years, the economist Robert H. Frank has become the main proponent of Hirsch's line of argument. He often repeats Hirsch's evocative phrase: when everyone stands on tiptoe, no one sees any better.[25]

These beliefs tend towards something of a Malthusian logic: just as Thomas Malthus thought that, given the rate of population growth, the earth would soon run out of resources, these critics claim that because of the positional nature of consumer goods, one soon runs out of elite space, which is by definition limited. Upward mobility gives people the impression that once they can afford the lifestyle they imagined for themselves, they will finally feel immense satisfaction. But when (if) they finally get there, they realise that the goods they sought are either of a limited number, like paintings of Old Masters that have been priced out through demand, or that they are prone to crowding, like the Piazza San Marco, which teems with tourists trying to snap a selfie away from the other selfie stick-wielding tourists. In a world competing for positional goods, Hirsch argued, only a small group can ever derive the satisfaction of being on top. Everyone else is assured frustration.

But just as Malthus got it wrong – because he badly underestimated the earth's bounty, when combined with human ingenuity – so too do these arguments underestimate our ability to generate new objects of aspiration. Paintings by Titian may be in limited supply, but the contemporary art market keeps producing new art that keeps fetching ever higher prices (regularly outbidding those Old Masters). For better or worse, we continue to discover new holiday destinations. In other words, economic growth can also be used to relieve congestion, akin to adding extra lanes to the motorway. So while there are indeed social limits on how much economic growth can contribute to well-being, these do not come down to competition over the same positional goods, because the market, in its inventiveness, keeps generating novel planes of comparison.

Rather, the limits on the gains from consumption are the result of social learning. As we get better at detecting others' intent, we increase our efforts at disguising our own. Of course, everyone else is busy doing the same. An arms race results, with familiar results. For every person of means who has of late embraced a decluttered, minimalist life as a means of conveying an enlightened knowingness, there is an even keener observer who is quick to dismiss such flights to hyper-curated minimalism as just 'another boring product wealthy people can buy' – an obvious class signifier at best, morally dubious self-righteousness at worst.[26] The Veblen Treadmill moves faster than our ability to acquire the right material goods. The result is that those vying for social esteem can no longer purchase, capture, or reach for. Instead, they must be born into, come in with, and stumble on. In a market society such as ours, this leads to an obvious problem. Market actors are good at saving, planning, and reaching for; they are less good at stumbling on.

Turnips vs Transcendence: The Evolving Basket of Goods

Eventually, affluent consumer societies become byproduct societies. The Veblen Treadmill is one reason for this: products become byproducts as the audience clues into the intent behind their acquisition. The other reason is simpler still. In a subsistence economy, individuals are content with trying to get by. But through economic growth, a decreasing portion of individuals' basket of goods is made up of subsistence goods like food and physical safety. As Adam Smith observed of the wealthy landowner, 'The capacity of his stomach ... will receive no more than that of the meanest peasant.' The remainder of their wealth is dedicated to less tangible, and more elusive goods. But these are also more likely to operate as byproducts: they elude direct will and are impervious to purposeful efforts at attaining them.

As societies grow more affluent, they climb Maslow's hierarchy of needs. I still remember learning about Abraham Maslow and his pyramid in a high-school home economics class. It made a big impression on me. It was my first encounter with a theory capacious enough to account for all social behaviour. Maslow ranked five basic human needs in a hierarchical pyramid, with those at the bottom requiring satisfaction before the higher ones could be attended to. First come purely physiological needs, like water and food and shelter. Then follows the need for safety: a feeling of personal physical or financial security. But next come needs of an entirely different sort: the third rung is love and friendship, followed by Adam

Smith's basic human motivator: esteem. And at the very top is the most ambiguous of the lot, what Maslow initially called 'self-actualisation'.

Maslow kept updating his own hierarchy, and eventually added another need to the top of his pyramid, with a more ambiguous name still: *transcendence*. As I recall, my home economics class left that one out, presumably because explaining how the self might transcend itself to a group of twelve-year-olds proved too much for our teacher, who doubled as the PE instructor. But in a gesture that the nineteenth-century European Romantics and their American Transcendentalist cousins would recognise, Maslow came to think that transcendence was where the whole question lay.

For our purposes, the takeaway from Maslow's hierarchy of needs is that as we ascend the pyramid, we go from things that are readily obtainable – food on our plates and a roof over our heads – to needs that cannot be satisfied through direct exertions of the will. As societies grow more affluent, we thus spend more time and effort seeking to attain things that come to look increasingly like byproducts. Put another way, economic development shifts our attention away from the type of good that the discipline of economics studies – the type that is prone to scarcity – and towards goods that economics purposefully leaves out of its purview. In a fitting progression, Maslow himself became interested in progressively higher rungs on his hierarchy of needs, and he spent the last part of his work and career focused entirely on the very tip of his pyramid, asking how people might reach 'transcendence'.

A Recipe for Frustration

Running on Veblen's Treadmill and ascending Maslow's Pyramid, market societies turn into byproduct societies as they grow more affluent. An increasing portion of the things their citizens strive for become of the kind that eludes conscious effort. This, in itself, is cause for celebration. The door is opened to getting on to what Keynes called 'our real problems – the problems of life and of human relations, of creation and behaviour and religion'.

The issue, however, is that market societies reach this level of affluence by being market societies: devoting themselves to consumption, instrumental behaviour, and the growth these produce. This was Adam Smith's double insight: the consumption of baubles and trinkets by the well-to-do vying to impress one another may be absurd, but it also fuels economic growth, which benefits the rest of us; it is the very stuff that makes the wealth of nations.[27] Leaving aside the more recent appreciation for how the love of baubles and trinkets of some may have pernicious effects on the well-being of others, there remains an even more fundamental problem. If market societies progressively turn into byproduct societies, how do they wean themselves off the beliefs that led them to reach a state of material plenty in the first place? And what happens if the weaning fails?

Individuals striving towards goals make up the building blocks of market societies. They view all desirable states as attainable through planning, saving, and reaching for. The whole point is to be highly aware, to correct the trajectory in mid-air if it seems like it may be falling short. It is this goal-seeking behaviour that produces mission statements, company visions, performance targets, to-do lists, end-of-year resolutions. 'Never stop believing in your dreams,' we tell children. 'Keep your eyes on the prize. You can do anything you set your mind to!' But what if setting your mind to it is precisely what renders that 'anything' unachievable? What if the optimal strategy rules out the possibility of strategy?

Market actors continue to apply the means for obtaining the objects on the lower rungs of Maslow's hierarchy to the upper rungs. But in a byproduct society, this results in frustration. Relying on consumption to achieve social effects – once these can no longer be attained through simple consumption – leads to disappointment.

Much has been made of how consumer society feeds this confusion. To recast it in the terms used here, the advertising industry can be said to be in the business of promising values that operate as byproducts via consumer goods. Soda, perfumes, and mouthwash come with the assurance of social approval and devoted friends. The self-improvement business does the same with Goop jade eggs and expensive creams, thriving on the same ingenious combination of promise and let-down. They follow the lead of the conman who sells the same dog over and over, having trained it to escape and return home after a week.

Relying on the means developed during the industrial nineteenth century to attain twenty-first-century post-industrial aspirations generates brisk business for therapists of all stripes, who have long been tasked with picking up the pieces. The psychology profession is thus well placed to diagnose the social ailments resulting from treating byproducts as if they were readily attainable consumer goods. The psychoanalyst Leslie Farber describes the upshot: 'The consequence of willing what cannot be willed is that we fall into the distress we call anxiety.' And echoing the Romantics' cursed self, its doubting eye trained on itself, Farber warns, 'Since anxiety, too, opposes such willing, should we, in our anxiety about anxiety, now try to will away that anxiety, our fate is still more anxiety.'

This insight about the effect of willing what cannot be willed remains poorly understood, including by psychiatrists themselves. As I write this, the world is in the thick of the coronavirus pandemic. Newspapers have taken to offering advice on how to boost one's immune defences against the virus. Among other facts, there is an understanding that heightened stress is related to lowered immunity. This has led health authorities to order people to relax, as if the command could produce anything but its opposite. A professor of psychiatry and behavioural sciences at Northwestern University thus tells the *New York Times*, 'My general advice would be that people should try to reduce their stress over all ... Stress impacts your immune system, and the more you're stressed, the more you're reducing your body's ability to fight off infections.'[28] One's pulse is apt to rise just *reading* such advice. The failure of logic rests in the belief that understanding the desirability of the outcome is enough to bring it about, when the opposite is more likely. The command 'don't think of an elephant' is not made any more achievable by adding that your life depends on not thinking of the elephant. It would have been more useful to instruct people to remember to water all their plants, or work on touching their toes every morning – by deflecting their intent, they might become more likely to 'reduce their stress over all' than when making it their explicit goal.

Farber appears to view the issue as a peculiarly modern one. 'Increasingly we apply the will ... to those portions of life that not only will not comply, but that become distorted – or even vanish – under such coercion.'[29] The premise is that the will was once effective, and now no longer is; though Farber falls short of explaining *why* it is that wilful exertions would have grown less fruitful over time.

Like others, Farber uses the analogy of insomnia to represent a desirable state, deep sleep, that eludes direct effort: 'I can will ... going to bed, but not sleeping.' Similarly, I can buy a yellow convertible, but not the admiration of bystanders, even though the latter is my true intent. In both cases, the more forceful that intent, the less likely it is to bear fruit. The political scientist Jon

Elster picks up on the example of insomnia in such a mercilessly accurate passage that it is worth reproducing in full:

> First, one tries to will an empty mind, to blot out all preoccupying thoughts. The attempt, of course, is contradictory and doomed to fail, since it requires a concentration of mind that is incompatible with the absence of concentration one is trying to bring about. Secondly, upon understanding that this is not going to work, one tries to induce a state of pseudo-resignation to insomnia. One acts, that is, as if one were persuaded that sleep is going to elude one, by taking up a book, having a snack or a drink, etc. But at the back of one's mind there is always the idea that one can cheat insomnia by ignoring it, and that the cheerful indifference to sleep will make sleep come at last. But then, thirdly, one understands that this is not going to work either. Next, real resignation sets in, based on a real, not a sham, conviction that the night will be long and bleak. And then, finally and mercifully, sleep comes. For veteran insomniacs, who know the game inside out, the last stage never arrives. They know too well the benefits of resignation to be able to achieve it.[30]

Note how this account also features a treadmill effect. The more seasoned the unlucky insomniac, the more impervious to effort sleep becomes. And though the insomniac is nominally a single individual, Elster's account actually reveals two selves at work: the first tries to lull the second to sleep by various means, all the while trying to keep that second self from becoming aware of what the first self is up to. Once the second self is on to the first self's scheme, the game is up. Until all hope is truly lost, which releases the grip of the will, and sleep becomes possible anew. In fact, the process resembles nothing so much as a parent soothing a baby to sleep. That too works best if the parent is seen to be doing anything but what they intend to: telling a story, singing a song, taking a drive around the block. This multiple self, as I argue in the last two chapters, is an essential characteristic of byproduct states. It may even hold a key to addressing the paradox that interests us.

Another psychotherapist, Viktor Frankl, the author of the best-selling *Man's Search For Meaning*, identifies these as problems arising from what he calls 'hyper-intention', that is, excesses of will. Frankl also places insomnia in this category, together with a range of other ailments. He views patients dealing with sexual impotence, for instance, as victims of the same tragic conundrum: 'The more a man tries to demonstrate his sexual potency ... the less they are able to succeed. Pleasure is, and must remain, a side-effect or by-product, and is destroyed and spoiled to the degree to which it is made a goal in itself.'[31] As with social esteem and deep sleep, so too with physical lust. Intention proves counterproductive, as does all that accompanies it: the conceiving, the planning, and the striving. Here too, we are dealing with a divided self. The point of lust is that we cede to something beyond our control. This gives us both the angst of Frankl's impotent patients, and the symmetrically opposite torments of a St Augustine, trying in vain to be good, but powerless before his errant lust.

Frankl's diagnosis of the issue as one that arises from excessive will is revealing. The common response in market societies to failure of any type is precisely the opposite: it is seen as a *weakness* of will. Someone will say, 'They didn't want it badly enough. They should have tried harder,' they will sigh. The solution, as per St Augustine, is then to bolster intent, to steel our will. In this case, this proves exactly the wrong remedy.

A Persistent Idea

The stakes vary, but the game stays the same. The paradox of consumption, whereby we become less able to buy the things we strive for just as we grow better able to afford them, is of the same form as the paradox that befalls Elster's veteran insomniacs, or Frankl's sexually impotent patients. And all of these are but different versions of the quandary that J. S. Mill wrestled with in the 1820s, while in the grips of existential depression.

Ideas can hang in the air for decades, even centuries, before they are recognised for what they are, given a name, and put into service. So it was with this one. 'The only chance is to treat, not happiness, but some end external to it, as the purpose of life … without dwelling on it or thinking about it, without either forestalling it in imagination, or putting it to flight by fatal questioning.'[32] J. S. Mill's insight went largely unnoticed while it remained confined to that brief passage in the description of his period of depression.

Yet Mill kept seeing the same paradox in different guises. Take the benefits of education, a topic Mill considered at some length, likely because of the peculiarity of his own upbringing. As he wrote in an 1846 article, 'What shapes the character is not what is purposely taught, so much as the unintentional teaching of institutions and social relations.' The formation of good character, in this way, resists deliberate inculcation. It only lets itself be affected by lessons which do not appear to be lessons.*

---

* This rings true to me. The unspoken, second-order objectives of my political science courses, like developing a reflex for critical thinking, students' conception of themselves as citizens, an appreciation for how their incentives shape the incentives of those around them, often feel more important than the first-order lessons about, say, the history of mercantilism. But my suspicion is that these second-order lessons would be transmitted less effectively if they were presented front and centre as the intent of the class.

But it took another Utilitarian thinker to take up J. S. Mill's idea and render it fit for use, by giving it, for starters, a less unwieldy label. Henry Sidgwick makes up the third branch of the holy trinity of Utilitarianism, together with Bentham and Mill. His 1874 *Methods of Ethics* is usually thought of as the culmination of the Utilitarian school of thought, and it is widely considered one of the greatest books ever written on moral philosophy. It is there that we find the classic statement of what has come to be known as the *paradox of hedonism*. As Sidgwick writes: 'Here comes into view what we may call the fundamental paradox of Hedonism, that the impulse towards pleasure, if too predominant, defeats its own aim.' Ever since, having thus obtained its imprimatur among philosophers from Sidgwick, the paradox of hedonism has been taken up and remarked on with increasing frequency.

Here is a more recent formulation from the philosopher Peter Railton:

> The hedonist, looking around him, may discover that some of those who are less concerned with their own happiness than he is, and who view people and projects less instrumentally than he does, actually manage to live happier lives than he despite his dogged pursuit of happiness ... the hedonist, it would appear, ought not to be a hedonist.[33]

Similarly, the philosopher Thomas Scanlon invokes Sidgwick's refinement of J. S. Mill's idea when proposing what he calls the 'paradox of teleology', which Scanlon sees as operating with regards to friendship. We recognise friendship as valuable, he writes, but we can also see that it somehow defies Utilitarian reasoning: 'The fact that it is good that friendship should occur, but that in order for it to occur, people have to be moved by reasons other than the reason of promoting the occurrence of friendship, is an instance of what might be called a "paradox of teleology".'[34] The same could be said of romantic love. Loving and being loved comes with many benefits. But if during your wedding vows, you explain that you are entering into holy matrimony because you have read convincing studies showing that monogamous relationships increase life expectancy, and that being held by another human being produces spikes in dopamine levels leading to an increase in well-being, your new spouse may well throw their wedding ring in your face. The game of seduction is premised on a convincing claim of disinterest.

In all these cases, a purpose-driven approach to desirable things, by which we try to maximise what we find valuable, proves self-defeating. Make these your conscious goals, and they recede from view – as Mill wrote, they are 'put to flight'. If this sounds like some chestnut of Eastern philosophy, there is good reason for it. While much of Western thought has been concerned with our ability to alleviate scarcity and achieve states of plenty, Eastern traditions have long shown greater interest in *privative states*. These are states that are characterised by an absence, be it of distraction, pride, will, or consciousness itself.

As the French scholar of Chinese literature Romain Graziani observes, 'very early in the history of Taoist thought we find the intuition that the decisive actions and behaviours that can transform someone may only take place if they are not done consciously, that is, if they are not mentally represented as the voluntary purpose of the action. They are essentially indirect results of actions undertaken for other ends.'[35] So while J. S. Mill may have been the first figure in Western thought to explicitly state the challenge posed by byproducts, Taoist texts like the *Zhuangzi* had taken up a similar idea some 2,000 years earlier.

Graziani points to a passage from the Chinese political philosopher Han Fei, written in the third century BCE, which is so close to the central idea that interests us that it is worth citing in full:

> Those who hold non-action and non-thought as a state of emptiness constantly focus their mind on this state of emptiness without being able to forget it, and that is how they are still governed by the desire to make themselves empty. Emptiness can only mean that the will is not governed by anything. Now, being governed by the intention to become empty means not to be empty. Non-action that defines proper emptiness means, on the contrary, that one does not take non-action as a constant rule. It is only if you do not take non-action as a constant rule that you can have real emptiness.[36]

It's all there, isn't it? Von Kleist's doomed youth, Veblen's well-to-do, Veyne's Roman emperors. Kwakiutl aristocrats trying to out-gift one another, modern-day philanthropists vying for the same. Veteran insomniacs and the sexually impotent. To these, the coming chapters will add bakers and beer brewers vying for customers, poets searching for inspiration, Silicon Valley coders seeking a state of flow, and politicians trying to gain their constituents' trust. All of them confronting the same recurrent paradox: the thing yearned for becomes less attainable, the greater the effort expended to attain it.

The challenge posed by desirable states that operate as byproducts was already daunting in the nineteenth century, when the young J. S. Mill was undone by their implications for his inherited Utilitarian view of the world. But as I have tried to show in this chapter, the challenge has only become more vexing since Mill's time. What Mill, Sidgwick, Railton, Scanlon, and the more recent thinkers who have observed some version of the paradox of hedonism fail to appreciate is that the issue is becoming more of an issue. As market societies grow more affluent, they are increasingly confronted with the paradox of consumption: individuals find that fewer of the things they seek, like the esteem of others, can be obtained through consumption, just as their purchasing power increases. Having secured the necessities, these individuals find themselves increasingly vying for desirables that are not limited by scarcity, but by their resistance to wilful effort. Market societies turn into byproduct societies, but market actors continue to employ the same means to achieve their ends. Frustration results.

If our most dear aims are not attained through striving, but as unintended outcomes of unrelated actions, then this represents the prime flaw in advanced market societies. That flaw has never been as visible, or consequential, as it is today. Mill's Utilitarian caveat has never felt so current. How do market societies, ruled as they are by wilful intent and deliberate effort, adapt to their mutation into byproduct societies? This is the question we take up next.

3

Why Disinterest Pays

There is no neater encapsulation of the belief that self-interest makes the world go round than the alliterative line from Adam Smith's *Wealth of Nations*: 'It is not from the benevolence of the butcher, the brewer, or the baker that we expect our dinner, but from their regard to their own interest.'[1]

Adam Smith's baker goes through the trouble of waking early and kneading his sourdough because there is gain to be had from it, rather than out of any charitable impulse towards humanity.[2] Smith is saying that we all put our trust in bakers' recognition of their self-interest. By contrast, as he adds in a later passage, 'I have never known much good done by those who affected to trade for the public good.'

Yet today's bakers are more likely to claim they are kneading their sourdough out of an abiding passion, or a deep love for the craft of breadmaking – anything, in fact, but self-interest. Popular accounts play up such disinterested motives. 'It's a passion for both of us. We're not in it for the money,' says a baker in Clark County, WA.[3] 'While they say they're not in it for the money, they're taking the internet by storm,' gushes a headline in the *Israeli Times*. One half of the challah-baking duo agrees, assuring us that 'money isn't the reason she does it'.[4] Another story about another baker from my own hometown on Québec's Gatineau River plays the same tune. A former banker, this baker coyly confesses, 'A lot of people told me, you're out of your mind.' As the local news reports in a breathless article titled 'A Baker's Bliss', 'he knows he needs to grow, but doesn't want that growth to be at the expense of his product, or vision. "For me," says the banker-turned-baker, "it's about the craft."' And then comes the inevitable climax: 'I don't want to be a businessman. I want to be an artisan.'[5]

In part, these claims to passion reflect how most people do not set off for work with the sole intent of paying the rent. Wage work is only tolerable insofar as it's a site of interpersonal exchange and a source of self-fulfilment. But there is another reason for these avowals of passion: admitting that one's motivation is naked self-interest is somehow off-putting; it might even prove bad for business. That's because most consumers today, with apologies to Adam Smith, would likely opt for the passionate baker over the baker pursuing gain alone. There is a warm feeling, and reassurance, in believing our bread was kneaded by someone who was acting out of passion, rather than interest. Somehow, we trust the former more; we have an instinctive sense for which of the two breads is more likely to contain potassium bromate and added sugars, and we make our choice accordingly.

The advent of the passionate baker who's 'not in it for the money' is only one example of the artisan's baffling reappearance in contemporary commerce. What's odder still is that the figure of the artisan is flourishing at the very heart of those pockets of the economy otherwise devoted to high-tech knowledge and service industries. The management consultant turned maker of artisanal jam has become a trope. As one such convert put it, having redirected his skills and energy to making small-batch mustard, 'McKinsey was just not what I wanted.'[6] And it is knowledge workers who appear most eager to spend on and support passionate producers: craft bakers and farmer's markets do their briskest business, at highest mark-ups, in affluent coastal urban enclaves, far from the actual farms of the heartland.

As with Adam Smith's bakers, so too with brewers. The beer industry has witnessed a bewildering development over the last decades: from an oligopolistic chase for economies of scale through merging global conglomerates, it has given way to an industry where efficiency has actually been precipitously *decreasing*: with the rise of microbreweries, the cost and number of people required to brew the same amount of beer has grown by multiples. In a recurrent pattern, 'Goliaths are tumbling, Davids are ascendant.'[7]

Profit-seeking is inimical to the artisan's incentives. Products said to be 'artisanal' – a label the desirability of which has quickly corroded its meaning – are required to be born of passion rather than profit. For a brand of soft drink, pasta sauce, organic juice, or kombucha to go big, it must declare itself to be purposefully small, far removed from concerns of productivity, efficiency, or standardised production. It must have been started for its own sake, with no regard for its commercial success.[8] World domination is increasingly the preserve of those who manage to eschew ambition.

I have kept these examples purposefully quaint, yet the phenomenon goes far beyond the recent trends for artisanal bread and mustard in urban enclaves. Why does it seem that Adam

Smith's phrasing has lost some of its hold over us? Why are we drawn to claims of passion, rather than assertions of self-interested behaviour?

To be sure, the insight behind Adam Smith's baker remains valid in many aspects of the economy. Our belief in what constitutes others' self-interest still serves to reassure us. Just as Smith trusted his baker to provide his bread because there was gain to be had from baking it, the US economy was largely built on the enforcement of such trust through contracts. Part of the reason we trust aeroplanes not to go down, beyond government safety codes, lies in the knowledge that any accident does untold damage to an airline's reputation, and that airline executives therefore have every reason to keep a good record of safety, because retaining their jobs and year-end bonuses depends on maintaining value for the company's shareholders. We have a deeply internalised sense for how the economic-legal system has constructed a complex harmony between our interests and those of the producers of the goods we purchase, and we trust in that harmony. We board the plane because we rely on that system's self-enforcing nature.

Much of the formal economy thus remains based on such offsetting relations between self-interested actors serving as checks on one another's behaviour. In fact, much of the economy has no other purpose but the creation and maintenance of those countervailing chains of self-interest. And as I argue below, the sheer cost of this formidable institutional edifice actually contributes to the appeal of passion for self-interested actors.

But in the case of the passionate baker, something else is afoot. The baker's reluctance to embrace typical market incentives seems to carry positive market effects. In this case, disinterest pays: the market rewards those who reject it. Does the phenomenon matter beyond artisanal bread in wealthy urban enclaves?

Yes. In fact, the economic value of disinterest lies at the very heart of the founding myth of capitalism.

The Original (Reluctant) Capitalists

Another thinker, another mental breakdown. We are in 1897, in the German city of Heidelberg, one of the epicentres of the German Idealists and the Romantic thinkers. Max Weber was neither. He was, instead, a consummate workaholic, an insomniac prone to bouts of angst and depression. Working himself to mental exhaustion, he had to quit his enviable perch at the University of Heidelberg while still in his thirties, finding himself burnt out and unable to deliver his lectures.

But just as John Stuart Mill's mental breakdown led to the insight that would colour the rest of his life's work, Max Weber emerged from his own burn-out in 1904 to write one of the foundational texts of sociology, *The Protestant Ethic and the Spirit of Capitalism*. Weber spent the rest of his life revising, resentfully defending, and adding ever more content to it. The replies to his critics that accompanied later editions were soon longer than the original book. How fitting, then, that *The Protestant Ethic* is likely the greatest scholarly treatise ever written on workaholism.*

---

* Several biographers have suggested that Weber's sensitivity about *The Protestant Ethic* and the defensive tone with which he lashed out against critics were due to how he viewed their critiques as attacks on his own personal manic character. Weber's wife, Marianne, complained that their wedding had to be scheduled around a work project. Weber himself let on that his work was a means of staving off his inclinations towards depression: 'After years of dreadful torment I feared a profound depression would set in. It did not happen, and I believe it was because I worked constantly and did not let my brain or nervous system get any rest. Quite apart from my natural need to work, this is one reason why I am so very reluctant

Weber's Exhibit A is Benjamin Franklin, whom Weber holds up as the embodiment of the 'spirit' he was investigating. *The Protestant Ethic* begins with a lengthy quote from Franklin, taken from his *Advice to a Young Tradesman*, written 150 years before Weber's time, in 1748. It is to this sermon that we owe the phrase, 'time is money':

Remember, that time is money. He that can earn ten shillings a day by his labour, and goes abroad, or sits idle, one half of that day, though he spends but sixpence during his diversion or idleness, ought not to reckon that the only expense; he has really spent, or rather thrown away, five shillings besides.

Weber was trying to account for a long-standing puzzle: since ancient times, commerce had been an object of disrepute, condemned as greed and avarice. So how was it that it came to be seen as virtuous in parts of Northern Europe and then America, where it flourished like nowhere else? As Weber sets out in the book's opening passage: 'How, then, did what was, at best, behaviour which was morally no more than tolerated, become a "calling" as understood by Benjamin Franklin?' And secondly, how was it that New England Puritans and their descendants, Franklin among them, did so astonishingly well at the money-making game?

The story Weber tells is among the best known in all of social science. Few books have been as thoroughly pored over and rehashed as *The Protestant Ethic*. It has become permanently fused with the founding myth of the United States. And like all such myths, the story told by Weber has been bent to the needs of

to make a really perceptible pause in my work.' Letter from Max to Marianne Weber, 20 July 1894, in Joachim Radkau, *Max Weber: A Biography*, Polity Books.

every faction in every age. It has been enlisted both as a warning against a culture of mindless consumption, and as its opposite; a managerial thesis on how to succeed in business, and an explanation of why some societies prove better at it than others. This malleability is precisely what has led to the book's continued relevance: every generation has rewritten the Weberian story for its purposes, emphasising the angle most relevant to their time and place.

Allow me to rewrite it in turn. In Weber's account, the Spirit of Capitalism was borne aloft in an unlikely way by the Reformation. Only an insurgent set of religious ideas could dislodge the sinful image of moneymaking etched into Christian thought since its beginnings. As products of seventeenth-century Calvinism, the English and Dutch Puritans advocated a sober life of hard work and self-discipline as the only means of assuring themselves that they were among the elect.[9] These were Ben Franklin's ancestors. Franklin's father, as Weber never tires of reminding us, was himself a Calvinist minister. The Puritans carried these Calvinist ideals of toil and restraint with them across the Atlantic, to New England, where they applied themselves to their respective tasks with historically unprecedented zeal. The result was the transformation of work from an unfortunate necessity — what it had been for centuries — to a religious *calling*.

The Puritans' convictions served them well. The colonies of New England prospered like no other. The Puritans abhorred luxuries and condemned all pleasures of the flesh. They were also partial, as those who have read Margaret Atwood's *The Handmaid's Tale* will know, to a rather cheerless sense of style.*

---

* Weber saw in this preference for unadorned, uniform-like clothing the spiritual underpinning of capitalist standardised methods of production: 'The powerful tendency toward increasing uniformity of lifestyle, which today is encouraged

Their ascetic compulsion to save meant they had little to spend, so they reinvested all their profits into their budding enterprises. Wearing the same scratchy linen shirt day in and day out, the Puritan baker used the proceeds to open several other outposts, until he found himself at the head of a chain of bakeries that spanned the county. The Puritan baker's peers, the butcher and the brewer, all did the same,[10] and before long, the Puritans found themselves the prosperous American sons of industry we paint them as today.

Such is the conventional narrative: the Puritans grew prosperous because they spent little, and saved much. And yet this misses the most interesting bit of the story. Deferring gratification and reinvesting profits makes for pretty pedestrian business advice; it's not exactly a great secret of management. Insofar as it is an effective instrumental strategy, it can be readily emulated.

No, the secret of the Puritan baker, which business management textbooks are not well placed to grasp, lies in the nature of his *intent*. It lies in the fact that profit never occurred to the Puritans as being the object of their pursuit. The irony of the originators of the Weberian capitalist spirit is that making prosperity the goal of their toil would have been viewed as deeply reprehensible. Luther and Calvin had been unequivocal in their condemnation of usury and lust for lucre. In pursuing their calling with blind determination, the Puritans never intended to give birth to any Spirit of Capitalism. They were aiming at something entirely different. They sought to increase God's glory and subject themselves to his purpose, and in so doing, to

by the capitalist interest in the "standardization" of production, has its spiritual basis in the rejection of the worship of the creature.' It seems equally likely that a natural kinship between Utilitarianism and efficiency was at the basis both of the Puritans' sartorial preferences and the convergence of capitalist industry towards standardised methods of production.

convince themselves that they were destined for salvation rather than damnation. The Puritans were so unbeatably good at the business of money-making because they were the only ones for whom making money was beside the point.[11]

Weber turned Adam Smith on his head. The Puritan baker worked hard not because he stood to gain financially, but because making bread from early morning was his *calling*, and by applying himself to it, he assured himself and those about him that he was among God's elect. Just like for Larry, the baker from Clark County, WA, baking was indeed a passion, in the fullest sense: an activity that transcends all worldly motivation. The blind aspect of the calling obliterated any consideration of efficiency, and increased output in the process.* The Puritan baker would have got up early and toiled away even if there was no money in it. Except that there was, and so his profits grew handsomely.

It just so happened that Benjamin Franklin's ancestors had inherited a belief system according to which the certainty of one's salvation was attained through hard work. As a result, the accumulation of wealth was tolerated as a side-effect of hard work and asceticism – but only ever as a side-effect. The Puritans did not stumble onto capitalism, as the conventional story goes. It was capitalism that found them. Capitalism realised what ideal market agents the Puritans were – precisely because they were not driven by market incentives – and it embraced them.

---

* Considerations of efficiency carried no sway, since the Puritan cared for the maximisation of *input*, rather than output. Along these lines, Ernest Gellner writes of the 'rigid attachment to the notion of a calling, an attachment which, through that rigidity, was itself impervious to instrumental considerations of efficiency'. Gellner, Ernest, 1987, 'The Gaffe-Avoiding Animal', in *Relativism and the Social Sciences*, Cambridge Paperback Library, p. 75.

What's more, had the Puritans been in fact motivated by market incentives, had they simply been trying to maximise their earnings, they would not have fared nearly as well. Weber suggests as much himself when he notes the prosperity of the Northern states as compared to the relative poverty of the Southern states. The rich New England colonies were founded by preachers fuelled by religious motivations, while the neighbouring colonies of the Southern states 'had been founded by great capitalists for business purposes'. The reluctant capitalists proved better at the capitalist game, while those who single-mindedly sought out profits continued to struggle.

Why might this be? What was it about the reluctance of the original bearers of the Spirit of Capitalism that proved the secret to success? For an answer, let's return to Weber's Exhibit A: Ben Franklin, the presumptive personification of the Spirit of Capitalism. The 'sermon' which Weber quotes from at such length turns out to be mostly interested in how a tradesman might attain and maintain his *credit score*:

> The most trifling actions that affect a man's credit are to be regarded. The sound of your hammer at five in the morning, or eight at night, heard by a creditor, makes him easy six months longer; but if he sees you at a billiard table, or hears your voice at a tavern, when you should be at work, he sends for his money the next day; demands it, before he can receive it, in a lump.

And Franklin goes on: 'It shows, besides, that you are mindful of what you owe; it makes you appear a careful as well as an honest man, and that still increases your *credit*.'[12]

Franklin's tradesman aspires not so much to honesty, as to projecting a convincing image of it – in this case by literally hammering it home: 'I am diligent, hear me toil.' The insistence on honesty is amusing, since Franklin makes plain that the hammering is a performance, and one meant for a specific audience: the creditor.

We are reminded of the great quandary of Veblen's gentleman of leisure from the previous chapter. How to communicate the expanse of his ease when no one is there to witness it? Perhaps Veblen's gentleman might, taking a leaf from Franklin's sermon, sing loud enough for all passers-by to hear and appreciate the extent of his idleness. This also brings to mind our current-day selfie-takers, who worry that if a moment has not been captured so that it may be posted and broadcast for their own audience, it's as if it hadn't really happened.

We find two common elements across these cases. The first is that the behaviour of all three characters is instrumental: Franklin's tradesman toils so as to appear reputable and increase his credit. Veblen's gentleman of leisure displays trophies as evidence of his leisure time. The contemporary selfie-takers post images on social media that are consistent with the personal identity they are trying to cultivate, as adventurous travellers or loving parents. In each case, the action is not done for its own sake; it serves as a means to an external end.

Which leads us to the second aspect these three characters hold in common, namely, the nature of that end. In each case, they are trying to convince an audience that they are in fact what they want to be seen as: an honest tradesman, a high-status gentleman, an adventurous traveller or a loving parent. All three characters are desperately trying to be believed: they are vying for *credibility*.

It's fitting that Benjamin Franklin's tradesman is so preoccupied with securing and maintaining his credit. 'Credit' comes from the Latin *creditum* and its root *credere*, which means to believe or to trust. In all these instances, that is what's at stake: to be believed. One needs credibility to obtain credit. Franklin understood that when it came to the Puritans, God was on the creditors' side, and the creditors knew it too. By tying themselves to God, the Puritans invested in their credibility. As a result, creditors doted on the Puritans.

That is where the key to the Puritans' commercial success lies. In striving for proof of their divine salvation rather than for economic gain, they benefited from an unprecedented level of commercial credibility. Just imagine doing business with a New England Puritan: knowing that work was the point of their existence, rather than a means to an external end, you could be entirely confident that they would never seek to exploit you or run away with your money. Because why would they? When they promised to pay you next week, you would readily believe them. In fact, you might believe them more than you believed yourself, knowing the lesser purity and greater shiftiness of your own motives. Similarly, you would never have to worry that your Puritan business partner was taking any shortcuts to save time at your expense, because in the Puritans' view of the world, effort was not an unfortunate requirement of work; it was the point.

Now, imagine two Puritans dealing with one another. They could fully trust in one another's integrity and diligence. They would not hesitate to perform a service now for payment later, nor would they need to check on the diligence of one another's work. Such was, in fact, the relation of Puritan employers to their workers. When the Puritan baker hired others like himself to help out as the bakery franchise grew, these made for unspeakably good workers. Weber saw this: 'The power of religious asceticism made available to [the Puritan employer] sober, conscientious, and unusually capable workers, who were devoted to work as the divinely willed purpose in life.' What more might a capitalist wish for? Here were labourers who toiled away regardless of the earthly rewards, whether or not they were supervised.

They were holding out for a far greater heavenly bounty; they were more concerned about God's stern look than the foreman's. They toiled under the spell of a system of belief that 'glorifies the faithful worker who does not look for profit, but lives according to the example of the apostles and is thus endowed with the charisma of discipleship'. In other words, a manager's dream!

In a single stroke, the Puritan ethos offered not only an army of devoted disciples-cum-workers, but it also absolved their masters from any ill feelings over the exploitation of their toil, since it was all being done to a holy purpose. As Weber put it, 'it also legalized the exploitation of this characteristic willingness to work by interpreting the employer's moneymaking as a "calling" too'. Looking over their accomplishments, these reluctant capitalists saw in their fortuitous prosperity the one sign they had of their divine election.

Using the terms introduced in the previous chapter, the Puritans owed their earthly success to treating wealth as a byproduct, rather than as a product of their work. Prosperity was a side-effect of an unrelated, and in fact entirely opposite end. We have encountered this logic before. To use J. S. Mill's phrase, the Puritans grew rich en passant: by happenstance, without aiming to – and precisely *because* they did not aim to.

This is why the view that the New England descendants of seventeenth-century Calvinists stumbled into capitalism has it backwards. The Puritans proved to be exemplary agents of capitalist ideas because they lacked capitalist motivations. It was capital that found and actively wooed the Puritan. And by Ben Franklin's time, the seduction was complete, the union fully consummated. God had been eclipsed, but the profit motive remained. Wealth, which until then had been an unanticipated byproduct, was turned into the intended product.

As a result, Franklin was left with advocating tricks that amounted to subterfuge. A convincing performance of honesty in the place of actual honesty, helped by the fact that honesty had once genuinely been the point. The very title of Weber's magnum opus contains this dance of opposites: The 'Protestant Ethic' and the 'Spirit of Capitalism' are like two magnets attracting and repelling one another in turn.

Weber himself witnessed parts of this dance with his own eyes. In a later essay on American churches, he described seeing an adult baptism in North Carolina, an event which made a great impression on him. Ten men and women, fully dressed, were submerged by a minister in the icy water of a mountain stream. Weber enquired after one of these new converts, an 'intelligent-looking young man', asking what had led him to undergo this 'procedure'. In response, he was told that the young man 'intended to open a bank in Mount Airy and needed a substantial loan'. As he pressed for an explanation, it came out that 'admission into the Baptist church was so important not so much on account of the potential Baptist clientele but rather to attract *non*-Baptist clients'.[13] The young man knew what he was doing: by being seen to take on the rigorous religious rites and beliefs of the Baptist church, he earned himself credibility in the eyes of his future customers – *especially* the non-Baptists among them, who presumably were all the more impressed by a degree of devotion which they themselves could never pretend to.[14]

The dance of opposites plays out in three moments. In the first, the original Protestant Ethic of Luther and Calvin condemns any hint of the profit motive, which it views as sinful. In the second, the belief that tireless work was proof of salvation among the New England Puritans proves to be an accidental key to economic success. In the third moment, by Franklin's time, the Spirit of Capitalism has swallowed the Protestant Ethic entirely, as the tradesman is reduced to mimicking the Puritan's gestures to advance his interests. Behaviour that was once spontaneous has grown affected. What had been performed to increase God's glory is now performed for the sake of convincing the creditor. Through this transmogrification in three parts, Puritan ascetism manages to turn itself into what Weber calls a 'philosophy of avarice'. The ascetism functions as a handmaiden to ambition, only to be eventually snuffed out by it.

But let's stay on the second moment of that dance for now. The very reluctance of the original capitalists proved the key to their economic success. How unusual was this? Far from being an exceptional case, the rewarding of a disinterested attitude with economic success turns out to be a mainstay of capitalism.

Why Disinterest Pays

The current-day Brooklyn baker and the original Puritan baker have much in common. They are both passionates, for starters. The Puritan baker is pursuing what Weber called a *Beruf*: a calling, in the religious sense of the word. But the Brooklyn baker claims to pursue a passion, too, one that has for its object the artisanal craft of breadmaking itself. And in both cases, they may be surprised to see how their passion pays off. Creditors trust them, as do their customers. Their passionate behaviour seems to mimic market incentives, but the similarity is pure happenstance. They have found themselves living out Robert Frost's vision, from what may be his most famous stanza: 'My object in living is to unite / My avocation and my vocation / As my two eyes make one in sight.' The two happen to coincide, and both our bakers are the better for it.

Neither the Brooklyn baker nor the Puritan baker is motivated by the incentives that Adam Smith would attribute to a baker, that is, those incentives imputed to market actors engaged in breadmaking. And benefiting from the same paradox, they both reap greater gains than Adam Smith's baker, who is motivated by gains alone. Creditors offer them easier terms, customers are willing to pay a premium for their sourdough. What's more, they owe these advantages to the same reason: they are believed. And the reason they are believed is that they are *disinterested*.

Disinterest, in this case, does not mean indifference, far from it. After all, both the Brooklyn baker and the Puritan baker are passionates. But their passion is pitched towards the activity itself – as religious calling or love of craft – rather than the advancement of their self-interest that might come from it. This is akin to the term's legal usage, where one might speak of a 'disinterested party' as a neutral arbiter in a dispute, that is, one who has no external stake in either side prevailing.[15] The arbiter is not without interests; she simply does not have a dog in that particular fight. As a result, both parties trust her to offer an impartial opinion. One thus pursues an activity in an 'interested' fashion when it is performed in order to reap some external gain. One remains 'disinterested' whenever one lacks such external ends, and engages in an activity for its own sake. It's useful to draw a connection here to the notion of byproducts from the prior chapter: disinterested entrepreneurs are those for whom commercial gains are merely the unintended byproduct of some non-commercial purpose – a passion, a calling, a vision.[16] That this genuinely disinterested entrepreneur is an ideal type, and that this ideal type remains a rare occurrence, does not take away from the commercial payoff of coming across as such.

The Brooklyn baker and the Puritan baker thus knead their dough *disinterestedly*, motivated by ends unrelated to commercial gains, while Adam Smith's bakers are *interested* insofar as they bake bread 'from their regard to their own interest'.* Now, where things become interesting is when self-interest and passion happen to coincide. It seems an enviable outcome, and

---

* Here, one might object by observing that the Puritan baker is also pursuing an external end, namely, reassuring himself of his status among the elect. Similarly, is

one that today is sought out by many. Ray Dalio, the billion-aire investor, is among them. As he advises in his best-selling *Principles*, 'make your passion and your work the same thing'.[17] It has become the mantra of a growing class of creative freelancers and entrepreneurs. But as the coming chapters show, anyone who actually tries to follow this advice, by wilfully making self-interested and disinterested motivations coincide, runs into a tricky problem.

We can already imagine who one such individual might be. Adam Smith's baker may be self-interested, and driven only by gain, but he is also a sensible businessman. He will soon see that the passionate baker is drawing more customers. As a result, the self-interested baker will have reason to pass himself off as passionate. The question is, can he pull it off? Can any calculated attempt at passion be convincing? When customers are choosing where to buy their sourdough, which of the two bakers will they believe?

the Brooklyn baker not in fact pursuing personal gratification as an external end? And thus are these two not pursuing their self-interest, in the same way as Adam Smith's baker? The risk of such a reading of (dis)interest is that it amounts to a familiarly circular conception: any action performed for any motive is then said to be performed in furtherance of that motive. Yet a meaningful distinction between interested and disinterested commerce can be preserved on the basis of how intrinsic to the task the individual's motivation is. In the case of the Puritan baker, religious beliefs turned work into a *Beruf*, a calling. The very notion of calling rests on this intrinsic aspect: a calling provides its own motivation. Similarly, the passionate Brooklyn baker is motivated by the love of the baking itself. And though Adam Smith's baker may well derive some gratification from his labour, it is the resulting commercial success that is his prime motivation, and it is to that motivation that Smith directs his trust. Personal gratification arises after the fact; it does not turn the baker's concerns for profit into an unintended byproduct.

'Believe Me': The Cornerstone of Capitalism

I have been referring to 'the market' in the way it is used in common usage: as an impersonal force, the water we all swim in. But now is a good moment to be more precise. What exactly do we mean by 'the market', and what is its relation to interest and disinterest?

To borrow the Romantics' favourite trope from Chapter 1, in the Garden of Eden, no market exists because none is needed. Adam and Eve have only to extend their hand if they desire a ripe fig, because a ripe fig is always hanging just within reach. They have no reason to exchange anything between the two of them. If Adam says, 'Eve, I'll give you two figs if you give me an orange,' Eve will reply, 'Whatever for? I can have as many figs as I want, and you can have as many oranges as you want.' But as soon as they are banished from Eden – via the consumption of another fruit, as it happens – things change.

The punishment that came with the Fall was that Adam and Eve would, from then on, have to toil for their daily bread. 'In the swaete of thy browe shalt thou eate thy breade,' God promised in anger. It was a bad day for humanity, but a very good day for economists: their discipline was born.

Economics arises from scarcity. Its classic definition, offered by Lord Lionel Robbins in 1932, goes simply as follows: 'Economics is the science which studies human behaviour as a relationship between ends and scarce means which have alternative uses.' As soon as there aren't enough ripe figs for everyone, it becomes interesting to study which humans get to eat how many, and how it's determined. Suddenly, those people who happen to be living under a fig tree have many figs, while others have none. Luckily, those other people may have spotted an orange grove nearby. The combination of scarcity and differences in endowments creates the potential for beneficial exchange: 'I'll trade you two

fresh figs for an orange.' In the face of scarcity, efficiency suddenly becomes relevant: we want the biggest output from the
least amount of input, the most breade from the least swaete on
our browe.

But as it turns out, scarcity and differences in endowments are
not sufficient for a market to form. It is not quite true that, as the
economist Oliver Williamson put it, 'in the beginning there were
markets'.[18] To extend our allegory, once humanity is banished
from Eden, it finds itself in a different state of nature: something closer to a Hobbesian world, where everyone is fearful
of everyone else, and everyone must look out for themselves.
Insofar as life is 'nasty, brutish and short', it is in part because
everyone is reliant on themselves alone to meet their susten-
ance needs.

The challenge that must be overcome is the fear of being
exploited. As soon as we go beyond ourselves, or our smallest
unit – the family, or at most the tribe – that fear of exploitation
makes any exchange difficult. I have no guarantee that you will
hand over the figs in exchange for my oranges. Especially since as
it happens, figs ripen three months later than oranges: if I deliver
my oranges now, how do I know that you will keep your end of
the bargain by delivering your figs three months from now?

As the size of the market grows, so does the fundamental
problem of credibility. There are suddenly greater gains to be had
from expanding to faraway markets, where people have never
seen oranges before, but the risks are greater, too. I often need
to rely on strangers to reach those faraway markets. I may trust
a cousin, or maybe a neighbour, to deliver my figs in exchange
of oranges, but I will certainly not entrust my shipment of goods
to some unknown ship's captain who promises to ferry them to a
distant port and bring back the proceeds in a month.

Crucially, the ship's captain has as much to gain from convincing the merchant as the merchant has in believing the ship's

captain. The same goes for Ben Franklin's tradesman and the creditor. Since the exchange is by definition mutually advantageous, both stand to gain from coming up with a way to believe one another. This proves to be an exceedingly difficult challenge to solve. Yet doing so is a requirement for any market to function.

Social scientists conceive of credibility as convincing others of one's 'type'. I may be the good type of tradesman: steadfast, diligent, 'good for it'. The trouble is that there also exists another type of tradesman, who will abscond with any money he is entrusted with and never be seen again. The resulting challenge for the diligent tradesman is that as much as he would like to communicate that he is of the good type, there is no credible way of doing this, so long as the cheating tradesman could mimic it perfectly. Merely loudly announcing one's honesty, for instance, won't do, since the bad type could make the same claim just as loudly. The mantra of credibility is that *talk is cheap*. 'Cheap talk', in fact, is the technical term that game theorists use to describe empty commitments.

The problem of credibility underlies the formation of political markets, too. Would-be political leaders want citizens to entrust them with power, but they have no way of credibly demonstrating that they are the type of leader who will not abuse that power. Those citizens realise that if they *are* in fact dealing with a despot in disguise, any power granted may never be ceded again. History is littered with would-be benevolent leaders who proved to be despots in disguise, taking office through democratic means and then refusing to step down, dragging their countries into chaos in the process. Fearing this, citizens may refuse to delegate power in the first place. Everyone is worse off as a result: citizens lack a leader, and the leader is unable to rule. So what is a would-be non-tyrannical leader to do?

The problem is a general one. All transactions include some element of risk: the figs may be poisoned; the ship's captain may abscond with the cargo; the benevolent-sounding leader may quickly turn tyrant. Much of the game of seduction that takes place both in commerce and in politics comes down to an attempt at being believed: 'I am the dependable and committed type, rather than the fickle and unfaithful alternative.' But mere words may not be enough, since those words are cheap: they can be spoken by anyone. The problem only grows with the size of the market, as we come to know less and less about any given individual. All our dealings become impersonal exchanges. To distinguish themselves from the 'bad types' – be they cheating tradesmen, secretly lazy workers, or tyrannical leaders – the good types must act in a way that the bad types are unable to mimic.

There are only two known solutions to the problem of credibility. The first is the solution favoured by economists, and it consists of putting down a *costly stake* of some kind. That is, in making it pricey to break one's vow. If others see that I stand to incur a significant penalty from being anything short of honest and hardworking, then they are more likely to believe that I will be honest and hardworking. The existence of such costs requires a system: it can be an informal system that allows me to stake my reputation on being reliable and faithful, or one that formally sanctions anyone who breaks their commitments. The cost comes from dirty looks and social opprobrium in the first case, and fines, jail time or debarment in the second.

A second solution relies not on a costly stake, but on persuading others of one's intent, or lack thereof: if the Puritan tradesman, or the passionate baker, can sufficiently convey their Puritanism or the passion for their craft, then others will expect them to be honest and hardworking, since they will know them to be driven by something other than material self-interest. That trick of persuasion, in turn, entails behaving in a way that non-Puritans or non-passionates could not perfectly mimic. In other words, the second solution to the problem of credibility, the fundamental challenge of market capitalism, is to convey one's *disinterest*.

Two Sorts of Commerce

In his *Treatise of Human Nature*, David Hume, the pre-eminent figure of the Scottish Enlightenment, distinguished between 'two different sorts of commerce, the interested and the disinterested'. Disinterested commerce was the older kind. It relied on natural feelings of obligation arising from a sense of gratitude, as one might expect between close friends or loved ones. But in a modern society, Hume recognised, most human dealings took place between strangers, on the basis not of gratitude, but the expectation of some mutual advantage. In such situations, as Hume put it, 'I have no kindness for you, and know you have as little for me.' Lacking the natural basis of friendship or affection, two strangers may be useful to each other, yet never be able to consummate their profitable union. You could use my help, and then I could use yours in turn, but since I cannot be assured that you will reciprocate once I have kept my end of the bargain, I choose not to assist you. We both end up worse off. Or as Hume had it: 'Here then I leave you to labour alone: You treat me in the same manner. The seasons change; and both of us lose our harvests for want of mutual confidence.'

Hume was making the distinction between interested and disinterested commerce because he saw that the modern form of interested commerce led to a problem that had not previously existed. As long as favours had been offered to familiar people out of goodwill, exchanges had arisen naturally. But once the size of the market demanded impersonal exchanges between strangers,[19] there appeared a new problem, that of *credibility*.

Hume recognises that a market that relies on transactions between strangers requires constant leaps of faith, since my oranges ripen three months before your figs: 'These mutual performances cannot be finished at the same instant, it is necessary that one party be contented to remain in uncertainty.' Similarly, we may want to lend each other our labour, but we can never do so simultaneously. I cannot help you move house at the same time as you are helping me move house; one of us has to help the other first.[20] Nature made people mutually useful to one another, but that isn't enough to ensure that those benefits will be taken up.

For that to happen, we also need to be believed, which proves supremely difficult. And that's because as Hume saw, there is nothing natural about the making of promises. We cannot appeal to any fundamental human quality that might convince others of our commitment, as with a parent's devotion to a child. When we give our word to someone, or promise to help them move house once they have helped us, we must create something out of nothing: an obligation. Hume, the consummate empiricist, was full of awe over this: how could a sense of obligation appear *ex nihilo*? He described it as 'one of the most mysterious and incomprehensible operations that can possibly be imagined', comparing it to 'TRANSUBSTANTIATION, or HOLY ORDERS' (that is Hume's own exuberant capitalisation). So how is this process, as mysterious as bread being turned into the body of Christ, ever accomplished?

Through a transformative human invention. A series of agreed-upon words, of 'certain symbols and signs', which, once spoken, give rise to an obligation. 'Cross my heart and hope to die,' or else a notarised affidavit. And a curse on anyone who would break them: 'After these signs are instituted, whoever uses them is immediately bound by his interest to execute his engagements, and must never expect to be trusted any more, if he refuse to perform what he promised.'

It is a typical Enlightenment move: Hume split the world neatly into two spheres of human activity, and the dividing line between them was drawn by a human invention, the promise. Without the ability to make promises, markets failed to emerge, and strangers were unable to be of service to one another. And although Hume drew most of his examples – corn harvests, trade in wine, house sales – from economic exchanges, the implications reached far beyond the economic sphere. Indeed, the term 'commerce', in Hume's time, had a broader meaning than it does now. It encompassed all types of human exchange, from conversation to romantic entanglement.[21]

It's tempting to see in the convergence of the term 'commerce' to its current strictly economic meaning a broader phenomenon. As the next chapter shows, the commercial sphere has a way of progressively incorporating all other types of human activity. Activities that had no economic aspect progressively cede to economic incentives. Tellingly, it is often those pursuits that are not only indifferent to, but squarely opposed to economic motives that are incorporated most eagerly, precisely because their disinterested nature is catnip to economic actors.

'Interested Commerce' in Early Markets

Economic historians have retold Hume's stylised story by comparing the emergence of real markets in different parts of the world. Most often, these accounts turn on the ways people came up with to make themselves believed. In a small market where everyone knows each other, like a village, simply giving one's word might suffice, since the social opprobrium of being seen as a cheat is a high enough penalty to ensure that no one breaks their word. The result is what economists call 'self-enforcement', where no one has an incentive to flout the rules.

But in bigger markets, like the cross-continental spice trade of the Middle Ages, or the dense trading network that developed between countries around the Mediterranean Sea in the fourteenth century, relying on first-hand knowledge of commercial partners became impossible. Merchants had to resort to more elaborate means of being believed.

Going as far back as the fourteenth century, Genoan merchants thus created an elaborate system of letters of exchange and bills of lading: each ship carried a clerk who kept a register of all the goods on the ship, which was used to confirm receipt of the goods by the ship's captain, who was then liable for the goods until they were checked and received by the consignee at the port of destination.

An alternative system aiming to resolve the same problem was simultaneously in use among Maghribi traders, starting in the thirteenth century. Instead of formal commitments recorded by dedicated clerks, they relied on an informal network of reputation. This system proved highly efficient at home. But eventually, the Maghribi traders' reliance on personalised relations imposed limits on the scale of their trade network. According to the economic historian Avner Greif, this difference accounts for why the descendants of the Genoan merchants eventually expanded their operations across the Western hemisphere, while the Maghribi traders did not. The Genoans had come up with a scalable means of resolving the credibility challenge; it proved the difference between world dominance and being limited to a small regional market.

The Maghribi traders' enforcement system effectively required chains of gentlemen's agreements, where each gentleman needed to know the other. The Maghribis were initially able to rely on reputational chains because they were a tight-knit minority, the descendants of Jewish traders who had fled the area of Baghdad for the more secure lands of Tunisia.

This initial advantage eventually proved their limitation. Not having to rely on elaborate legal instruments came as a net benefit in domestic trade, compared with the Genoan system, which required complex book-keeping and the hiring of clerks aboard every ship.[22] But as soon as the Magrhibi traders reached the limits of their network, trade became impossible. There was no good way of being believed. Capitalism halts where credibility can't follow.

This is especially so because as the scale of the market increases, so does the temptation to break one's promise: not only is it easier to get away with transgressions because the parties to an exchange are unlikely to know each other personally, but the fruits of cheating also increase. As the economist Douglass North puts it, 'returns on opportunism, cheating, and shirking rise in complex societies'.[23] Whereas earlier, you could cheat your neighbour out of a cow, at best, in modern societies, skilfully applied dishonesty might yield increased market share in a large industry, or control of a privatised state enterprise. The increased temptation to cheat made it harder to be believed; everyone suddenly had even more reason to suspect everyone else's motives.

The problem of credibility in capitalist markets remains. To this day, a lack of credibility represents the greatest obstacle to the development of modern markets. The huge literature on 'social capital' records countless examples of what happens when credibility is lacking and people are unable to believe one another. In one of the most famous studies in the subject, the Harvard political scientist Robert Putnam contrasted the differences between northern and southern Italy. To this day, Italians living in the north display significantly more social trust than Italians living in the south: they are more likely to say that they would trust a stranger in an emergency, and less likely to think that other people would try and take advantage of them if they got a chance.[24] Putnam links this back to divergent cultural traditions dating back a millennium, the effects of which continue to be felt today.

In fact, the very institution of trade credit – the chief concern of Ben Franklin's sermon, as cited by Weber – was invented in the northern medieval Italian republics, during what is often called the Age of Dante.[25] As in other settings, the use of credit was made possible by the entry of the state, and its willingness to play an enforcement function through the courts.

We have a handy measure for the extent to which people believe one another's promises, and that is the rate of interest on loans. The greater the average level of suspicion, the higher the rate charged for lending out money, or entrusting funds to strangers. In some settings, the implicit rate of interest was so high as to be prohibitive; this was the case in southern Italy during the medieval period and in the centuries that followed. As a result, the impersonal use of credit was effectively unheard of in the southern towns of Bari and Palermo, where it was often impossible to obtain credit at all, at *any* rate of interest. Meanwhile, the interest charged steadily dropped in the north as the financial–legal edifice grew more sophisticated, and the state took on a growing role as enforcer. It became progressively easier to be believed; the spot price of credibility declined.

Fast forward to the present, and northern Italians find it easier to engage in exchanges with strangers; whereas those living in the south are confined to smaller circles of people they can truly trust, mostly members of their extended family.

One frequently cited lesson from studies of social capital is that 'strong ties' like those between family members are ultimately less important to prosperity than 'weak ties' between, say, business partners.[26] What's more, in places and cultures where people put all their faith in strong ties and rely on kinship in resolving the credibility problem, the emergence of weak ties becomes less likely, and the development trajectories of whole societies are affected as a result.

Credibility and Transaction Costs

The takeaway from the diverging destinies of the Genoan versus the Maghribi traders, and northern versus southern Italy, is that being believed is invaluable. But it requires costly contrivances, like clerks and courts. Economists refer to the sum of these as 'transaction costs'.

Transaction costs are to the economic world what friction is to the physical world: an unfortunate but seemingly unavoidable hindrance. Much of the capitalist system today consists of such costs, and exists solely to manage the credibility of market agents. A hedge-funder can make a king's ransom by finding one broken promise before anyone else does: the financial system provides incentives for anyone who can ferret out signs of fraud or other deceptive practices in a firm to bet against that firm, and reap a windfall if their suspicion proves right. This is to say nothing of all notaries, underwriters, middlemen, tribunals, and rating agencies, all devoted to the functions of monitoring, enforcing, and scoring. All these actors are in the business of making the promises of others believable. That is often the only justification for their existence.

Markets rely on these actors to solve the credibility problem. Though the corporate world has a habit of griping at excessive monitoring and regulation, it would swiftly come apart in the absence of such institutions: successful firms desperately want rating agencies to go through their books and assess their claims, because otherwise no one would know the difference between them and the mismanaged, floundering enterprise next door. Demonstrating their 'type' requires a complex financial system that rewards an entire set of market actors – analysts, accountants, insurance companies – for denouncing any broken promises by other market actors. Because as Hume knew, there is nothing natural about the making of promises; they had to be invented. As did the contrivances we rely on to enforce them.

Economists talk about the need for such contrivances as belonging to a 'second-best' world. What they mean by this is that although we might wish for a 'first-best', frictionless world in which mistrust of others' intentions doesn't arise, and although most people may in fact have good intentions most of the time, for markets to function, we must assume everyone's ill intentions at all times. So we design human institutions under the premise that, as Hume puts it, 'every man ought to be supposed a knave, and to have no other end, in all his actions, but private interest'.*

Of course, the idea of a first-best world is make-believe. In the words of the economist Avinash Dixit, 'the whole world is second-best, at best'. Some degree of inefficiency is inevitable, as rules are put in place to deal with human imperfections, and guards are appointed to enforce them. Unless, that is, we somehow find a way of transacting in a frictionless setting, a

---

* Hume made this point by acknowledging how odd it was that political institutions would be built on a premise that was demonstrably false, namely that society was made up of immoral egoists: 'Political writers have established it as a maxim, that, in contriving any system of government, and fixing the several checks and controls of the constitution, every man ought to be supposed a knave, and to have no other end, in all his actions, but private interest. By this interest we must govern him, and, by means of it, make him co-operate to public good, notwithstanding his insatiable avarice and ambition ... It is, therefore, a just political maxim, that every man must be supposed a knave: Though at the same time, it appears somewhat strange, that a maxim should be true in politics, which is false in fact.' (Hume, *A Treatise of Human Nature*).

capsule devoid of gravity, where all those notaries and bailiffs and rating agencies are unnecessary.[27]

That world does in fact exist; Hume was clear that it did not go away by virtue of the appearance of modern markets. If anything, it was elevated by contradistinction to interested commerce. Despite his awe for the human inventiveness spurred by modern markets, Hume betrays an evident preference for the older form of commerce: 'But though this self-interested commerce of man begins to take place, and to predominate in society, it does not entirely abolish the *more generous and noble intercourse* of friendship.'[28]

By a game of contrasts, the two forms of commerce are etched into sharper relief by the existence of the other: disinterested commerce is now defined, and elevated, by the absence of instrumental ends. It is a form of exchange that is not done to procure any gain, and which therefore has no need for promises. We recognise it by actions taken without expectation of reciprocal benefit. This is the world of friendship, of gifts, and of spontaneous exchange. It's the world of the New England Puritan and the passionate Brooklyn baker.

Disinterested commerce is an ideal form of frictionless exchange. It is devoid of fear or risk, and it thus has no need for the elaborate means we go through to suss out one another's true intent. What disinterest offers, improbably, is *efficiency*. It is the economist's unattainable first-best world.

Venture Capitalism and Disinterest

Though we have come to accept and rely on a set of second-best legal institutions devoted to constructing and maintaining the credibility of economic actors, the market has never forgotten the dream of a frictionless commercial environment.

And it heaps large rewards on whoever can best approximate it. This is why potential business partners seek out the passionate baker – both the seventeenth-century New England kind and the twenty-first-century Brooklyn kind. It's because they can trust the baker's 'type': they can count on the baker not slacking off, or worse, running off with the cash from the register. If they can ascertain the presence of genuine passion, they can do away with that costly edifice that capitalism relies on to render promises believable.

For the same reason, all passionate employers look to hire similarly passionate employees, rather than ones merely interested in earning a living. Hence Max Weber's observation about how the Puritan employer had at his disposal a retinue of 'sober, conscientious' workers 'who were devoted to work as the divinely willed purpose in life', and thus required no oversight.[29] The same, it turns out, goes for modern investors. Among today's venture capitalists looking to place their millions, 'passion' has become a byword for a promising investment.

In August 2019, the company WeWork, the world's fastest-growing player in the game of shared office space, was preparing to launch a $65 billion initial public offering. WeWork had become the world's biggest landlord: its business model consisted of buying up office space in dozens of cities around the world, outfitting these spaces according to a common aesthetic with pinball machines and beer on tap, and leasing them out to tech companies looking for an all-inclusive solution to house their employees. WeWork's dazzling rise was fuelled by investments from Masayoshi Son, a Korean-Japanese investor who sits on the $100-billion Vision Fund, which invests in tech start-ups. Son did not invest in WeWork the company, as much as in its CEO and co-founder, Adam Neumann.

Masayoshi Son first saw Neumann speak at a start-up conference in India in 2016. There, Neumann signalled his type from the start of his talk: 'For such a spiritual country, I'm surprised [by] the amount of talk I heard about valuation and raising money and bubbles and building big companies. That is not the goal. The goal is finding something that you truly love.'[30] Neumann was making it clear that he was no Adam Smith baker; he was the passionate Brooklyn type. Yet Son entrusted him with his dinner, and then some. The next year, Son invested $4.4 billion into WeWork. The following year, he put in another $4.25 billion.

Neumann had managed to turn what was at its core a property-management business into an exalted enterprise where profits appeared to be merely an unintended byproduct of a higher purpose. 'We are here in order to change the world,' he declared. Neumann made much of his upbringing on an Israeli kibbutz – another setting where prosperity is not the goal, but a byproduct of a shared vision. He spoke of a global 'capital-istic kibbutz' where workers are united by a common purpose rather than individual self-interest.[31] To match this vision, he cultivated an unhinged outward appearance. As the *Financial Times* reported, 'Neumann sometimes showed up [to negoti-ation meetings with Masayoshi Son] barefoot, or encouraged his team to hold hands and pray.' These were dismissed as idio-syncratic antics, but another possibility is that Neumann was giving the market exactly what it wanted. The exuberance was by design. As one business paper headline gushed, 'Focus On Passion, Purpose, Funding Will Follow: Adam Neumann'.[32] It was all made to appeal to the staid investment banks that were pursuing the ultimate dream of capitalism in a time of liquid markets and high information, where conventional investment opportunities have either dried up, or yield trifling returns: the dream of harnessing disinterest to interested ends.

Today, of course, WeWork is worth a fraction of its value, its IPO plans have been shelved, Neumann has been ousted from the company he founded, and Son has been left handling the fallout. It is the corporate crash-and-burn story of the decade. The company's rise and fall have been gleefully portrayed as one more tale of capitalist hubris, but it's more interesting than that. It's a story of self-interested investors being swayed by the glow of disinterest.

Investors looking to make abnormal returns by betting on disinterested behaviour are not the exception; the notion of investing in passionate founders, rather than in their companies, is the standard mantra of venture capitalism. There are too many stories like Neumann's to think that this is an aberration. It is, rather, a predictable effect of existing incentives. If female peacocks select on the vividness of the males' feathers, those males will evolve to develop absurd plumages that appear irrational on all other evolutionary grounds. So it is with the trappings of passion in the contemporary marketplace.

As Taizo Son, the brother of Masayoshi Son and a venture capitalist himself, put it: 'My criteria to invest are the founders. So I won't check any business plans, any economic projections, spreadsheets; but (instead) I focus on the founder's mindset (and) passion.'[33] Nor is this merely a family preference. As one study from Stockholm found, among the most sought-out personality traits that venture capitalists look for in making investment decisions, the 'first one is "passion."'[34] As the authors conclude, 'venture capitalists look for an entrepreneur that burns for what he is doing'. An investor from the Icelandic state-owned fund NSA Ventures used an Icelandic word to describe it: *eldmóður*, which denotes 'a combination of fire in the belly of the entrepreneur and his passion'. As the study goes on to explain, *eldmóður* 'translates into stamina and commitment'. Therein lies the difference between the passionate baker and the profit-driven one: the latter will stop when the effort no longer seems worth it, while the former will keep going until she burns herself out entirely. What investors want to hear is that founders are pursuing a set of essentially non-economic goals; that they will not abide by common economic incentives; and that they will surround themselves with other, like-minded individuals, all driven by a vision, rather than profits. What they want is a Puritan baker, rather than a Smithian one.

The Aesthetic of Credibility

When social norms become established, they often congeal into moral and aesthetic codes. These are at the source of our fastest evaluations: a single glance is enough to judge the man sporting an oligarch watch: what a douchebag. The nineteenth-century merchant taking on the airs of a well-bred gentleman: plainly an *arriviste*. We need not go through the motions of evaluating sincerity vs competence; we react instantly. Verdicts of vulgarity feel to us instinctive, unthinking, as immediate and non-cerebral as judging a dish too salty, or a drink too bitter. They carry an emotional valence. We grow indignant. The striver, if found out, is dismissed not merely as overly ambitious; he is reprehensible, disgraceful, downright sinful.

The doggedness of our collective efforts at determining credibility, at distinguishing between the spheres of interested and disinterested commerce, has yielded a number of peculiar moral and aesthetic categories. Perhaps none is more noticeable today than the contemporary cult of *authenticity*. Today, the label is used less for claims of truth, as when judging whether a painting is an authentic Rembrandt, and more to describe travel that feels meaningful, experiences that seem unmediated, foods that taste homemade, clothing labels with a storied 'heritage', and celebrities that avoid make-up.

Across different settings, the common element of authenticity claims is the attempt to demonstrate disinterested intent. Straining for authenticity is a sure sign of its lack. Big brands run costly market surveys to learn that consumers want more 'authentic' products, but those consumers immediately dismiss as inauthentic anything that smells as if it came from a market survey. As a wine trade publication warns, 'When something looks overly focus-grouped ... customers balk.'[35] The point of focus groups, of course, is to find out what people want in order to offer it to them. But doing so in an overly transparent way backfires because the eagerness to please is itself a liability. Suddenly, winemakers are facing incentives similar to those of contemporary artists; they do well by appealing to their audience without ever betraying a desire to appeal to their audience. They strive, but must hide the striving.

Yet strive they do, because the market rewards of successfully performing authenticity are immense. As with the concept of credibility, our elevation of authenticity reflects the recurring difficulty of being believed when others have an incentive to mimic all the signs one may offer as evidence of one's believability.

This is also why, as we will see in the coming chapter, fakers pay such a high cost if they are found out, falling even lower than the explicitly self-interested. Adam Smith's baker, driven by profit alone, may thus be judged less authentic than the passionate Brooklyn baker, but the least authentic of all is the baker who tries to pass off as passionate, and fails. It is not the naked attempt at self-advancement, but its denial that most irks us. By analogy, we have come to value the label of authenticity more than what the label is applied to. To be seen doing something in an authentic way is more important than what it actually is that is being done.

On the harmless end of the spectrum, we thus get the emergence of such things as celebrities who are famous for being famous. A puzzling phenomenon at first, the celebrity who does not produce anything of cultural value – no movies, or songs, or plays, or books – begins to make sense when considered through the lens of a cult of authenticity which rests on a collectively held suspicion of intent. In an age such as this one, the production of any actual *product* becomes suspect. Not producing anything of obvious worth actually becomes a selling point. The absence of an identifiable product refutes any charge of trying to please. Suddenly, a celebrity who neither acts, nor sings, nor writes, proves unexpectedly appealing. Instead of trying to peddle some product, this crop of celebrities offer up their very selves. Which is the one non-negotiable demand of their fanbase: that they make themselves fully available, at all times.

If the cult of authenticity were limited to twisting the incentives of pop celebrity, there would be little to worry about. But the 'aesthetic of the real' manifests itself in more worrying ways. In the wake of the Great Recession of 2008, democracies across the world fell prone to a wave of political populism. The United States, Brazil, India, the UK, Poland, Hungary, and the Philippines are among the countries that turned to a similar strain of right-wing political entrepreneur.

Populist leaders succeed by leveraging the cult of authenticity in political life. Political scientists usually define populism – a concept with many competing meanings – as the pitting of a genuine, 'authentic people' (the populist's audience) against an inauthentic people (made up, as the case may be, of coastal elites, immigrants, or sexual and ethnic minorities). The core claim of populism is that 'only some of the people are really the people'.[36] And the populist leader stands for the real people among the people, in opposition to the 'other'. We thus get repeated invocations of the 'real Americans' living in the heartland. Consider Nigel Farage, the former leader of the UK Independence Party, declaring Brexit 'a victory for real people'.

The populist rides to victory on the attempt by political audiences to detect intent. The populist's currency is credibility. This may seem an extraordinary claim to make, given how often populist leaders, drawing on the recent American exemplar, deal in lies and misrepresentation. But what unites them is a willingness to say the unsayable. Followers marvel at how only the populist leader 'says it like it is'. And this willingness, by itself, becomes of greater importance than the content of the 'it' which is being said. The label of authenticity thus attaches itself more readily to appearance, tone, demeanour, and swagger, than to the content of the political message itself. Social media serves as a great enabler of both the famous-for-being-famous and the populist politician. Both rely on a perception of unmediated reality, something that the unbridled aspect of late-night tweets can offer – spelling mistakes and exclamation marks included.

And just as putting down a costly stake is a means of attaining credibility in economic settings, the willingness to incur mainstream censure for making outrageous claims is a testament to the populist's authenticity. It is the way by which populists disassociate themselves from the realm of calculating, run-of-the-mill politics. Naked lies thus register as more genuine than the centrist politician who must hedge her message to meet the demands of the truth, not to mention the constraints of courtesy or respectability. A devotion to the truth becomes a compromising position. The ultimate irony, then, is that the perception of authenticity may pass through untruth: the willingness to break existing codes by telling lies is interpreted as a form of loyalty. When the label becomes more important than the content it is affixed to, lying can become an investment in believability.

The elevation of an aesthetic of authenticity in politics hits mainstream career politicians particularly hard. In debates, they must roll out carefully planned messaging under the guise of spontaneity. While they may fool some by feigned ad libs, others will dismiss these efforts as 'overly focus-grouped'. In response, and failing to grasp the paradox of intention, their political consultants have been known to react by rolling out a 'spontaneity strategy', oblivious to how such efforts inevitably backfire, fuelling the audience's misgivings.[37]

The value attributed to authenticity partly accounts for another puzzling aspect of electoral politics in democratic societies, which is that it is the rare field that does not reward professionalisation. In most domains, people pick an area, acquire experience in it, build on that experience over their career, and profit from it. They become specialists, *experts*. It is often a condition for plying their trade. We want to know how many surgeries our surgeon has performed before we submit ourselves to the scalpel; we don't value their coming fresh to the task, untarnished by past experience. This is also why a mechanic cannot decide to become a cook overnight, or an engineer suddenly turn into a nurse. But politics seems impervious to expertise; it rewards self-professed dabblers, and sometimes real ones. Owing to a prevalent incumbent advantage, most high-level politicians are in fact career policymakers, but they rarely admit to it. Why is this?

Politics is an exercise in persuasion. It's 'the art of making your selfish desires seem like the national interest'.[38] But who is willing to be persuaded by a suave expert at persuasion? We fear being had by a well-honed pitch. Instead, we prefer to be persuaded by bumbling amateurs who happen to have a good case.

More recently, the sociologist David Riesman observed how 'this focus on sincerity, both in popular culture and in politics, leads the audience tolerantly to overlook the incompetence of performance ... Forced to choose between skill and sincerity, many in the audience prefer the latter. They are tolerant of bumbles and obvious ineptness if the leader tries hard.'[39] When it comes to changing people's minds, the appearance of incompetence can be reassuring.

Populists count on this effect. As in the case of celebrities famous for being famous, with no product to hustle other than their unmediated selves, the populist politician often boasts of a lack of actual political expertise. Incompetence appears comforting if it represents an absence of calculation, because calculation has come to be seen as posing the greatest risk. The cult of authenticity, and the attendant hunt for signs of inauthenticity, translates into a set of aesthetic codes, and these can have frightful effects.

(Dis)interest in Political Markets

The appeal of disinterest is not the newfound discovery of today's populists. Disinterest actually plays a central role in the history of political thought. Just as the expanding scale of commercial markets requires ever greater specialisation and risky exchange, so too does an enlargement of society require ever more delegation of power. The fundamental idea of the social contract comes in a wide range of flavours, but it boils down to an abiding need and a corresponding fear. No sooner are we freed from an insecure state of nature by delegating power to a leader to enforce a set of ground rules, than we begin to worry that leaders will abuse that power at our expense.

The risk in political markets may be even greater than in commercial markets. In the case of commerce, one might lose the value of one's cargo if one entrusts it to a duplicitous tradesman. In the case of politics, delegating power to a leader who turns out to be a tyrant might mean losing one's freedom.

The fundamental question of politics is, 'Who will guard the guards?' This famous phrase, which today gets trotted out by serious people in serious times talking about regulation and oversight, actually has its origin in a skit about adultery. It comes from a satirical comedy by Juvenal, the Roman playwright, who lived in the second century CE. In that 2,000-year-old play, a group of soldiers are going merrily off to war, but they worry about their wives cheating on them in their absence. Luckily, one of the men comes up with a brilliant solution: let them appoint guards to watch over the wives! Then, someone raises the obvious problem.

Whether the stakes are adultery or tyranny, the issue once again comes down to credibility: a leader is needed, yet as soon as we appoint one, we expose ourselves to their perfidy. The problem of credibility is just as bothersome from the would-be leader's standpoint. A benevolent leader who in their heart of hearts knows they will be fully devoted to the public good and never abuse their newfound power nonetheless has no credible means of conveying their benevolent nature: they can solemnly swear all they want, but it all amounts to cheap talk, since all solemn declarations can be readily mimicked by would-be tyrants.

The common solution is exactly analogous to the case of commercial markets: a second-best set of rules and institutions that recognise the existence of friction in the social world. Thus we get the separation of powers; an upper house checking a lower legislature, both checking the executive; all of them looking to regulatory agencies for common standards, and to courts for the adjudication of disagreements over their interpretation. Together, these various checks and balances form the political analogue to the economic edifice that supports capitalism. In both cases, this edifice arises in response to the difficulty of being believed.

These institutions represent the best set of solutions we have arrived at, but all this wilfully created inefficiency also comes at a necessary cost. Grandstanding legislatures, filibusters, congressional gridlock: these are all unavoidable parts of the package. From there, we get the oft-cited notion of democracy as the worst form of government except for all the other forms that have ever been tried. What is often missed is that the second-best aspect of democratic politics is *by design*.

And yet, that hasn't stopped us from dreaming. The vision of a frictionless political system is as old as political thought itself. It is, in fact, the animating fantasy at the core of the first work of Western political philosophy, Plato's *Republic*. In it, Plato proposes a quasi-frictionless solution to the problem of 'who will guard the guards?' It comes down to the way by which the guards are chosen in his imagined Kallipolis, 'the beautiful city'.

Plato's philosopher-king has had a bad rap in the intervening millennia, and for good reason. The history of the twentieth century has chilled us to the idea of a hierarchical society with a class of guardians-cum-benevolent-dictators, calling on citizens' trust in their far-sighted wisdom.[40]

Yet in our eagerness to reject Plato's notion of the philosopher-king, we often overlook one of its most interesting aspects. Plato's main criterion for leaders is that they *must not want* the job. All who would volunteer themselves for the post are immediately barred from consideration: 'Surely it is those who are not lovers of ruling who must do it,' Plato tells us. 'Otherwise, the rivalling lovers will fight over it.'[41] So Kallipolis selects its leaders from among the uninterested. The only suitable leaders are those who are desperate to cede the office to anyone but themselves, because they do not see ruling as an attractive means to power or personal enrichment. Unwillingness becomes the criterion. Generating the right type of leader falls to Kallipolis' educational system, which is designed to imbue would-be rulers with passions beyond ruling. The city instils in its future rulers a yearning for values like beauty, contemplation, and philosophy, and then forces them, against their will, to rule the city instead. As Socrates argues in the dialogue, 'If you can discover a better life than ruling for the prospective rulers, your well-governed city will become a possibility.'[42] Disinterest is not a bug, but a feature: the aim is to create a class of reluctant leaders.

And yet, just as in commercial markets, we have had to settle for something less than a first-best, frictionless political system.[43] In fact, in coming up with a solution to the credibility problem, our current democratic system inadvertently generates the very opposite incentives to those Plato imagines for Kallipolis' rulers. We have made running for office an exercise in selling, hand-shaking, baby-kissing, and money-raising; a tedious game that could only appeal to those for whom the prospect of holding office is so valuable, that they are willing to put up with the pains of getting there. We are casting around for the opposite of reluctance. It comes as little surprise, then, that these individuals are often in it for something over and above the inherent gratification of public service. We find ourselves selecting for 'lovers of rule', for those who see in it a means to self-aggrandisement, self-enrichment, or both.

Yet the game of coy reluctance has not disappeared entirely; it continues to play out in smaller political settings, from neighbourhood co-ops to parent-teacher associations. Every three years, my own university department must elect a department chair by majority vote. And every time, all the potential candidates begin by claiming they do not want the seat, that they have no time for it, that they lack the required administrative skills, that they are fully consumed by their research. This show of unwillingness has come to be the first criterion for the job. Anyone who would offer themselves up too quickly would be voted down immediately, from fear of what their eagerness reveals about their motives. The result is that until the last moment, it seems as if no one will come forward. And yet, somehow, the position always gets filled.

Twisted Incentives

Hume was right in guessing that as markets grew larger and more complex, they would give rise to a split between an interested and a disinterested sphere. He was also right in identifying the fundamental problem of interested commerce: how to be believed? The solution he described, the human invention of promises, continues to be the most prevalent solution employed today. It is the stuff modern society is made of: rules, contracts, institutions. But where Hume was misguided was in thinking that the separation between the two spheres – the interested realm that relies on formal promises, and its disinterested counterpart that has no use for them – would remain clear-cut.

In Hume's telling, the emergence of interested commerce distinguished the modern market from the older, 'nobler' zone of disinterest. As the historian Pierre Force puts it, the market, with its affidavits, its underwriters, its middlemen, and its notaries, 'clears up any ambiguities regarding the nature of the transactions taking place'.[44] Within this setting, we agree to address ourselves to one another's self-interest: 'Self-interest is, *by convention*, the engine of modern commerce.'[45]

But what Hume never saw coming is that people might have every reason to break this convention. The result might then be the very opposite of what was intended: ambiguities between the two spheres could increase, rather than dissipate. Who might have thought that one day, interested commerce would have an incentive to present itself as its disinterested counterpart? That despite the availability of the remarkable human invention of the promise – which accomplished the impossible-sounding trick of making something out of nothing – an *even better* trick would be to do away with the need for promises altogether, and to run on passion alone. Or on a divine calling, or love, or friendship; anything, in fact, but self-interest.

Hume thus assumed good faith twice over. First, he took for granted that everyone would keep their promises so long as they understood that others have an interest in keeping theirs.[46] As it turns out, armies of lawyers and auditors are required to make this happen. Two hundred years later, this legal edifice constitutes an enormous portion of developed markets. But more importantly, Hume also assumed that the norms around when to resort to the convention would always be respected; people would commit to *using* this novel technology of promises, and thus declare their intentions as resting on self-interested rather than disinterested motives. Whereas, in fact, both types of commerce are constantly sliding into each other. What Hume failed to see, in other words, was the value of *faking*. The faker acts as if a formal promise were unnecessary, because, the faker self-righteously insists, the situation falls under 'the more generous and noble intercourse of friendship'.

Nor did Hume ever imagine the opposite form of temptation, that of *selling out*. Indeed, to be nobly disinterested is to be constantly tempted by the prospect of switching one's allegiance; from passion to profit; from disinterest to self-interest. That temptation exists because markets recognise the limitless gains they stand to reap from disinterest, and they seek to capitalise on it. What's worse, this temptation only keeps increasing. The longer one persists in the disinterested realm, the more credible one's disinterest appears, and the greater the potential gain from crossing over to the other side of the divide. The *faker* and the *sellout*: these are the two tragic characters that arise in response to the high wages of disinterest.

4

On Fakers

We have established how disinterest pays: it is a source of credibility, and credibility is what underpins market society. In the market, to be perceived as disinterested attracts business partners seeking reliability, investors seeking resolve, and consumers hunting for authenticity. It even lowers one's cost of credit. In politics, disinterest helps would-be rulers attain power when the ruled are hesitant to give it up from fear of tyranny.

Since investors' money, consumers' business, and the attainment of power are of interest to the interested, we end up with a paradoxical set of incentives. The self-interested have reason to appear disinterested, and to do so convincingly. If the passionate baker inadvertently prospers through his passion – if not being in it for the money proves to be a recipe for commercial success – then a dispassionate rival baker in the Adam Smith mould, motivated by nothing but profits, may look on and draw certain conclusions. Watching the passionate baker prosper through passion, the self-interested baker has an incentive... to become passionate in turn.

The effect is of a snake eating its own tail. Pursuing interested commerce to its fullest extent requires turning into, or else least passing itself off as, its disinterested counterpart. Self-interest passes through its own suspension.

Fakers are the creatures born of this paradox. Their emergence is not a mere possibility; it is a necessary consequence of market actors acting on market incentives. That is to say, those who act wholly out of self-interest will at a certain point find it in their interest to suspend their own interest. In doing this, they are faced with a problem we have seen in other guises: the self-interested baker must somehow will himself to forget about his goal of profit – *in the service of that goal*. This is, to say the least, a difficult trick to pull off. That a conversion to passion is motivated by an attempt to reproduce the inadvertent commercial success of passion would seem to preclude any genuine conversion. The greater his yearning to pick the fruits of passion, the less likely he is to succeed. So the self-interested baker is limited to feigning disinterest. The baker becomes a faker.

Fakers come in many forms: the striver and the poser; the *arriviste* and the *parvenu*; the hipster and the humblebraggart. We have seen the faker at work among Veblen's middle classes aspiring to upper-class status. And among today's nouveaux riches trying to buy their way to esteem. The fact that we hold such an elaborate mental catalogue of fakers speaks to how socially valuable detecting fakers is, and how the process of social evolution has made us all experts at it.

By definition, fakers are all intent, but they know better than to admit it. And it's here that the faker is confronted with paradox. Because the faker may be motivated by instrumental ends – prosperity, advancement, power, influence, good credit – but to admit to that motivation is to lose any chance of obtaining it fully. It is to lose the edge offered by disinterest. To achieve his ends, the faker must strip himself of the intention that defines him.

Is this even possible? By some accounts, no. William James, the father of modern psychology, congratulated himself on being able to spot a faker, one who would try to mimic the insouciant manner of the true gentleman, a mile away. Even with unlimited financial means and professional advice, James claimed, the faker's case was hopeless. He actually set an age limit past which it could no longer be done.

In William James's view, the styles of the well-bred gentleman are like the tones in Mandarin Chinese. If one has not been fully immersed in the mores of polite upper-crust society by the age of twenty, James held, then all is lost. Past that point, the required demeanour cannot be learned convincingly, and one can never hope to 'pass for'. James made good fun of those who tried in vain to prove him wrong:

> Hardly ever, indeed, no matter how much money there be in his pocket, can he even learn to dress like a gentleman-born. The merchants offer their wares as eagerly to him as to the veriest 'swell,' but he simply cannot buy the right things. An invisible law, as strong as gravitation, keeps him within his orbit, arrayed this year as he was the last; and how his better-bred acquaintances contrive to get the things they wear will be for him a mystery till his dying day.

Suffice it to say that to have a fine enough nose to discern this, to possess the ability to spot the faker, is the sure sign of a true gentleman. In recognising the codes that were broken by the *arriviste*, William James was implicitly suggesting where he himself belonged on the totem pole. Spotting fakers must have been something of a family pastime. William James's younger brother, the writer Henry James, was a close reader of Veblen's *Theory of the Leisure Class*, and made a career of drawing literary characters who desperately try to fake their way into higher society.

The faker, then, is a tragic hero: he tries in vain to 'pass off', but he is doomed to failure. We have seen this form of tragedy before. It results from the fact that the faker is after something that cannot be willed directly, but which can only be obtained as the byproduct of actions undertaken for other ends. And yet fakers persist in spite of the difficulties. This is likely because there is so much to be gained from pulling it off.

A popular insight from game theory holds that the most desirable situation for a rational, self-interested individual is to be the one defector in a society of cooperators. Conversely, the greatest fear is to be on the other end: to have one's benevolence exploited; to keep cooperating as others are defecting away. In the Prisoner's Dilemma, the most elemental game in game theory, it is this interplay between the temptation to be the single defector and the fear of being the single cooperator that drives the incentives of the game, and ensures that everyone defects, leaving all of society worse off. The dream, in other words, is to be the wolf in sheep's clothing: the one interested party in a world where everyone else believes themselves to be engaged in disinterested commerce. To achieve this is to reap infinite rewards.

This is the idea behind *The Invention of Lying*, a middling romantic comedy from 2009 with a clever premise. The film is set in a parallel guileless world, where everyone is always taken at their word, and no one is capable of deception. Until a screenwriter, named Mark, accidentally tells the world's first lie. Since everyone readily believes everything they're told, the credibility problem does not yet exist. Mark makes the most of it: he invents God, religion and the afterlife. Turning himself into a prophet with direct access to 'the man in the sky', he becomes rich and famous and tries to win over Anna, the woman of his dreams. More on which later.

The people in Mark's parallel society are powerless against his lies, since they cannot conceive of misrepresentation. Luckily, this is not our case: we have a range of built-in defence mechanisms against would-be schemers trying to exploit others' guilelessness. In fact, as we have seen in the previous chapter, the institutions of capitalism exist in large part to assess the validity of the claims we make to one another. This benefits the 'true' types, the genuine articles, the William Jameses of the world: those who seek to distinguish themselves from would-be fakers. The members of the in-group, like Veblen's well-to-do, thus invest in elaborate social practices designed to ensure that members of the out-group are duly kept out.

When the existing codes fall short, and the social barriers prove too porous, and too much of the out-group finds a way in, it is time to redraw the boundaries – time for a *Reformation*. The Puritans were so called because they aspired to greater 'purity' than their fellow Protestants – who of course were after greater purity than their Catholic brethren. So too with Veblen's idle rich, who continually tried to outrun the rising bourgeoisie, until at some point in the wake of the First World War, they were eaten up by it entirely.

The Risks of Faking

But even if we are not among Veblen's idle rich, we too have armed ourselves with sophisticated means of spotting fakers. So practised are we in these gatekeeping exercises that we hardly think of how we are taking part in them. But just as predators have evolved to the point where they can smell their prey from two miles away, so too have we developed acute social sensory faculties, an ear for the sound of strategic calculation in others.

In recent years, behavioural scientists have demonstrated just how sophisticated these social radars of intention can be. Since Ervin Goffman's foundational work on self-presentation in the 1950s, social psychologists of various stripes have become increasingly interested in how the audience for the attempt at self-preservation adapts to these tricks. All this work, in turn, serves to illustrate the countless pitfalls involved in trying to make a favourable impression.

Ovul Sezer, of the University of North Carolina at Chapel Hill, and her colleagues Francesca Gino and Michael Norton, of Harvard Business School, recently conducted a series of nearly a dozen experiments on a specific form of self-presentation, humblebragging. Humblebragging is a pervasive tactic that people adopt to disguise their boasting under the guise of humility: 'I can't believe they all thought to nominate me for this award and want me to give a talk in front of thousands of people... I'm more surprised than you are!'

Humblebragging is thus an attempt to have it both ways: to elevate one's status ('I've won an award and have been invited to give a talk in front of a huge audience') while simultaneously projecting humility ('I can't believe that', 'I'm more surprised than you are'). The boast is aimed at self-advancement, while the show of humility is meant to disguise the boast's self-interested nature. It is, in short, a tool in the faker's arsenal; the question is whether it's an effective one.

The authors of the study came up with two intriguing results. First, they showed just how pervasive the practice is. In a national survey, they found that 70 per cent of respondents could recall a recent instance of humblebragging: these tended to concern physical appearance, wealth, and career achievements. Not surprisingly, social media proved to be especially fertile ground for the practice. As the authors concluded, humblebragging is 'ubiquitous in everyday life'. The suggestion is that people believe it to be an effective tool of self-presentation; otherwise they would not engage in it.

To test whether this is so, the authors then ran a series of survey experiments. They split their sample in half, and offered the first group of respondents examples of people humblebragging, while the second group got examples of straightforward bragging ('I've won an award!'). They then asked all respondents to rate how much they liked the person, and how competent they considered them. Most interesting from our standpoint, respondents were also asked, 'How credible do you think this person is?'

The results suggested that for all its ubiquity, humblebragging appears 'uniquely ineffective'. Those who tried to have it both ways did less well on each: they were seen as both less likable *and* less competent than those who engaged in outright boasting. Crucially, it was the perception of insincerity that drove these negative evaluations. The loss of credibility proved most costly of all. In other words, attempts at disguising self-interest in the trappings of disinterest failed so badly as to undo any benefit of conveying one's achievement – and that failure was due to the perceived attempt at disguising intent. No one likes a braggart. But what people *truly* can't stand is a humblebraggart.

A number of other studies have produced analogous findings. Successful self-presentation hinges on the perceived intent. For it to be effective, self-promotion needs to successfully 'conceal the ulterior motive [making a favourable impression] to be seen as sincere'.¹ The lesson of these studies is that people are good at detecting self-interest behind gestures that pretend at disinterest, and they punish those who try to have it both ways. The punishment, moreover, is so high as to undo any of the benefit from the self-interested attempt at self-advancement. The faker's calculated attempt backfires: it would have been better to stay squarely in the realm of self-interest, and avoid all the effort of pretence.

Much of the exotica of 'late capitalism' can be traced to this attempt at navigating the paradoxical incentives facing the faker: the realisation that disinterest pays, coupled with the considerable risk of posing as disinterested for self-interested reasons and incurring the punishment meted out against unsuccessful fakers. The very worst sin in a society that elevates authenticity above all other values is to be seen trying to impersonate an authenticity that one does not possess.

Detecting the Faker: A 350-Year-Old Tradition

David Hume might have missed the possibility that interested commerce would seek to pass itself off as disinterested. And social psychologists at Harvard Business School have only recently begun to measure our ability to detect inauthentic self-presentation tactics like humblebragging. But the insight had been fully grasped by a group of writers skewering social practices some 350 years ago.

Writing in the seventeenth century, the French duke, famous wit, and consummate cynic François de La Rochefoucauld made a career of piercing the calculated efforts of fakers who tried to feign disinterest to advance their interests. La Rochefoucauld's aphorisms have the effect of gunshots. He was aiming at the hustlers of aristocratic circles and courtiers in princely courts. 'Interest speaks many languages, and plays all types of characters, even that of the disinterested.'[2] Neither kindness nor even friendship, the paradigmatic instances of disinterested commerce according to Hume, was beyond cooptation to self-interested ends: 'Yet kindness is actually the quickest possible way for self-love to reach its goals: it is a secret pathway that brings it home with greater wealth and prosperity; it is a kind of disinterestedness from which it earns a flurry of interest.' In this vein, the most poignant of these witticisms actually comes from a close friend of La Rochefoucauld's, the lesser known Jacques Esprit: 'Kindness is a type of magic that a man uses to appear to be elsewhere, though he remains still at home.'[3] It is difficult not to feel exposed by such unerring accuracy.

The French Moralists, as they were known, were unveiling the workings of what they called *amour-propre* (self-love)[4] before political theorists homed in on self-interest as the fundamental driving force of human behaviour. In this sense, it is these French wits dreaming up scintillating epigrams to wow the patrons of Parisian salons who ushered in the modern notion of self-interest.*

The setting of the aristocratic court thus functioned as an early laboratory for the observation of disinterest deployed towards self-advancement. Once based on aristocratic honour,

---

*Consider that La Rochefoucauld's *Maxims* appeared – to considerable popular success, as it happens – a decade before Spinoza excoriated political philosophers for 'conceiv[ing] men not as they are but as they would like them to be', which became the touchstone for all positive political theory in 1676. And we are a full half-century before Bernard Mandeville's *Fable of the Bees*, which showed how 'private vices' turned into 'publick benefits', and which remains the first reference for what came to be called the doctrine of self-interest.

the Moralists showed it to have become a setting of continuous intrigue, one where scheming insiders acted on self-love, albeit under the guise of appearing pleasant, accommodating, and full of grace.

In this line of social scientists of the court, the French Moralists did have one illustrious predecessor, who was interested precisely in the means of attaining the coveted state of grace. At the height of the Italian Renaissance, more than a century before the appearance of La Rochefoucauld's *Maxims*, there came a little book titled *Il Cortegiano*, or *The Book of the Courtier*, by one Baldassare Castiglione. Written in the form of a dialogue, and pitched as a manual for ambitious courtiers seeking to move up in the cut-throat setting of a princely court, it became from its very publication the Renaissance version of a runaway hit, and it proved to be among the most influential Italian texts of the period.[5] Castiglione himself was a courtier in the tiny dukedom of Urbino – not to mention a clothes whore, a pedant, and frequently short of funds. In *Il Cortegiano*, he set out to describe the 'perfect courtier', who would earn his Prince's esteem, and rise in rank within the court.

How *does* the courtier get ahead, when everyone else is vying for the same? By appearing not to try. If he talks, his speech must look improvised. If he dances, he must do so with spontaneity. If he plays music, he must introduce some dissonance and avoid 'a harmony which is too affected'. Far worse than being seen as unskilled is coming across as self-conscious or strained in the deployment of that skill. The court hustler must try, by any means necessary, to come off as disinterested.

Today, *The Book of the Courtier* is best known for the term Castiglione coined to describe this state of grace: *sprezzatura*. How appropriate that the term used to describe this feat of effortless effort is itself an expression which it is impossible today to pronounce without affectation. *Sprezzatura* is an Italian word more commonly employed by a certain set of English speakers vying for an air of sophistication than by any actual Italians, who in my experience rarely know the word. What is in common usage is its root, *sprezzare*, which means to disdain. The object of disdain, in this case, is any sign of effort or intent. *Sprezzatura* is often featured in lists of 'untranslatable' words; in English it is usually rendered as 'nonchalance', which indeed fails to convey all that Castiglione had in mind. The term makes its first historical appearance in the following passage:

> I have discovered a universal rule which seems to apply more than any other in all human actions or words: namely, to steer away from affectation at all costs, as if it were a rough and dangerous reef, and (to use perhaps a novel word for it) to practise in all things a certain nonchalance [*sprezzatura*] which conceals all artistry and makes whatever one says or does seem uncontrived and effortless.[6]

By contrast, Castiglione goes on, labouring at producing an effect 'shows an extreme lack of grace and causes everything, whatever its worth, to be discounted'.

What becomes evident is that Castiglione is more interested in dissimulation than in attainment: 'True art is what does not seem to be art; and the most important thing is to conceal it, because if it is revealed this discredits a man completely and ruins his reputation.' It follows that the greatest danger of all is to appear forced in the attempt at faking nonchalance. Describing the dancing style of a known acquaintance, Castiglione opines, 'His nonchalance is affected and inappropriate, and it has exactly the opposite effect of what is intended.'* The implication is that in the setting of the court, everyone is vying to make an impression; some are simply better at hiding their effort, and they are the only ones to succeed.

What is merely implied in *The Book of the Courtier* is made explicit by the French Moralists. Everyone is trying to produce an effect, even as everyone must admit that the best effect would be produced by someone who would not be trying. Grace is merely the term by which we recognise the most able faker. The problem that dogs the ambitious is that it is impossible for them *not* to try to get ahead. The French Moralists may not have invented egoistic ambition, but they were the first to place it at the centre of human behaviour, and the setting of the court provided the first site for their field survey.[7]

There is something irreversible in the verdict of the aristocratic court writers. Once the masks are lifted, there is no use putting them back on: the revelation is self-fulfilling. Because

---

* If we allow the snake to swallow one more section of its tail: Castiglione follows up the discussion of *sprezzatura* with an explanation of his own decision to write *The Book of the Courtier* in his native Lombardian vernacular, rather than the more erudite Tuscan dialect. As he lays out with no small irony in the book's preamble: 'I confess to my critics that I do not know this terribly difficult and recondite Tuscan language of theirs; and I admit that I have written in my own, just as I speak, and for those who speak in the same way.' Later, this decision to use plain spoken language rather than more formal language is taken up in the dialogue itself as an instance of the very lack of affectation that the entire book is concerned with: 'Affectation is a vice of which only too many people are guilty, and sometimes our Lombards more than others, who, if they have been away from home for a year, on their return immediately start speaking Roman or Spanish or French, and God knows what. And all this springs from their over-anxiety to show how much they know.' Aptly, the same concern now applies to the contemporary usage by English speakers of the term *sprezzatura* itself, usually reserved for effortful attempts of self-presentation.

an act of kindness *can* serve our self-love, all such subsequent acts must necessarily be thought to do so. Out of a concern for self-preservation, we must for evermore disguise our attempts to stay ahead, and suspect everyone else of doing the same.

Perhaps unbeknownst to himself, La Rochefoucauld does leave one door unlocked, which we will attempt to pry open in the last chapter. Here's his Maxim 119, which expresses a recurrent idea among the Moralists: 'We are so accustomed to pretending to others, that we end up pretending to ourselves.'[8] La Rochefoucauld meant this as further demonstration of how deeply the hypocrisy ran. Yet acting on ourselves in this way, if carried out in full, may also function as a type of salvation. Let's stick a pin in this thought for now, and return to it later.

We recognise the sting in these maxims, because we have all seen fakers at work, and we have observed similar impulses in ourselves. In La Rochefoucauld's view, we are all fakers. And for this reason, we suspect others of the same. We are reflexively wary of claims of friendship when we feel we might lose from the bargain. We scrutinise the moves of a lover for signs of hidden intent. We recognise in others our own foibles.

By splitting all human dealings into interested and disinterested commerce, Hume meant to eliminate ambiguity.[9] Instead, by its effect on the faker's incentives, the division threatens to achieve the very opposite. The greatest gain suddenly comes from belonging to one while seeming to be of the other; by appearing to be elsewhere, while remaining very much at home. There's a sinister implication to this: if the payoff from coming across as disinterested proves sufficiently large – and as I argue below, it eventually does, like a lottery prize that keeps swelling so long as no one claims it – then interested commerce threatens to swallow disinterested commerce entirely. Far from the emergence of the modern market bringing about a clear separation between two spheres of activity, and thus preserving a zone for friendship, love, and passion, the risk is that one comes to capture the other. And as we shall see, it isn't a fair fight.

Between the incentive for misrepresentation on the one hand, and for its detection on the other, can disinterested commerce survive? La Rochefoucauld did not think so: an interested motive can always be found, and any claim to the contrary is invariably an attempt to maximise one's social dividend. Even a far less cynical thinker like Rousseau also believed that the disinterested transaction may not exist, though he arrived at this conclusion through a different reasoning. In Rousseau's view, it isn't so much that the awareness of self-love reduces every gesture to some version of it. Rather, Rousseau arrived at the fanciful, if oddly coherent belief that the only untainted transaction is the one that never takes place. As the historian Pierre Force writes, 'It is as if a truly pure gift could only be an intent to give, which becomes impure once it is acted upon.'[10] It isn't just that 'the intention is what counts' – it's that the intention is *all* that can count, and thus all that should be offered.

It goes without saying, moreover, that one could never boast of having had the intention to give and having desisted from doing so, in order to preserve the gift's purity: that would be worst of all, an obvious instance of self-advancement. So the only thing left to us in the disinterested sphere, according to Rousseau, is the exchange of never-consummated and never-shared intentions. What a pity.

Nietzsche also thought it was a pity. He was highly influenced by his reading of La Rochefoucauld, whom he called 'the greatest master of the psychological maxim', and his own writings often bear a resemblance to the French Moralists. And while no prig when it comes to revealing truths about human nature, Nietzsche was nonetheless uneasy with the piercing of disinterest for sport that the sixteenth-century French writers were engaging in:

> La Rochefoucauld and those other French masters of soul-searching … are like expert marksmen who again and again hit the black spot – but it is the black spot in human nature. Their art inspires amazement, but finally some spectator, inspired, not by the scientific spirit but by a humanitarian feeling, execrates an art that seems to implant in the soul a taste for belittling and impeaching mankind.[11]

Sometimes, no matter how sharp our aim, the shot is not worth taking. Instead, some measure of prudery, 'a sort of shame-facedness at the nakedness of the soul', might serve us better. Ultimately, training the inner spectator to spot self-interest in disguise might prove our undoing, if it disallows the very possibility of disinterest from the outset. Remarkably, Nietzsche was suggesting that the cultivation of a collective belief in 'a plenitude of disinterested benevolence', even at some resulting risk to ourselves, might ultimately prove more conducive to human happiness.[12]

After all, we also know true disinterest, for having glimpsed it within ourselves. Just as our internal observer, trained on our own lowest instincts, makes us doubt the authenticity of others' avowed passions, we also recognise that we sometimes fall prone to genuine moments of disinterested passion. If we sided with La Rochefoucauld entirely, we would be denying ourselves the possibility of whimsy, kindness, love – or, as we will see in the coming chapters, true leisure. As Nietzsche warned, that is unlikely to be the world we want to live in.

This point can be made more forcefully. We cannot *all* be fakers, for there would be nothing left for fakers to mimic.[13] That faking proves strategically worthwhile for some necessarily implies that others are behaving non-strategically – there must be genuinely passionate bakers who really *aren't* in it for the money; ascetic Puritans whose only purpose really *is* to pursue their divinely ordained calling; true friends whose devotion to us awaits nothing in return. Had we gone fully over to the Rochefoucauldian camp, we would have lost not only the possibility of falling in love ourselves, but the benefit from faking it for instrumental purposes.

Which brings us back to *The Invention of Lying*, the Ricky Gervais romcom. Its premise proves highly Rochefoucauldian: unable to lie, everyone reveals the base motives that animate them. Anna, the object of the lying protagonist's affections, openly admits that she is wavering between him and a better-looking rival. Mark may have convinced everyone that he has a direct line to God, but his egoistic and brutish rival is clearly, as Anna explains, 'genetically superior'. The joke is that all our romantic desires are nothing but a Darwinian search for good genes.

But the movie is unable to sustain its cynicism. In the final scene, God and the afterlife having proved no match for good looks, Anna has chosen the better-looking rival, and they are about to be married. At the wedding, Mark, the screenwriter, has an opportunity to interrupt the proceedings by lying, and claiming that God is opposed to the marriage. It's his unbeatable trump card, but he demurs, saying 'it wouldn't count'. This disinterested gesture proves to be the winning move: when Mark then confesses his secret ability, and Anna realises that he could have lied to capture her heart, but didn't, she truly falls in love with him. Happy ending.

Success in love, then, is the fruit of disinterest once more – even among the Rochefoucauldians. It beats the open egoism of the better-looking rival. But at the risk of submitting a lighthearted romcom to a critique it was not designed to withstand, we can ask how *The Invention of Lying* manages the recurrent paradox that interests us.

The movie tries to have it both ways: people operate on Rochefoucauldian self-interested grounds and never bother to disguise them, but they nonetheless appear able to fall in love. Yet if falling in love is to remain possible, it seems necessary that, though they may be unable to lie to one another, the inhabitants of this parallel society of truthfulness are able to lie *to themselves*. That is, the woman choosing a mate on the basis of genetic fitness will at some point need to convince herself that genetic fitness is not actually the basis of her choice. Otherwise, there is no 'falling' to speak of.*

Hollywood, of course, has always tried to have it both ways. And the conclusion of *The Invention of Lying* follows a familiar script. As Hollywood knows better than anyone, not only does disinterest pay, but stories of disinterest sell. That, to a large extent, is the very business that Hollywood is in. We cannot get enough of stories about practical people throwing away

---

* One might raise the following objection: Anna had not, in fact, fallen in love with the 'genetically superior' rival, but she does fall in love with Mark after his show of disinterest. In this way, the film remains internally consistent, insofar as Anna is the first person ever to fall in love in this parallel world, because she is the first to glimpse the possibility of disinterest. Indeed, since the film's Rochefoucauldian premise is that everyone behaves from transparently self-interested motives, disinterest cannot exist. The intriguing implication is that in the land of the Rochefoucauldians, falling in love only becomes conceivable as a result of disinterest, which only becomes possible through the invention of lying. That is, lying makes love possible.

their conventional careers and staid marriages one morning to pursue their true passions, and setting out on journeys of self-discovery, creation, and spiritual awakening, come what may. And so Hollywood serves it up, again and again.

The appeal is understandable. These stories reassure us that disinterest remains possible, even in our self-aware, instrumental, calculating age.[14] We pine for it, and happily part with our money in exchange for two hours of that reassurance in a darkened theatre.

Yet even in Hollywood, love must remain a byproduct. Much as with J. S. Mill's view of happiness, or the esteem sought by Veblen's well-to-do, love in Hollywood cannot be willed; it must be, well, fallen into. And in most cases, the choice of a life partner, insofar as it is a choice, is disinterested, or it eventually becomes so. Fooling others is difficult, and fooling oneself may be more difficult still. The required duplicity represents a long-term effort, and the self-interested maintenance of the necessary pretence is unsustainable over the long haul. Truly transactional relationships are a slog. It may be that the maximisation of individual utility – a partner with a good job, 'genetically superior' good looks, and family wealth – is what lies underneath all genuine-sounding affection, but the complete absence of genuine affection seems like impossibly hard work. The process of falling in love involves the sublimation of those Utilitarian assets into uncontrolled, non-Utilitarian feeling. One can will a wedding into being, but not love itself.

To borrow a line, the heart must be allowed its reasons, which reason does not know. That famous turn of phrase, from Blaise Pascal, the seventeenth-century French thinker, is invoked most often precisely in the romcom context, to describe, and often to excuse, the follies to which romantic desire pushes us. But it's something of a malapropism.

Fooling Others, Ourselves, and God

Pascal's wager is usually remembered more for its conclusion – yes to God – than for the challenge that the means of reaching this conclusion raise. Pascal himself was both a fervent believer and a systematic thinker. Eventually, the former won over against the latter, and he abandoned his ground-breaking work in mathematics to devote himself to a life of ascetic religious contemplation.

The thought experiment behind the wager represents a rare coming together of both dimensions of Pascal's mind. In wondering about whether faith in God is reasonable, Pascal has recourse to the first explicit instance of an expected value calculation in philosophy. It amounts to applying a business management cost-benefit approach to theology. The idea goes like this: if there is some outcome, the value of which is either infinitely good or infinitely bad, then even if the chance of its occurrence is truly very small, we should act as if this outcome will occur: an infinite quantity multiplied by a small probability remains infinitely large. Say there is some very small chance that an asteroid will hit the earth, but the result would be human extinction, then we should devote all our resources to thinking about how to avoid asteroids hitting the earth. In the theological case, the prize won by the faithful in the event of God's existence, Pascal argued, was infinitely great: 'There is an eternity of life and happiness.' So from an expected value standpoint, one ought to believe.

So far so good, and this is usually where the retelling of Pascal's thought experiment ends. But the most interesting bit actually comes next: if we are convinced by Pascal's reasoning, how do we bring about that soul-saving faith? Because faith, as any other form of belief, is a byproduct: it cannot be willed directly.

Stated in these terms, Pascal's wager becomes one more instance of the paradox faced by J. S. Mill following his epiphany in Chapter 1. To begin with, Pascal's wager is very much premised on a Utilitarian calculation: it is interested in the best likely outcome based on a consideration of the payoffs and their likelihood. But then an individual who would take Pascal at his word would be trapped by the approach, just as J. S. Mill senses that all Utilitarians will be trapped by theirs: having arrived at a conclusion through calculation, they must forget the reasoning that led to that conclusion. The ability to identify religious faith as the optimal outcome conflicts with the ability to achieve that optimal outcome.

It amounts to quite the challenge. Just like the citizens of the parallel universe depicted in *The Invention of Lying*, the individuals eager to carry through on Pascal's wager must fool themselves into believing that their belief is not instrumental – though we all know it to be just that. Similarly, Anna from the film, who first falls for the 'genetically superior' rival, would at some point need to successfully lie to herself, to convince herself that the real reason behind her choice was some ineffable, uncontrollable romantic feeling, rather than the Darwinian search for genetic fitness she knows it to be.

In both cases, the heart must be made to usurp the mantle, even as the head knows that it was the one to bring it to the podium. And this self-effacement itself seems the domain of reason, which needs to act as a hidden handmaid, performing her task without ever being seen to do so. Reason must whisper to the heart the reasons which she must then find a way of forgetting.

Did Pascal himself believe that this sleight of hand could be pulled off? The passage following the wager suggests so. There, Pascal offers advice to a hypothetical unbeliever who would be convinced by his reasoning, the implication being that unbelievers could be pushed towards faith by an appeal to reason.[15]

In Pascal's time, in the latter half of the seventeenth century, the role of self-interest in religious faith was a live question. It is no coincidence that just as thinkers like La Rochefoucauld were skewering the pretences of an aristocratic society formerly based on honour, revealing it to be driven instead by self-love, ambition, and greed, theologians of a mystical bent began applying similar reasoning to the pretences behind religious practice, revealing them to be equally self-serving.

The most eloquent among them was the mystic Archbishop of Cambrai, François Fénelon. If people turned to God in search of inner peace, or from a fear of death, or to assure themselves of a comfortable afterlife, how would God take to such instrumental behaviour? 'He will not receive it,' replied Fénelon. Faith as a means to personal happiness was unworthy of God. Instead, all believers needed to aim for what Fénelon called 'holy indifference': an utter lack of interest in one's salvation, other than as the carrying out of God's will.[16] As with today's consumers of sourdough, what God cared about was the underlying intent.

Religious authorities must have feared that this was setting the bar a little high for ordinary Sunday churchgoers. In 1699, both the Sun King, Louis XIV of France, and Pope Innocent XII condemned Fénelon's writings as heretical. If you're keeping track of your theological intrigues, this was the heart of the Quietist controversy that ripped through the European Church at the turn of the eighteenth century.

How are three-century-old theological spats relevant to our examination of the faker? Just as the best pre-Enlightenment art in Europe is religious art, so too was the sharpest human reasoning of the time devoted to religious questions. In this way, these mystical theologians' musings provided much of the scaffolding upon which later thinkers would build their own arguments about self-interest, and the ability to suspend self-interest in an attempt to advance it.

Fénelon, the archbishop, could thus be just as ruthless in his hunt for interested motives as La Rochefoucauld, the 'sharpshooter':

> You see him, he's not disinterested, however much he tries to seem it ... He wants to love so that others love him in turn, and so that others will be touched by his disinterestedness; he seems to forget about himself only to better engross the world with himself.[17]

And yet, Fénelon appears full of understanding for the faker's striving: how can anyone resist the draw of disinterest, he seems to say. What else can a rational self-interested individual do, upon seeing the benefits of passion? 'Self-renunciation appears so grand that self-love itself seeks to mimic it, and finds no greater glory than to seem as if it is not seeking any.'[18]

More than any other writer, past or present, Fénelon gives words to the Faker's ruminations:

> He does not say to himself: 'I want to fool the world by my disinterest, so that everyone loves and admires me.' No, he would not tell himself such crude and unworthy things; but he fools himself by fooling others; he looks upon his disinterest with smugness ... the illusion that he casts on others shines back on him.[19]

In the same passage, Fénelon applies the same cold-shower treatment to those who would portend to renounce material riches – they too are fooling themselves. Of one such ascetic, he writes,

> He cannot stand those who get drunk on their fortune; he wants, by his moderation, to be above wealth itself, and

thus to create a new level of achievement for himself ... it is to want, like Lucifer, to become equal to God.

The dilemma is by now familiar to us. But considering it in a theological context is useful because it poses the question in its hardest form: after all, we might fool others; we might even fool ourselves; but is it conceivable to fool God? If we are convinced by, say, the reasoning in Pascal's wager, perhaps we can make ourselves believe, and even forget the reasons for setting out to do so in the first place. But would God ever forget?

If we are of a Kantian bent, we may impose similarly theological strictures on ourselves when dealing with friendship or charity. We may try and deny ourselves the satisfaction of good deeds from fear that we carried these out from some hidden attempt at attaining this satisfaction. As Schiller quipped, 'I help my friends, and it feels nice / Until I fear that it's a vice.'[20] The only way to sustain the glow that comes from giving a friend a hand is to never become aware of its warmth.

Is the Faker Doomed?

We are thus back at our initial question: is the faker doomed to remain a tragic character? The stakes of the question could hardly be higher: the fate of the modern market rests on it, for starters. It will determine whether the baker can ever convince his customers of his passion, when they know full well that he also stands to profit from it. What conclusion observers draw whenever a posture of disinterest pays also holds implications for our ability to love truly, the possibility of genuine friendship, and the ability to attain religious faith. So having revealed the ways in which 'disinterest pays', are we destined to be frustrated fakers?

La Rochefoucauld thought so: any appearance of disinterested motivation should be seen for what it is, self-interest in disguise. And though Pascal held out the possibility of 'faking till you make it', in his later writing he also suggested that true faith could only be the result of grace: a gift from God. And Fénelon was suspicious of all efforts embarked on for the wrong reasons – Lucifer, the fallen angel, also tried to outdo God in his goodness. The political scientist Jon Elster, of Columbia University, is similarly pessimistic about the faker's prospects; as he puts it, 'It is of course possible to fake a belief, if what is useful is other people's belief that one has it rather than the belief itself, but I do not think one can fool oneself in the same way.'[21] Taken together, this makes for a bleak verdict.

And yet, a simple fact remains: disinterested behaviour does exist – we see glimpses of it in ourselves, and we know others who embody it in full. We all know some truly passionate brewers and bakers. It is, in fact, our skill at detecting fakers that allows us to also recognise genuine passion when we encounter it. These ascetics, obsessives, fanatics, they inspire awe in us. Then how unfortunate it is when, having finally come upon such a true passionate, one day they turn around and betray us. Because for all the hope we had pinned on them, passionates sometimes prove weaker in the face of temptation than we had hoped. We sigh: the passionate is a *sellout*.

5

On Sellouts

On his way to a promised Eden of profitable disinterest, the faker may encounter someone headed in the opposite direction: it's his counterpart, the *sellout*. And though, like the faker, the sellout gets a bad rap, it is often undeserved. Just as we all occasionally find ourselves in the position of the faker, there are also times when we find ourselves walking in the shoes of the sellout.

Selling out is borne of a revelation. Like Adam and Eve growing suddenly aware of their nakedness, the true passionates eventually come to realise how their passion is perceived by others. This newfound awareness marks their coming of age. Suddenly, they grasp that the market will reward them for the same actions they have been doing all along – and which they would have continued to do regardless of the gains.

From that moment onwards, the temptation to shift their allegiances can only grow. It's an imperceptible shift at first. Their actual behaviour may remain unchanged; but the underlying intent behind it begins to drift. The passionate brewer keeps at his microbrew, and the Puritan keeps at his calling. But they now do so with a new understanding: the realisation that disinterest pays.

When Heinrich von Kleist, the nineteenth-century German romantic writer cited in Chapter 3, describes the beautiful adolescent at the baths as 'manifest[ing] only the faintest first traces of vanity fostered by the favour of women', he has in mind that knife edge of transition between the two realms. The recognition of his beauty has only begun to dawn on the youth, who'd previously thought nothing of it. The friends who then clap and urge him to repeat the gesture which he'd performed innocently precipitate his undoing. He has passed from the sphere of disinterest to that of interested commerce. From an unthinking gesture done for no reason but to dry his wet foot, to one that he now attempts to please his friends. From action to performance. It purports to be the very same gesture; the youth tries with all his might to reproduce it faithfully. And yet, something is amiss. What exactly has happened from one moment to the other?

Here, Max Weber proves useful once more. Because Weber's subject is the original sellout to capitalism. It's right there in the title of his magnum opus: *The Protestant Ethic and the Spirit of Capitalism*. The first belongs squarely to the realm of disinterested commerce; the second is the animating principle of interested commerce. The sellout walks from the first over to the second. In Weber's telling, this is what all the New England Puritans ended up doing, shifting their aim from the pursuit of a religious calling to an economic one. 'Certainly,' he writes, 'these Puritan ideals of life could be defeated when subjected to an unduly strong pressure from the temptations of wealth.'[1]

It is often the case that the disinterested realm, the sellout's native land, is not merely indifferent to the lure of the market, but exists in explicit opposition to it. This is most clearly the case with the Puritans, who were outright repulsed by any hint of the money god Mammon – hence the drab clothing, and their pervasive suspicion of all adornment. As Weber put it, they 'saw in the striving for wealth *as a goal* the ultimate in what is reprehensible'.[2] Wealth was fine, commendable even, as long as it remained unintended.

Like the lapsed Puritan, the sellout confuses means and ends. What was done for its own sake is now performed instrumentally. Or, to be more accurate, what was an unintended byproduct of actions undertaken for some other end has now become the end itself. The baker still bakes his sourdough, but he now does it to grow the business, rather than out of intrinsic passion. Soon, to allow for greater economies of scale, the kneading is done by machine.

But we know what happens when a byproduct is sought as an end. We are back to J. S. Mill's original insight. We have returned to Sedgwick's paradox of hedonism, and Scanlon's paradox of teleology. When the object of our pursuit is a byproduct, our reaching for it only pushes it further away.

Such was the fate of the Puritans. They had the misfortune of conceiving of their divine calling in such a way that their day-to-day behaviour could remain ostensibly the same, whether the end being sought was spiritual salvation or profit-seeking. The shift from one to the other was almost imperceptible: wealth had been the unintended byproduct of a divine pursuit, now it became the goal itself. It was so swiftly done. Who would even know the difference?

We might ask the same of the countless music bands who, on the serendipitous path to success, irrevocably disappointed their earliest fans. I suspect that to most people, the term 'sellout' does not immediately conjure the image of Weber's New England Puritans. What's more likely to come to mind is a band we all loved in our youth, which was known only to us and to a small circle of devotees who happened to be our closest friends; a band we went to see once in a cramped sweaty bar and that we revered, until they had the gall to make it big.

From that day on, they were dead to us. We threw up our hands just like metalheads sighing at the mention of Metallica; hip-hop fans who covered their eyes when Snoop Dogg collaborated with Katy Perry; and rock 'n' roll audiences who cried out 'Judas!' when Bob Dylan went electric. All of them traitors, trading an original vision for radio plays, signing away their souls in exchange of greater fame, artists turning themselves into popstars.

The Artist as Sellout

Musicians are undoubtedly the most frequent targets of the term. There may be good reason for this. The temptation of mainstream appeal in an industry where the average band does not earn enough to make ends meet is great, though economic destitution is also the modal state of writers and painters. But music, more than any other medium, serves as an early means of identity formation for adolescents. Young listeners identify themselves with genres, bands, and musicians, and in so doing hitch their own credibility on the credibility of their musical icons. Mass appeal is also minutely tracked, with micro-movements of market success updated on a weekly basis. The Top 40, the Billboard Hot 100 Chart. No other artistic medium has as visible a ranking of changing popular approval.

All of which leads to a phenomenon that would seem inconceivable, were it not so familiar: an artist's success makes them suspicious in the eyes of the audiences that originally championed them. The mere fact of appealing to a growing number becomes cause for suspicion, and evidence of a shift in intent.

And that is the reproach that lies underneath all accusations of selling out: the artist is charged with having gone from doing their work in a disinterested manner, beholden only to the art itself, to caring about how their work is perceived. They have walked from one form of commerce to the other. Once they are seen to care about winning approval, and what is worse, pursuing its market rewards, they are for ever tainted.

The challenge the artist faces is the same as underlies all human commerce: how to be believed? Much like the passionate entrepreneur, they must convince the audience of their integrity. Persuade their audience that they are of one type, rather than the other; the one driven by an original artistic vision, rather than its earthly rewards. Tellingly, it is precisely the language of credibility that is used to denounce compromising moves: musicians have not 'stayed true' to their promise, their sound, their original vision. Often, those compromising moves do not even relate to the music itself, but to any gesture directed at financial gain: a musician collaborates with a mainstream act, plays a larger venue, sells the rights to its song to a Volkswagen commercial,* and their original fans turn on them in scorn.[3]

Just as a creditor might be less willing to lend to a lapsed Puritan than to the bona fide believer, so too will the discriminating listener be less willing to invest themselves in a musician whom they see as selling out for mass appeal. The currency of the Dylan coin or of the Snoop Dogg bond is then devalued. And this devaluation resembles monetary inflation in other

---

* No other company has done more to expose indie musicians to mass audiences, and thus earned as much scorn from the original fans for slaying their sacred cows: see Nick Drake's 'Pink Moon', Grizzly Bear's 'Two Weeks', and an entire catalogue of songs by Wilco.

respects: the greater an artist's fan base, the less valuable one's devotion to that artist is as a marker of discriminating taste and in-group knowingness.

The earliest use of 'sellout' carried a strictly positive connotation. Sellout crowds, a sold-out opening show. Its negative usage emerged first in the political context, to mean the act of giving in to pressure from powerful interest groups. One sold out to big business, or to the unions.[4] When the label's derisive meaning travelled to the music industry sometime in the 1950s, it was first used by Black audiences denouncing jazz musicians who were seen as trying to appeal to white listeners.[5]

It will come as no surprise that race was the major dividing line marking credibility claims in 1950s America. In a way that speaks to the opposition by symmetry between the sellout and the faker, the original usage of 'hipster', the label affixed to the prototypical cultural faker of the 2000s, emerged in the very same period. Just as the term 'sellout' was being thrown at jazz musicians catering to white audiences, 'hipster' was lobbed at white Americans in the 1950s who espoused 'black tastes' in an attempt to capture some of the exoticism and energy associated with black culture.[6] This hipster intersected with the Beats (think of Allen Ginsberg's 'angel-headed hipsters' from the poem *Howl*): a white middle-class movement reacting against white middle-class tastes. Jazz was at the centre of both these motions: sellouts producing, and fakers consuming, each accused of scheming for self-advancement.

The Sellout's Natural Habitat

Since what the sellout has to offer is their original disinterestedness, they most often emerge from those rarefied domains that purport to be devoted to principles and values that rise above

self-interest: the various fields of culture, from music to independent film and contemporary art, but also the fields of science
and public service. In each case, the sellout shifts from the pursuit of a disinterested aim – an original artistic vision, scientific
truth, the public good – to an interested one: money, fame, votes.
The sellout in the music industry lends a song to a car commercial; literary authors turn to genre fiction and sell the rights to a
Hollywood studio; film directors regarded as auteurs sign on to
a crowd-pleasing summer blockbuster.

There is no worse pan in the art critic's vocabulary than
the description of a piece of contemporary art as 'decorative'. In the realm of science, the scholar sells out by turning
into a 'public intellectual'. One overhears sneers at academic
conferences: 'Look at Paul Krugman, who used to be a good
economist, but then he won the Nobel Prize and became –
what, an opinion peddler?' Krugman is in good company. 'Joe
Stiglitz? Used to do serious work, then they handed him a
Nobel, and suddenly he's turned into some lefty activist.' Just as
with musicians scorned for softening their original sound to win
over radio audiences, public intellectuals are accused of compromising their scientific standards in an attempt to offer easy
soundbites to a mass readership. They are derided for valuing
flashy findings and zippy titles over careful method.

Even democratic politics, the very premise of which is to
appeal to majority preferences, is not immune from accusations
of selling out. In political markets, the sellout is the opportunist
who is willing to dilute their original ideals in pursuit of broader
appeal. For this reason, the political sellout usually originates
from the political fringes, where winning office was a sufficiently remote prospect that they could indulge in espousing
radical views. The unlikelihood of actually winning office is
seen as a licence for speaking truthfully. But when the outward
appearance of disinterest begins to pay off, when the political

'outsider' begins to reap rewards from her outsider status, and once the prospect of actually gaining power comes into view, the temptation to build on the momentum, to vie for the median voter by moving closer to the political centre, also comes at the risk of alienating the original base of ardent supporters. These politicians must walk a fine line, as they try and remain the outsider even once they are inside. One increasingly common tactic is to project a sufficiently softened image to appeal to mainstream voters, while dog-whistling audibly enough for the original base to hear. If different audiences can interpret the same speech in their own preferred way, then the political sellout can have it both ways, courting mainstream voters while retaining their more radical base.

Faker and Sellout Meet

The challenge faced by the outsider-on-the-inside politician illustrates how our two characters, the faker and the sellout, frequently end up converging on the same behaviour. The savviest sellouts, realising that their market appeal rests on their disinterested origins, continue to gesture towards these even as they cross the threshold of self-interest.

Consider Benjamin Franklin, Weber's Exhibit A. Weber realised Franklin had crossed the threshold: 'The religious foundation [of asceticism] had already ceased to exist at the time of Ben Franklin.' Temptation had proven too strong; the Puritans had given in. At some point, their descendants, Franklin among them, had lost sight of the ultimate goal – spiritual salvation – and had instead set about attaining its outward manifestation: material prosperity. Weber saw this as the narrative arc of all spiritual radicals: 'The entire history of the monastic orders is, in a sense, one of constant wrestling with the problem of the secularizing influence of wealth.'[7]

But secularisation also meant giving up the source of their unique credibility. Ben Franklin realised this. That's why he advocated performance, advising the young tradesman to start hammering at 5 a.m. – not in order to repair his roof, but as a way of fooling creditors. The original Puritans had had no need for such artifice. They were readily believed by creditors, precisely *because* they did not play by the market's rules and actively rejected its tenets. Then, as soon as they adopted the market's goals as their own, as soon as the creditor recognised them as his brethren, he regarded them with newfound suspicion. He demanded a risk premium on his loan, additional guarantees on his investment, more equity in the partnership. He now wanted signed documents, affidavits, bona fide contracts: the friction of interested commerce. The Puritans had gone soft; by no longer denouncing Mammon with their old vehemence, they had fallen out of Mammon's favour. Their market advantage was squandered.

The savviest sellouts realise this, and they know to avoid crossing over fully. They remain as if suspended between the two realms. Their intent may have shifted, but they still gesture to their disinterested origins. In this way, Ben Franklin continued to speak the language of Puritanism. In his wildly popular *Poor Richard's Almanach*, built around a compendium of folk sayings, Franklin reiterates the tune of hard work, asceticism, and saving. He sneers at sleep ('How much more than is necessary do we spend in Sleep! forgetting that The sleeping Fox catches no Poultry, and that there will be sleeping enough in the Grave'); laziness ('Sloth, like Rust, consumes faster than Labour wears'); and frivolities of all kinds ('Women and Wine, Game and Deceit, Make the Wealth small, and the Wants great'). Even that most famous saying of Franklin's, 'time is money', which Weber cites with such scholarly glee, marks the passage from one realm to the other. Historians agree that the phrase does have its roots in

Puritanism – with the notable difference that what the Puritans were maximising was not money, but time for prayer.[8]

The very crest of the transition from disinterested to interested commerce appears as Franklin readily takes the religious counsel of his father, a Calvinist minister, and turns it around into a business-school axiom. As he writes in his autobiography, 'My Father having among his Instructions to me when a Boy, frequently repeated a Proverb of Solomon, "*Seest thou a Man diligent in his Calling, he shall stand before Kings, he shall not stand before mean Men.*"' And Franklin concludes: 'I from thence consider'd Industry as a Means of obtaining Wealth and Distinction.' Just like that, from one sentence to the next, as a magician turns a bird into a coin, Franklin has swapped the object of pursuit from salvation to affluence.*

The tastes of the Franklin household underwent a similar transformation, from asceticism to more capitalist-friendly forms. In his autobiography, Ben Franklin begins by boasting of the simplicity of his early ways, of how he would eat breakfast out of a 'twopenny earthen Porringer with a Pewter Spoon'. But then he lays blame on his wife, Deborah – like Adam accusing Eve of ceding to temptation in both their names – for introducing luxury into their home. It's a playful, self-deprecating passage:

> But mark how Luxury will enter Families, and make a Progress, in Spite of Principle. Being Call'd one Morning to Breakfast, I found it in a China Bowl with a Spoon of Silver. They had been bought for me without my Knowledge by my Wife, and had cost her the enormous Sum of three and twenty Shillings, for which she had no

---

* And to good effect: as Franklin goes on to note, his father's counsel proved prescient. He did in fact stand before five kings, and even had dinner with one of them, the King of Denmark.

other Excuse or Apology to make, but that she thought *her* Husband deserv'd a Silver Spoon and China Bowl as well as any of his Neighbours.

We are reminded of Adam Smith poking fun at the aspiring middle class encumbering itself with 'baubles and trinkets' and devising new pockets in their coats just to hold these in. The motivation in both cases is to earn the esteem of one's neighbour. 'To be observed, to be attended to, to be taken notice of with sympathy, complacency, and approbation.'[9] What better way of paying tribute to the Spirit of Capitalism than by trying to keep up with the Joneses through the purchase of silver spoons?

From that moment on, Franklin cheerfully admits, all was lost: 'This was the first Appearance of Plate and China in our House, which afterwards in a Course of Years as our Wealth encreas'd, augmented gradually to several Hundred Pounds in Value.' And indeed, there would later be a harpsichord and a large library and lace curtains, and so many other goods that the Franklin family eventually had to move to a large three-storey brick house on Market Street to contain it all.[10] They had run out of pockets in their clothing.

And yet notice the lighthearted tone of Franklin's 'confession'. Rather than beating his breast in penance, he seems altogether amused at seeing the change in himself. In his choice of an exemplar for the spirit of capitalism, Weber picked the wrong horse. Because for a sellout to capitalism, Franklin proved exceptionally adept at turning his back on market incentives. He retired happily at the age of forty-three, selling his printing business and devoting himself to a life of fruitful leisure. As he explained,

When I disengag'd myself as above mentioned from private Business, I flatter'd myself that, by the sufficient tho' moderate Fortune I had acquir'd, I had secur'd Leisure during the rest of my Life, for Philosophical Studies and Amusements.[11]

It's hardly the picture of a capitalist unable to quit market incentives. But that is the fate Weber envisions for those under the sway of Capitalism's spirit. In the last pages of *The Protestant Ethic*, which are likely its most famous, Weber abandons his usual value-neutral scholarly demeanour and, in a much-cited line, laments how we are all imprisoned in the 'iron cage' of capitalism, from which there is no exit: 'the outward goods of this world gained increasing and finally inescapable power over men'. The Puritans *chose* to devote themselves to their calling, Weber concludes, while we have had it imposed on us.[12]

From this angle, Ben Franklin appears to have belonged to a far rarer breed than the common sellout. Even once Franklin converted from the dogma of his Calvinist father to that of the market, he remained able to see capitalism as merely a means to an end. As he wrote his mother, 'I would rather have it said that "He lived usefully" than that "He died rich".'[13] Not quite the motto of a spirited capitalist. By his early forties, he was out of the game, and on to another. And then another one yet. He went from commerce to pursuits in science, and then moved on to politics and diplomacy, leaving behind remarkable achievements in each. Franklin was able to pull off that rare feat: to step back and alter the object of his pursuits.

The New Puritans

So the New England Puritans sold out, abandoning their calling, with its single purpose of salvation, for its outward marker: material prosperity. Many, like Ben Franklin, very likely became more agreeable human beings in the process. Yet the

Puritans continued to inspire subsequent American generations. For the next two centuries, New England, in particular, remained a breeding ground for a wide range of Utopian and Christian-socialist communes – all of them self-declared zones of exception, pockets of resistance founded on sexual egalitarian, vegetarian, transcendent ideals.

Though they fashioned themselves after different schools of thought, from Fourierism to Owenism, the nineteenth-century American communes tended towards shared property and a rejection of capitalist modes of production that had arisen under the industrial revolution. In many cases, these ideas extended to sexual property, giving renewed meaning to the archaic usage of the term 'commerce'. The American communes engaged in various forms of industry, but they did so to sustain the life of the community, and never with the accumulation of wealth as their goal. Yet, remarkably, a number of these utopian communes grew prosperous.

The Oneida Community is one such example. Founded in 1848 in the town of Oneida, in upstate New York, it was founded around principles of 'complex marriage', which its members believed were divinely ordained. Monogamy was considered a sin; couples that paired up were publicly chastised. To sustain the community, Oneida began making silverware, animal traps, and silk products.[14]

As is often the case, an intensely shared ideology helped the commune's members reach high levels of cooperation. What is more interesting is that this internal trust also spilt over into commerce with outsiders. Those who engaged in business relations with the commune often referred to their reputation for honesty and reliability. The utopians' social weirdness was the source of economic credibility. And as with the Puritans, disinterest turned out to be a uniquely effective way to affluence. By seeking to dismantle capitalism, and by scorning profits, they too became unusually reliable economic partners. Of course, not all nineteenth-century American utopian communities prospered financially. But among those that did, many regularly credited their success to the disinterested devotion of their members and their outward perception of reliability.

As one citizen of the town in which the Oneida Community was located wrote in a letter to the local newspaper, 'Every department of their business is a model of neatness and order. They are a hive of industry; they make the best goods in the market in every department which they manufacture. They have a model farm ... I wish all the people in the world were as honest as they are.'[15] In an article about Oneida, the *Sunday Register* in New Haven, Connecticut concluded, 'In many respects their habits are commendable. They are thrifty, industrious and honest – qualities all too rare.'[16]

In a country where the Spirit of Capitalism had come in in full, the American communes thus held out, for a while, as pockets of disinterested commerce: more concerned with utopian ideals of Christian love, or its free love alternatives, than in material prosperity. Those that prospered did so not in spite of their disinterest, but seemingly thanks to it. Yet, a recurrent pattern would then take hold. A utopian ethic would cede to a capitalist spirit.

Oneida continued to prosper for a quarter of a century, though its sexual practices drew opprobrium and made it a target of the local clergy, until, in 1879, Oneida's members voted to reorganise themselves as one of the first joint stock companies in the US. Free love took a back seat, and the thriving business that had been a mere byproduct of their 'joyous' work now became the point.[17]

Many communities built as social experiments eventually drifted from their first principles, and shifted from disinterested commerce to its interested counterpart. But the savviest among them tried to preserve at least the appearance of the traits that led them to prosper in the first place.[18] In 1902, years after the Oneida had gone commercial, the author of a study on the American utopian communities, and former member of Oneida himself, wrote, 'The reputation of the old [Oneida] Community for honest work and honest dealing is rigidly maintained; and altogether the future prospects of the new organization are full of encouragement.'[19] He guessed right. Nearly a century later, Oneida Limited was making more than half of all the flatware in the US, and it eventually grew into the world's largest manufacturer of stainless-steel cutlery. If you sit down in an American diner today, the Oneida name is still the most likely to be stamped on the backside of your spoon, a lasting testament to the commune-turned-corporation; an illustration of the dividend of disinterest, and of the resulting temptation to convert it into interested commerce.

Again and again, hostility to market ideals proves irresistible to market actors; disinterested commerce is embraced by its interested counterpart. Incentives change, until the markets' former dissidents are converted to its ideals. The same irony played out with the original Puritans, their descendants in nineteenth-century communes, and then once more, during the next wave of American utopianism, in the countercultural movements of the 1960s.

This time, the young people who fled cities for rural settings favoured the West Coast over New England. They shared similar views on property and sexual freedom. And just as in the past, some of the hippy communities that had defined themselves by opposition to market ideas then redefined themselves around the budding enterprises that had initially been meant only to sustain them. Among these was the Kerista Community, founded in the 1970s in Northern California as a free-love 'scientific utopian community'. As a sideline to keep itself afloat, the community began distributing Apple computers. Given their convictions around 'Total Rationality' and principles of human progress through science, they were early believers and fervent evangelists of the computing revolution.

Kerista did well. As with Oneida, observers attributed this success to their 'hippy business ethic': far in advance of the techno-utopian ethos of today's Silicon Valley, they called themselves 'A Vision with a Business'. They worked hard; as a fawning *Wired* article summed up, they were 'not just promiscuous, [but] extremely industrious'.[20] They too were not in it for the money; what they wanted was to usher in a technological utopia. Within five years of the commune's founding, their side-business was generating $35 million in sales. 'Not bad for a bunch of hippies,' one former member of Kerista reflected, adding what is now the standard axiom of the Bay Area tech community: 'All we wanted to do was change the world.' As in past social experiments generating an economic byproduct, once their disinterested approach began to pay off, the goal shifted. 'We went from being an artist community to a computer business ... The whole culture changed. It became workaholic, yuppie cyberculture.'[21]

The dance of disinterest and temptation still proceeds through the same steps today. The mere mention of Burning Man suffices to make the point: it was initially devised as a modern-day, explicitly anti-capitalist gathering in the Nevada desert in the late 1980s, fashioning itself after the potlatch concept of giving away rather than accumulating wealth. From that felicitous premise, the event has turned into something more akin to a corporate retreat, attracting Silicon Valley entrepreneurs and Fortune 500 execs with their staff in tow, all seeking networking opportunities in an innovation-inspiring setting. As one participant quipped, 'I've tried to write it off on my taxes for many years, considering how much business I get done out there. But my accountant won't let me.'[22] From an event carried out for its own sake – culminating with the burning of the great wooden structure of the 'man', a gesture akin to the erasing of the intricate sand mandalas made by Buddhist monks as soon as they are completed – the coming together in the desert has become a means to all sorts of ends: connections among innovators, corporate bonding, the recharging of creative energies, all of them designed to be redeployed towards greater productivity once back in the Valley.

Burning Man's organisers have half-heartedly tried to preserve the event as a space of disinterested commerce, by banning any barter or exchange of money. But, fortunately, one can prepay for one's helicopter rides and luxury camp ahead of time. And while the event's commodification is a frequent target of ridicule, what is notable, if anything, is the way interested commerce continues to extract real value from the original premise of disinterest. Seed rounds of venture-capital funding are sealed with a hug, and the pretence of a zone of exception to market rules continues to prove beneficial to business dealings. The event remains sufficiently suspended between the two Humean poles of commerce to reap market rewards that cannot be found in regular boardrooms. Disinterest continues to pay its dividend.

Looking back, the progressive encroachment of market forces into a space of purported disinterest 400 miles away from Silicon Valley has an air of inevitability. The glow given off by Burning Man was always going to prove irresistible to the self-interested sphere, who descended like moths drawn to a light.

Tragedy Once More?

Though they have opposite origins and opposite destinations, we have seen how the sellout and the faker often meet in the middle, suspended between the two realms. The sellout keeps gesturing towards her native land of disinterest, while the faker is unable to fully shake the mannerisms that betray his self-interested origins. The sellout wants to persuade us that she has not crossed over entirely; the faker assures us that he has, though he is ultimately unable to.

Our two characters share something else in common. We have seen that the faker's destiny is a tragic one: in setting out to appear disinterested, the faker's initial intention would seem to preclude the possibility of success. But the sellout's trajectory is no less marked by tragedy. Like Oedipus running away from his foretold destiny, the sellout shuns the market, only to grow irresistible to it. Eventually, the temptation to cede to the very ideals she initially shunned becomes too much to bear. It is the sellout's initial disinterestedness that marks her ultimate downfall – by the very standard of her original ideals.

As with the Puritans and the utopian communes of the 1800s, so too with the hippies of the 1960s. By trying to espouse values squarely opposed to the Spirit of Capitalism, they proved overwhelmingly captivating to market society. Disinterest is a draw. And this appeal to the sphere of interested commerce is what creates the incentive to sell out, which in turn kills off the source of the initial market appeal. In elevating passion, the market precipitates its eventual devaluation. Music bands cannot help but care about their growing audience, just as Puritans cannot help but shift their view of prosperity, from a byproduct to the goal itself. And passionate entrepreneurs 'not in it for the money' eventually find that, as their passion begins to pay off, money may not be such a bad thing to be in it for.

Does Selling Out Matter?

So does it matter? Does it ultimately make a difference whether an entrepreneur is moved by passion or profit, as long as they keep offering their product? Should the creditor really care about the Puritan's purity? Does that Puritan actually become less dependable once he goes from toil-as-the-goal to toil-as-a-means-to-prosperity? Were we right to lash out against our favourite band when it hit the Top 10 chart and sold the rights to its songs to a car commercial? Did their music sound any different for it? In other words, does the cult of authenticity have any basis? Is our inkling to trust passion over profit well grounded, or did Adam Smith really know best, and should we instead simply put our trust in one another's 'regard to [our] own interest'?

In the discussion of fakers, we saw how recent experiments conducted by behavioural scientists can throw light on the social costs incurred by those who would try, as the faker might, to conceal their strategic attempts at self-presentation under a veneer of humility. Similar experimental approaches can illuminate what happens when individuals drift in the opposite direction, from an activity performed disinterestedly to one performed out of self-interest.

This recent crop of behavioural scientists conceive of Hume's two sorts of commerce in terms of 'intrinsic motivation' versus 'extrinsic motivation'. The term 'intrinsic' refers to inherent rewards, of the kind that, say, friendship provides. As a seminal study from 1971 explained, 'One is said to be intrinsically motivated to perform an activity when he receives no apparent rewards except the activity itself.'[23] In other words, the task is an end in itself. It is what T. S. Eliot once called an 'autotelic' activity, from the Greek *auto* and *telos*: self-goal. By contrast, extrinsic motivation represents an activity done instrumentally, with some other goal in mind, be it money, recognition, or the esteem of others.

And while economic markets are usually built upon extrinsic motivation – wages, merit bonuses, performance reviews, score cards – laboratory experiments have repeatedly shown that this may not be the most effective, and certainly not the most efficient, means of getting the most out of people. More generally, what emerges from the study of intrinsic versus extrinsic motivation is the extent to which behaviour *does* change when individuals shift from one to the other.

In one such study by James Heyman of Berkeley and Dan Ariely of MIT, subjects were asked to repeatedly drag a circle onto a square on a computer screen for five minutes. Half of the sample was paid, the other was not. Among those who received money, some were paid a little (fifty cents), while others were paid a lot ($5). The effort of each subject was then measured by the number of circles they had dragged over in the allotted time. The question was, who would try hardest? It turned out that those who got paid more did make a greater effort than those that were paid little, but those that were paid nothing actually made the greatest effort of all.

This counterintuitive inverse relationship between reward and effort turns is in fact one of the oldest findings of behavioural science. Half a century ago, Edward Deci, a psychologist at the University of Rochester, showed that it seemed to apply to his psychology students: those offered monetary compensation put less effort into solving a puzzle than those who were offered nothing in return. It turns out pre-school-age children respond in similar ways to psychology undergrads: offer them material rewards, and they abandon hard tasks sooner than if they get nothing in exchange.[24] The conclusion across these studies is that rewards risk undermining effort if they shift the type of motivation, from doing a task for its own sake to carrying it out for some external end.

A half-century of such experiments led Ariely to conclude that 'we live in two worlds: one characterized by social exchanges and the other characterized by market exchanges ... Moreover, introducing market norms into social exchanges, as we have seen, violates the social norms and hurts the relationships.' Poor David Hume never gets a mention in any of these studies, though he had reached similar conclusions about 'two sorts of commerce', each one with their respective norms, some 300 years earlier.

We now also know that the mere *mention* of money is enough to prompt a shift akin to selling out. In fact, even fake money will do: when subjects brought in for an experiment were primed with a stack of Monopoly money lying in their field of view, they adjusted their behaviour, and became less willing to help an undergraduate student who later asked for their assistance with a five-minute task.[25]

These findings operate beyond the lab. When an association of retirees asked a group of lawyers if they might offer legal services to its members for a reduced fee of $30 an hour, most refused. When that fee was lowered to nothing, and the lawyers were asked to offer their services entirely for free, they disproportionately agreed. The effect also works in the opposite direction: when Steve Jobs returned to Apple, he famously worked for an annual salary of $1. Then, in 2000, the board of directors suggested he finally be paid; they were stunned by Jobs' demand of a Gulfstream V jet and 20 million options, a larger compensation package than the board had the authority to offer.[26]

Mouthwatering Market Implications

The first takeaway from these studies is that some of the suspicion of sellouts is in fact warranted. When working within the realm of disinterested commerce, we may actually put greater effort into tasks. The passionate artisan who turns his mind from passion to profit may continue to ply his craft, but there is actual reason to believe that the product may be affected by the shift in allegiance.

The market itself may suggest some of these changes – sometimes it outright imposes them. And subtle though they may be, we have a keen intuitive sense for these transformations; we see them coming. If a supermarket wants to capitalise on the passionate baker's passion, it may offer him a large licensing contract. The smaller margins on the bigger order may then require a little less marzipan in the almond croissants, and fewer raisins on the brioche; the increase in scale means the production must become more standardised, and each strudel now appears a little more similar to the next. The baker himself becomes more occupied with questions of marketing and distribution, and we never see him at the bakery any more, though a photograph of his face now adorns all the shop's packaging. We say, 'I used to go when it was still a tiny hole in the wall – they made the best sourdough, but then they went big, completely sold out, and now no one buys their bread any more.' So when the baker at the corner assures us that they're 'not in it for the money', they are actually attempting to credibly signal, 'my sourdough tastes better'. And behavioural science backs them up.

Similarly, creditors may be right to put more faith in the original Puritans than in their descendants, who came to regard prosperity as a goal, rather than an unintended byproduct. Just like the subjects of lab experiments who stopped working on a puzzle sooner when they were earning a fee for it, the lapsed Puritan may break his commitment earlier than his progenitor when the going gets tough. The creditor may be right to doubt what social scientists call his level of 'resolve': the likelihood of carrying through on commitments made.

But these findings also hold another lesson, and this one has a darker side. In Ariely's experiment, it takes a $5 reward for a five-minute task to approach, without actually surpassing,[27] the level of effort that subjects put into doing the same task for no reward at all. That amounts to the handsome wage of $60 an hour... In the case of Steve Jobs, once Apple's board got him to shift from one realm to the other, it took a private jet and millions of dollars-worth of stock options to get Jobs to keep doing the same task he'd been doing for its own sake for two and a half years. The takeaway is that it is of course possible to replicate the commitment and keenness of workers operating within the realm of disinterest by offering them material incentives – it's just very expensive.

Consider how this is likely to sound to a dyed-in-the-wool capitalist. If an employer can manage to convince workers that their work ought to be thought of as belonging to the realm of disinterested, rather than interested commerce, the gains to the employer are immense. Not only does the pretence of disinterest hold out the promise of the economist's dreamed-of frictionless transacting – no need for contracts, affidavits, or protracted wage negotiations – but workers are likely to work harder and longer than if they are driven by self-interest alone. In other words, a world where tasks are performed for their own sake rather than for instrumental ends is a capitalist utopia – as long as the market gets to decide which tasks these will be.

What an unexpected twist. Wasn't the market meant to be a space of alienation, where workers were mere cogs in the machine, disconnected from the fruit of their labour? Isn't commerce the world of thoughtless accumulation for the sake of accumulation? And aren't those rarefied worlds where things are performed for their own sake, the worlds of art, science, and friendship, spaces that exist by opposition to commerce, profit, and the unbending logic of capital markets?

Suddenly, market incentives seem oddly aligned with Aristotle's definition of the good life: pursue your calling; do it for its own sake – we'll even throw in a free lunch. Remember Robert Frost's line, quoted in Chapter 3, where he describes his goal in life as uniting his vocation and his avocation, 'like two eyes make one in sight'? It turns out the market couldn't agree more. Because uniting the two may just be where the greatest gains lie.

The required exercise in persuasion – convincing workers that they ought to consider their vocations as a passion, performed in the market but for its own sake – seems like a difficult trick to pull off. We have seen people's strong built-in reflexes against the manipulation of disinterest for interested ends. Yet as the coming chapter demonstrates, that difficult trick is precisely what the market has accomplished in recent years: interested commerce has successfully dressed itself in the garb of disinterested commerce. Aristotle's definition of the good life has been taken up as the workaholic's rallying cry. The realm of *work* has embraced the fruits of *leisure*. And what's more, this trick of cooptation has been unknowingly facilitated by the very people who have been most actively warning against such an encroachment.

6

The Anti-Instrumentalists

As you sit on the toilet, you feel an irrepressible urge to check your phone. Perhaps a new email has come in? You could use this time to respond to it. Maybe you could see how your latest online post is faring, or check the weather for tomorrow to plan the day accordingly? That way, you might make the most of this free time.

As we reach for our phone in that moment, how far we are from the toilet as a 'place of spiritual repose', a daily 'physiological delight' famously described by the Japanese aesthete Junichiro Tanizaki, in his small and perfect 1977 book, *In Praise of Shadows*. As Tanizaki rejoiced, 'No words can describe that sensation as one sits in the dim light, basking in the faint glow reflected from the shoji [paper screen], lost in meditation or gazing out at the garden.'[1] By comparison, it always proves tricky to dig out our phones from the front pocket of our trousers when these are bunched at our ankles.

Until recently, even if we lacked the good fortune of an open-air Japanese outhouse 'surrounded by tranquil walls and finely grained wood, [where] one looks upon the blue skies and green leaves', the toilet nonetheless remained a safe haven of disinterested activity. That is, the time spent sitting on the toilet was time spent for its own sake; we pursued no goal other than the physiological ones specific to the place.

There were always stories, I suppose, of titans of industry yelling across the partition to a secretary taking down dictation as they sat doing their business, though most of us lacked that option. Now, thanks to technology, we all have it – and how many of us take up the chance. I can also attest to how often, in a riskier move and for seemingly smaller gain, some men insist on bravely checking their phones while standing at the urinal.

That there is a gain to be had is undeniable: we now can, in fact, make the most of our time, not to mention banish any impending boredom that might creep up during those minutes. The dopamine rush that comes with the momentary distraction of retrieving a new email, or checking on a new notification, is well documented.

But as a growing chorus of voices has been telling us, something is also plainly lost. To express this in the terms developed in the past chapters, there exists a unique benefit, otherwise difficult to attain, that is lost in the passage from disinterested commerce (in the case of the toilet, a rare daily communion with ourselves), to that of interested commerce (maximising that time for other ends, as we dig out the phone from our bunched-up trousers).

We know of such spaces of disinterest that they often yield unsuspected payoffs. Tanizaki knew this too: 'Here, I suspect, is where haiku poets over the ages have come by a great many of their ideas.' Perhaps because our phones still perform poorly when wet, the proverbial inspiration in our own age usually comes in the shower – maybe the last remaining bastion of disinterested attention, until the waterproofing of our technology catches up.

Tanizaki's observation sends us back to desirable objects that operate as byproducts. You can sit at a desk, composing either dreamy haikus or a brilliant screenplay, and will yourself to be hit by a bolt of creativity; yet try as you may, no lightning results. That's because creativity is a typical byproduct state: it is attained through the disinterested pursuit of some other end. It's a common trope of the booming 'creativity industry' that lightbulb moments strike us precisely in those interstitial gaps of boredom or idleness. When we are not actively searching for solutions, these seem to appear of their own accord. Neuroscientists speak of an 'incubation period', characterised by the absence of task-directed effort, that often precedes illumination. As we stand waiting in a queue at the supermarket, or as we sit on an open-air toilet listening to the insects around us. So always carry a notebook, the creativity manuals instruct, because you never know when some revelation might descend upon you unbidden. That is benign enough advice, but it would be silly to then purposefully go and wait in a queue at the supermarket waiting for a lightbulb moment to strike you – the intent kills the ploy. Similarly, those haiku poets over the ages did not deliberately flock to the toilet in search of their best ideas. Rather, they sat in their open-air toilets, listened to the insects, and inadvertently discovered (en passant) that the place proved fruitful in unsuspected ways.

That the toilet itself is now fair game for the selling-out of disinterest speaks to how pervasive the option has become. The blame for this change is heaped squarely on technology. But for all the focus there has been on smartphones as the proximate cause, there is a prior, and more fundamental factor. The reason why such technologies have been developed and hungrily adopted in the first place is that they satisfy an underlying urge. The courtship of disinterested commerce by its interested counterpart plays out within all of us: we are constantly tempted to give over our time on the toilet, during the weekend, or on vacation, to productivity. It feeds an internalised desire to 'maximise', 'optimise', and 'make the most of': the sweet song of interested commerce.

Almost half of the US workforce is now employed in the knowledge economy.[2] When growing numbers of people earn their keep not by the strength of their bodies but by the ingenuity of their minds, untapped free time represents more than the sum of those additional minutes that can be transferred to the work side of the ledger. These moments are the source of that unbidden creative reflex within us; if Tanizaki's poets found their inspiration there, why not purposefully harness this source for our own instrumental ends?

Yet for as long as this courtship of the disinterested sphere by its interested counterpart has been conducted, there has been a parallel effort to resist it. This resistance is made up of a group of dissenters pushing back against the encroachment of market incentives into the few remaining zones of disinterested commerce. What they seek is to preserve a space devoted to family, play, and other non-productive pursuits. The space of *leisure*.

The Changing Fortunes of Leisure

The good name of leisure has gone through many seasons. Elevated as the space of 'highest virtue', it was then scorned as sloth, then elevated again, and scorned once more. Is it any wonder that we are now seeing a countervailing push to reclaim it?

We have seen the occasion for some of these shifts, and we can recall them here in broad strokes. When Weber asked how moneymaking activities, which until the modern age had been 'at best ethically tolerated', then turned into a 'calling', he was motioning to all of Western thought leading up to that point. Indeed, the pre-modern period was, almost without exception, characterised by a critical outlook on commercial activity and work, and an elevation of leisure as the preserve of free thought and the good life. Whereas leisure today is viewed as a reprieve from work – the week is the rule, the weekend its exception – in the classical period it was the category of reference: there is no specific term for 'work' in Latin, other than *negotium*: 'non-leisure'. Work is defined as a negation of leisure, rather than leisure being the exception to work. The same is true of the Greek: the term for work, *a-skholia*, is the negation of *skhole*, or leisure.[3]

The modern reversal of the relation between the realms of work and leisure took place in at least two ways. Weber laid out the first: an idiosyncratic set of beliefs about salvation and predestination generated a historically unique elevation of toil and commercial activity among a pious people. What was initially a byproduct of one's calling soon became the proximate goal: even as its religious origins fell away, the conception of prosperity as an outward sign of respectability remained.

But another story may account for a greater part of the explanation of how, sometime in the late seventeenth and early eighteenth century, the active pursuit of interest gained respectability, and leisure lost some of its social pre-eminence. In this telling, like in Weber's, the busy pursuit of commercial gain and self-advancement were not initially viewed as noble in and of themselves. Rather, they were seen as a useful check against the overall more destructive passions of the medieval period: the lust for glory and honour. These prior passions had driven rulers to war with each other for centuries, dragging their populations along with them and causing untold suffering. In the words of the economist Albert Hirschman, who has told this story most convincingly, the adoption of capitalist institutions emerged as a means of 'avoiding society's ruin'.[4]

This countervailing passion, which until then had been known as the sin of avarice, now took the name of 'interest'. And since war is bad for business, the interests of merchants came to oppose the whims of belligerent rulers. Capitalist institutions that tied together the fortunes of enterprising individuals across national boundaries thus exerted a pro-social effect. The merchant caught up in his nickel-and-dime concerns was suddenly promoted to agent of national prosperity, stability, and peace. Not coincidentally, this is also the point at which David Hume divided human dealings into the two spheres of interested and disinterested commerce.

The mid-nineteenth century saw another inflection point for leisure. With the advent of the industrial revolution, the commercial class gained further prominence, to the point where it began threatening the established social order. This is why so much of nineteenth-century literature is given over to intrigues surrounding the sons and daughters of rich merchants marrying into impoverished aristocratic families, trading one form of capital for the other. In reaction to this invasion from the masses, elites tried to preserve their distinct status by adopting the practices that Veblen drew in such vivid colour. The upper class became the leisure class. A state of leisure was once more something to be aspired to, but for reasons that were at least partly instrumental. It was valued not only as an inherent good, but also as a useful signal of status. The true gentlemen of means was recognised by his ability to devote himself to idle pursuits.

Much waste resulted, for waste was largely the point. Out of this waste occasionally came something of extraordinary value, though the signal-to-noise ratio remained low. As Bertrand Russell put it, 'The [leisure] class might produce one Darwin, but against him had to be set tens of thousands of country gentlemen who never thought of anything more intelligent than fox-hunting and punishing poachers.'[5]

Russell's reference to Charles Darwin is right on the mark. The famously obsessive savant was able to devote himself to a lifelong study of earthworms because he was in every way a 'gentleman scholar'. Darwin inherited a fortune from his mother's family, the Wedgwoods, which was tied to one of the great industrial fortunes in England, and he then did it once more by marrying his first cousin Emma Wedgwood, heir to the same Wedgwood ceramics fortune. We owe *On the Origin of Species* to a felicitous birth into money combined with an endogamous marriage, which together provided ample servants and free time for the scrutinising of earthworms.

But the gentleman scholar's days were numbered. As we know from Chapter 2, leisure as a means of social distinction could not last. The Veblen Treadmill kept running. By the interwar period, the aristocratic class had bowed out for good, their sons and daughters married off to merchant families aspiring to dyn-astic crests. The attendant social effects followed as expected; by 1950, the economist John Kenneth Galbraith could take stock of the shift by observing that 'in the United States, the leisure class, at least as an easily identifiable phenomenon, has disappeared. To be idle is no longer considered rewarding or even entirely respectable.' Gentlemen scholars, alongside their fox-hunting peers, were enlisted into the professions. They became lawyers, lobbyists, bankers, and commercial estate agents. The ownership of land gave way to the management of capital as the principal means of wealth accumulation.

The Current State of Leisure

From the postwar period on, leisure grew ever more suspect. The trend has only kept up since the time of Galbraith's writing. Idleness is now vaguely reprehensible; the busy, single-minded pursuit of goals we have set for ourselves is the only virtuous path.

The data on working hours bear out this puzzling pattern. As with so many other socio-economic trends, this one saw a turning point in the mid-1980s. Until then, as countries grew richer, average working hours decreased, and leisure hours increased. But sometime around 1985, the trend reversed: leisure hours started falling. Tellingly, this reversal affected the most well-off within wealthy countries, the very people who had previously made up the leisure class.[6] What has been dubbed the 'Veblen in reverse' pattern has been observed across the developed world, and most recently in emerging economies.[7] The richest and the most educated are now working more than they did twenty years ago, despite having gained the most in terms of wealth over the same period.[8] Income inequality is increasing, but as the economist Robert H. Frank observes, ' "leisure inequality" – time spent on enjoyment – is growing as a mirror image, with the low earners gaining leisure and the high earners losing'.[9]

Even as the data show losses in hours of leisure by those presumably best able to enjoy it, they miss the harder-to-measure associated loss in the *quality* of leisure. Among the handful of studies that do look at leisure quality using diary records, the findings are even more sobering. Hours of 'pure leisure', which social scientists define as 'leisure time that is not "contaminated" by other non-leisure activities', have fallen across the board, affecting all income and education levels.[10]

Much attention has been paid to the role of policy in this respect, emphasising differences in paid vacation time or parental leave between, say, the US and Western European countries. Yet for all the attention on policy reform, the determining factors may lie deeper. Shortly before the pandemic, a study run jointly by Oxford Economics and Ipsos found that in 2018, more than half of Americans had not availed themselves of all their paid vacation days. All told, Americans failed to use 768 million days of paid time off.[11] That was an increase of 9 per cent in forgone vacation from the previous year. The socio-economic pressures on individuals that this figure implies also say something about the likely quality of leisure during the same period: it suggests that even when those employees *did* take the free time they had earned, they might have felt an overpowering urge to log in to their work email while paddling their canoe.

Economists often claim that the trends of rising income and declining leisure are related: it is *because* the wealthiest have gained the most materially that they cannot 'afford' any time off work. The opportunity cost of leisure, or the income that people have to give up to free up a marginal hour of leisure, has increased the most for the well-to-do. But this only defers the question: what end are these wealthy classes ultimately pursuing? That is, insofar as their extra hour of work undeniably yields more income than anyone else's, the question is, more for what?

The reputation of leisure has thus come and gone. In the very societies best able to afford leisure, its stock has been declining for the last half-century. There is now less of it, and what there is has been degraded. But it bears repeating that for the greater part of human history, leisure has been the (often unattainable) goal, and work but a means of attaining it. The current age has reversed this order: by and large, it considers work and exertion as wholesome, and the enjoyment of 'pure leisure' as a symptom of decadence and moral dissipation.

Starting in the interwar period, a wave of thinkers have sought to remind us of how historically unusual our current attitude towards leisure is. The call for reclaiming leisure from market capitalism has been rising as the stock of leisure has continued to deteriorate. It is now the stuff of bestselling books and widely shared newspaper editorials. These writers style themselves as a resistance movement against dominant market forces. The most far-thinking among them also acknowledge that this defence of leisure, as we will see, is not without its pitfalls.

Voices of Dissent

The twentieth century's most probing thinking on work and leisure arguably comes from the German philosopher Josef Pieper, in a series of lectures he gave in Bonn in 1946. I mention the year not only to situate Pieper in time, but to underscore a recurring pattern. One might have expected that serious thinkers would concern themselves with such questions in times of ease, when leisure itself was in greatest supply and there was time for musing about how best to employ it. Yet the opposite seems true.

Pieper himself acknowledged this incongruity. He was writing in Germany less than a year after the end of the Second World War. It was a time when the ability to engage in meaningful, 'authentic leisure' was the last thing on anyone's mind. Germans were busy grappling with their nation's wartime deeds, and trying to rebuild an economically devastated country. As Pieper admitted in the opening lines of his lectures:

a time like the present seems, of all times, not to be a time to speak of 'leisure'. We are engaged in the re-building of a house, and our hands are full. Shouldn't all our efforts be directed to nothing other than the completion of that house?[12]

But as Pieper went on to argue, rebuilding that house entails not only material betterment, but the reordering of an entire intellectual and moral heritage. And that, in turn, required above all the defence of the space that has been at the basis of culture since ancient times: the space of leisure.

Pieper was not the only one worrying about leisure in the midst of hard times. It was during another turbulent period that Bertrand Russell, the logician, social critic, and one of the century's greatest minds, turned to considerations of leisure. At the start of his 1932 essay titled *In Praise of Idleness*, Russell expressed the hope that 'reading the following pages, the leaders of the Y.M.C.A. will start a campaign to induce good young men to do nothing. If so, I shall not have lived in vain.'

Russell was writing shortly after the economist John Maynard Keynes produced his divinatory essay, *Economic Possibilities for our Grandchildren*. Tellingly, there has never been as much interest in this short piece as there is today. Its premise is by now well known. Keynes, who was writing in 1930, predicted that a century hence, the world would be about eight times better off economically: the 'economic problem' of scarcity would thus be, for all intents and purposes, resolved. As a result, we would finally be free to devote ourselves to what had been the goal all along: leisure. As we now know, one of those two predictions turned out to be remarkably accurate; the other was bizarrely off. We are now, almost a century later, about six times better off, economically speaking, than we were in Keynes's time. Yet if anything, attitudes towards leisure have gone in the opposite direction.

Again, I want to emphasise *when* Russell and Keynes were writing. The interwar period had just turned sour, and no one realised this better than Keynes himself. The crash of 1929 was on everyone's mind, and the Depression was about to reach its deepest trough. The Nazi party in Germany was the largest in the Reichstag, and Hitler would be named chancellor three years later. The world was entering the low phase of what the British historian E. H. Carr dubbed 'The Twenty Years' Crisis'.

As Keynes admitted, 'We are suffering just now from a bad attack of economic pessimism. It is common to hear people say that the epoch of enormous economic progress which characterised the nineteenth century is over.' Yet Keynes was looking ahead past this moment, which he knew would one day end. At some point, he knew, economic prosperity would return. And with everyone's minds set on how to achieve this recovery, now was the time to ask, to what end?

The grandchildren whose economic possibilities Keynes so accurately predicted, but whose wants he so badly misjudged, are now fully grown. By Keynes's definition, in many parts of the world, the economic problem has been effectively solved. This is not to say that there is no economic suffering, far from it. But what Keynes called the 'economic problem' of scarcity has in fact been resolved in sufficient respects during the twentieth century, and for large enough segments of the population, to allow us to see that this technical solution has not provided an answer to the fundamental problems of advanced societies.

Against Keynes' expectations, the grandchildren whose economic possibilities have expanded much as he expected have not taken him up on his second prediction. They have not reduced their work to the fifteen hours a week that he'd prophesied, nor to the 'four hours of work out of the twenty-four' that Russell envisioned. Few can claim to be part of those people who, as Keynes put it, 'do not sell themselves for the means of life, who will be able to enjoy the abundance when it comes'.[13] Instead, as the studies cited above suggest, the very people who have reached a state of abundance have instead doubled down on the toil that Keynes saw as a mere means to an end.

It should not surprise us, then, that the thinkers who pointed out an essential confusion between means and ends, writing amidst the interwar crisis, and then amidst postwar devastation, should speak to us today with novel urgency. Keynes's essay, which his pre-eminent biographer Robert Skidelsky described in his 1992 tome as mostly a 'provocation', has gone on to enjoy a surge of renewed interest in the wake of the Great Recession, when a group of the world's top economists came together to revisit its implications.[14] These economists were wise to the parallels between the two eras. Those parallels have only grown closer in the time since.

Even prior to the pandemic, it had become common for economists to talk about a permanent 'fall of American growth'. According to that view, the era of high growth from the industrial revolution to the 1970s was actually a period of exception, rather than the historical norm.[15] A global pandemic that has put the world economy on hold has not helped global growth trends. But it may facilitate a fresh outlook on them.

We are living through another period of economic and moral angst. In such circumstances, the most urgent concerns of recovery, rebuilding, and a return to growth might seem to be the sole thing to focus on. And yet, as Keynes and Pieper both intuited, now may be the time when the question of leisure, and the reordering of our shared social objectives, are in fact most pressing. Shocks like the one the world has undergone can have catalysing effects. They serve as the moments of 'awakening' that reformist thinkers from St Paul ('now it is high time to awake out of sleep') and St Augustine ('Awake, thou sleeper') to Marx ('workers awaken!') are forever hanging their hopes on. Unexpected shocks do often lead to a re-evaluation of our objectives, whether these shocks come in our own individual lives, as with the death of a loved one or the birth of a child, or whether they are society-wide, as with an economic collapse or a global pandemic. Such re-evaluations, as with J. S. Mill's 'reprogramming' of himself, can prove revelatory.

As the economic recovery from the pandemic leads us to renegotiate the contours of work – the places and times in which it takes place, the wages it fairly deserves – the question of leisure is being posed anew. We have been forced to hit the reset button on the world economy; it is also an opportunity to reset our relation to the objectives of work – to ensure that the goals we are pursuing are still the goals we want to be pursuing. Just as our minds are consumed by the most immediate concerns, we should settle on the ends towards which we want to direct the recovery, so as to avoid confusing those ends with the means we must take to attain them.

The Apostles of Leisure

The battle lines are drawn. The natural dwelling places of leisure – in the private sphere, at the family table, on weekend mornings, and yes, on the toilet – are under threat. Joseph Pieper wrote of the need to 'defend' leisure from a 'take-over'. Meanwhile, in 1932, Bertrand Russell thought the game was already lost. The productivity credo had been too deeply internalised: 'Men would not know how to fill their days if they had only four hours of work out of the twenty-four. In so far as this is true in the modern world, it is a condemnation of our civilisation.' And Keynes, of course, was equally pessimistic about our ability to eventually deal with a world where the problem of scarcity had been resolved: 'There is no country and no people,

I think, who can look forward to the age of leisure and of abundance without a dread. For we have been trained too long to strive and not to enjoy.'

Hannah Arendt, the twentieth century's great theorist of *doing*, had a similar inkling. Anticipating some of the current discussions of the impact of artificial intelligence on wages and employment, Arendt saw ahead to a time when automation would drastically reduce the need for labour. Writing in the late 1950s, Arendt could already see around her 'a society of labourers which is about to be liberated from the fetters of labour, and this society does no longer know of those other higher and more meaningful activities for the sake of which this freedom would deserve to be won'.[16] The breakthrough of automation, 'like the fulfilment of wishes in fairy tales', she feared, would turn sour and fail to deliver on its promise of greater freedom. There was no doubt about what was being done for the sake of what, and what a reversal of the natural order this represented. 'What we are confronted with is the prospect of a society of labourers without labour, that is, without the only activity left to them. Surely, nothing could be worse.'[17]

Concerns from the 1950s over technology upending humans' relationship to work might seem quaint today, living as we do in the attention economy, where we pay for nominally free services by letting our limited attention be captured for the profit of advertisers. The looming prospect of artificial intelligence and automation now promises to transform the demand for labour in the decades to come. But in light of such developments, those past thinkers also read as remarkably far-sighted, and a new wave of thinkers have begun revisiting their ideas.

In the spring of 2019, the artist Jenny Odell put out a prescient book titled *How To Do Nothing*. Its tongue-in-cheek title notwithstanding, the book is a call for actively resisting usefulness and productivity, and paying attention to how our attention is instrumentalised for ends not our own. Odell's book was widely embraced. It launched countless thoughtful essays in high places, most of them joining in the breast-beating that laments our collective loss of attention. It was recommended by Barack Obama as one of his ten books of the year and stayed on the bestseller list for months.

Like Pieper, Odell has a weakness for martial metaphors. She speaks of 'resisting' the default onus of productivity, as a way of 'surviving usefulness'. She sees 'a similar battle playing out for our time, a colonization of the self by capitalist ideas of productivity and efficiency'. In her telling, 'doing nothing' does not mean being idle. 'Doing nothing is *hard*,' she admits. She describes it as an act of defiance against a market society that would have us constantly doing, striving, producing. And it's hard because the path of least resistance is actually to avoid doing nothing, or even being momentarily perceived as such. Instead, we seek productivity, and failing that, we seek distraction, which has never been easier, given its instant availability at our fingertips, at the mere cost of our unwavering attention. As one of the grandchildren whose economic possibilities Keynes was imagining, Odell usefully reminds us of the moment of conversion that Keynes's bargain anticipated, and of the challenge it represents.

Hers is only the most developed of a slew of recent critiques. In a similar spirit, a recent article by Derek Thompson in *The Atlantic* felicitously coined the term 'workism' to describe what its author described as the recent American elevation of work as a 'calling', and the attendant need to appear busy, productive, and *on* at all times. Workism, Thompson claims, 'is among the most potent of the new religions competing for congregants'. Never mind that rather than some new phenomenon peculiar to the millennial generation, driven as Thompson has it by technological change and unprecedented levels of student debt, 'workism' is actually a return to the past, a harkening back to the founding myth of the Puritan vision of work as an actually divine calling. The article touched a nerve, and set off a long string of mea culpas on the part of overburdened freelance journalists standing up and admitting (as did Thompson himself) that they too were blindly worshipping at the altar of work.

I like to think of them – Keynes, Russell, Pieper, Arendt, Odell – as the *apostles of leisure*. A group of thinkers writing throughout the last century, all similarly confounded by the same puzzling historical anomaly: the fruits are ripe, yet no one thinks of picking them. Instead, they continue to shovel manure around. I like to imagine them in some Socratic banquet scene, all sitting at a long table, drinking and breaking bread while gravely discussing the question of leisure. It would be an occasion for Keynes, the architect of the postwar order, to make amends for the sole regret he expressed in the last months of his life, when he is reputed to have sighed, 'I wish I had drunk more champagne.'[18]

As with the gallery of saints buttressing the original apostles, supporting characters might come in and out of the scene. Roland Barthes, the semiologist of Parisian cafés and Tokyo sushi bars, who once mused, 'I even wonder if there is such a thing as *doing nothing* in the modern Western world,'[19] might pop in over dessert to recite a Zen poem he was particularly fond of:

Sitting peacefully doing nothing
Springtime is coming
and the grass grows all by itself.

I like to imagine those lines composed one morning by a poet in an open-air toilet in rural Japan sometime in the tenth century, and I like to think Barthes would have liked this too.

Means vs Ends

What unites the Japanese poet listening to the insects in his open-air toilet and Darwin's obsessive study of earthworms? The apostles of leisure are a disputatious bunch; they are self-defined contrarians. Yet they happen to be remarkably of one mind as to the contours of leisure. Across their writings, leisure is recognised by the same criterion: it is what is performed for its own sake, rather than for some other end. It is why work is subservient to leisure: work is defined by an external purpose; leisure is defined by an absence of such purpose. Pieper put it most bluntly: 'Work is the means of life; leisure the end.'

They are also of one mind about the reasons we have witnessed a reversal of this ordering in the post-Enlightenment period. Arendt is the one who draws this transformation out most clearly. By looking to self-interest as the most tractable aspect of human nature – that universal drive which all individuals could best be seized by – Enlightenment thinkers imagined a society where the pursuit of individual interests could be aligned with the social good by means of laws and moral education. They recast every action as the furtherance of someone's individual interest; a means to an end that needed no defining. This legacy of the Enlightenment is with us still. It was embraced by neo-classical economics (which took up the study of means, while explicitly refusing to distinguish between ends) and then by the type of managerial thinking that has permeated so many aspects of our daily lives. The maximisation itself soon became the point. What emerged was a society of means, focused on the *how* over the *what*.

The wholesale adoption of self-interest as the cornerstone of human behaviour, initially motivated by its sheer tractability, percolated to individuals' perceptions of themselves. As

Bertrand Russell put it, 'The modern man thinks that everything ought to be done for the sake of something else, and never for its own sake.'

It is in reaction to this tendency that today writers like Jenny Odell call on us to 'suspend our tendency toward instrumental understanding – seeing things or people one-dimensionally as the products of their functions'. And it is also why leisure is so relevant, and why the apostles of leisure view it as worthy of defending: it represents the shrinking territory of non-instrumental behaviour.

In this sense, the apostles are *anti-instrumentalists*. Keynes decries the 'purposiveness' of those 'who will blindly pursue wealth'. Odell writes of the need to transcend 'usefulness'. Both draw our attention to how our time, our relationships, and our very imagination are increasingly applied to external ends. Keynes points to the capitalist who serves a useful social function, but only insofar as that function is not confused for the end itself: 'Regarded as a means he is tolerable; regarded as an end he is not so satisfactory.'

The term 'apostle' comes from the Greek for 'messenger'. And there is little doubt over whose message is being carried by the apostles of leisure. Some 2,400 years ago, Aristotle laid down his view of how to live 'the good life'. Reading the *Ethics*, I am always struck by how much Aristotle is at pains to acknowledge the banality of his thinking on the matter: he wants us to know that he is reiterating a set of ideas that were already well rehearsed those 2,400 years ago.* It's equally

---

* On the nature of the chief good: 'To say that happiness is the chief good seems a platitude' (I:7). On how 'the good' is whatever all things aim at: 'For we say that that which everyone thinks really is so'. Similarly, Aristotle's conclusions about happiness find confirmation not only through the sheer logic of his reasoning, but by 'what is commonly said about it'. (Aristotle, *The Nichomachean Ethics*, I:8.)

striking how little this view has been tampered with over the two millennia that followed.* For what might be considered the fundamental question we should all begin each day by asking – namely, what should we spend our life doing? – the sum total of human thinking on the matter delivers a striking degree of consensus: the things most worth doing are those that are done for their own sake. The further down the chain of means and ends, the less intrinsic value an activity has. Thus emerges the relation between work and non-work. As Aristotle puts it, 'We are not-at-leisure in order to be at-leisure.'[20]

To link to the previous chapter's discussion, we recognise leisure via the same traits by which we recognise disinterested commerce. In each case, the dividing line is the intent. Is the act done for its own sake, or in furtherance of some outside goal? Is the motivation, to use the behaviouralist's terms, intrinsic or extrinsic?

The lens of means vs ends is also what led Aristotle, and much of the Western thought that followed, to hold a dim view of commercial activities. Even Keynes, the economist who made a personal fortune in the markets (only to lose it all in the 1929 crash, and then earn it all back) viewed commerce as merely a means, albeit a necessary one 'for some time still'. For the goal of commerce is the accumulation of money, and money is the quintessential means: of no worth in and of itself (it can neither be eaten in a salad nor enjoyed on its own) and only valuable insofar as it procures us enjoyment – which often consists of 'baubles and trinkets' that Adam Smith recognised as means to other ends still.[†]

---

* For that matter, when the same question was considered in Eastern traditions during the same fourth century BC through which Aristotle lived, in texts like the *Zhuangzi*, the conclusions are, there too, strikingly similar.

† A notable complication arises. As Hirschman points out in passing (*The Passions and the Interests*, p. 55), money is oddly well suited to becoming a passion in itself, for the very reason that Aristotle condemned it: for some, no amount is ever enough.

According to the apostles, the commercial world, given its inherently instrumental outlook, is fundamentally opposed to leisure, defined by the absence of those external ends. They believe in a neat division between the two, and they believe they know exactly which camp they are in. They imagine themselves in those nineteenth-century battles where opposing armies had the courtesy of dressing their soldiers in vividly contrasting colours, so that everyone would know exactly whom to shoot at.

But the truth is thornier, owing to a reason that the apostles themselves highlight. As Tanizaki tells us, the state of leisure, sitting there among the buzzing insects, is unexpectedly fruitful. And the market is quick to recognise and reward fruitfulness. The apostles thus overlook one possibility, which is that there might be value in deception. One side might have reason to don the opposing side's colours.

This becomes all the more likely given how an activity taken up as work and one taken up as play might look much the same from the outside. The engineer plodding away at their desk on the company's new energy-saving widget and looking forward to the weekend camping trip is said to be at work. The hobbyist working on the same contraption in their garage is said to be at

---

For those individuals, money appears immune to the law of diminishing returns. It then becomes a genuine end unto itself, *provided that* it is not spent on things. The miser, in this sense, is on to something, having turned money into an object valued for its sheer existence, the appreciation of which has become downright aesthetic. Having 'bought into' the concept so much as to forget its original function as a means of exchange, money presents itself as an intrinsic good. This is the illusion for which Keynes reserved his greatest scorn. He held out the hope that 'the love of money as a possession – as distinguished from the love of money as a means to the enjoyments and realities of life – will be recognised for what it is, a somewhat disgusting morbidity, one of those semi-criminal, semi-pathological propensities which one hands over with a shudder to the specialists in mental disease'. Perhaps so, but this morbidity shares more with the satisfactions of the aesthete or the ascetic than Keynes cared to recognise.

play. Both appear to be engaged in the same activity, yet their motivations differ. The hobbyist toils away even without pay, and we know the market assigns special value to such peculiar passion. Insofar as there is an incentive to capture that value, we face a familiar issue: one camp might have an incentive to pass itself for the other. Suddenly, the anti-instrumentalists' call for the defence of leisure appears unexpectedly fraught.

7

The Place of Leisure in a Market Economy

W hen I mention the decline of leisure among the individuals best able to afford it, one common reaction of those concerned is to say that they love their work. They love it so much, in fact, that they hardly consider it work. It's their *passion*.

The outward resemblance between some types of work and leisure is the premise of Robert Frost's aforementioned classic poem 'Two Tramps in Mud Time'. There, it is chopping wood that can be both work and play, and the narrative tension of the poem runs on this twin possibility. Frost is another character we might imagine dropping in at the table of the apostles of leisure. Everyone present, of course, would already know the poem's final stanza by heart:

My object in living is to unite
My avocation and my vocation
As my two eyes make one in sight.
Only where love and need are one,
And the work is play for mortal stakes,
Is the deed ever really done
For heaven and the future's sakes.

Frost's 'object in living' has become the rallying cry of freelancers everywhere, who dream of blurring the divide between their day jobs and their passions. But what comes before that last jubilant stanza is often left out, and it proves more troublesome.

The poem's narrator is happily chopping wood in the chill of a sunny April day when he notices two wage-labourers looking on, eager for the work. Their presence gnaws at his conscience. He recognises, 'I had no right to play / With what was another man's work for gain.' His pleasure is another man's privation. 'My right might be love but theirs was need.' Yet ultimately, he lets his own claim win out. Blurring the divide between interested and disinterested commerce is his right; it is, we are made to understand, the poet's prerogative. Yet there remains a sense of compassion for those who are forced to disassociate their 'love' and their 'need'.

The one comment Frost himself ever made about the poem is that he considered it to be 'against hobbies'.[1] This might seem unexpected. On first read, it appears more likely that Frost would have considered it to be 'against work'. It is leisure that gains from being treated seriously, rather than work that benefits from being treated as play. At the very least, the remark complicates the usual reading of the poem's last stanza as a freelancer's motto.

I confess that I have always thrilled to Frost's call for uniting vocation and avocation. My work consists of academic writing, and for the most part it examines various political aspects of economic rules. Yet I start most days by spending an hour or so writing fiction. Occasionally I publish a short story somewhere, and I like having a larger piece of fiction to wrestle with. It brings me joy in the mornings, and it adds some propulsion to the rest of my day. But I also have friends for whom writing fiction is a vocation; it's their livelihood. Every weekday, they get dressed and put shoes on and sit in Montreal cafés for hours and *work* at it. I have always felt a vague sense of guilt towards these friends, an unease that comes from dabbling for pleasure in what is their means of making ends meet.

I wonder whether they too think that all writing should fall to those who do it for a living, the way the two strangers of the poem 'thought all chopping was theirs of right'. I also fear that they may feel what I feel, which is that in this case, dilettantism, or electing to walk the ridge between work and leisure just on this side of leisure, confers an advantage – and that this advantage is an unfair one. Just as in Robert Frost's case, to be able to unite one's vocation and avocation is a luxury that may be conditional on economic opportunity, as it was in Darwin's time. One can afford to dabble all the more when one has a pension fund and a health-insurance plan to fall back on. And there is something about the dabbling, about the ability to remain just on this side of the divide, that may well be freeing, in ways that manifest in the final product.

Additional unease comes from wondering whether dabbling may have greater social repercussions, by contributing to a view that the luxury of successfully linking vocation and avocation is such that it deserves no real monetary compensation. A hidden clash between individual and social incentives is revealed. The individual is undoubtedly best off finding work that can be performed as play. What could be better? Think of those obsessives who work at their craft from morning till night – composing, coding, researching – but who are still able to boast, 'I've never worked a day in my life.' Well, lucky them, we think. Sure, all else being equal, uniting one's avocation and one's vocation is the individual's 'dominant strategy'. Except that all else is not equal. Because the emergence of a creative class that yearns to unite work and play, to take up activities for their own sake that also happen to pay the bills, inevitably changes everyone else's market incentives.

Consider what might happen if a neighbour came along in Frost's poem and yelled out to him, 'Since you love it so much, come see all the blocks of beech in my yard: why don't you come round and knock them hard?' A market would be brought into being. It would count only two market actors, but right away, the problem identified in Chapter 5 would arise. If chopping wood can be preserved within a zone of disinterest, then the employer, that neighbour with blocks of beech in his yard, stands to reap limitless gains. This is why the self-interested employer has every incentive to hire passionate workers.

Non-passionate workers know this; if they want to secure work, they have every incentive to present themselves as passionates. They may have to claim that they all chop wood in their off hours, too. Here, the incentives around passion are arranged in such a way that the aggregation of individually dominant actions – everyone pursuing their passion – leads to a socially questionable outcome: why bother paying any of these passionates?

So I worry that through my happy mornings writing fiction, I inadvertently contribute to a generalised sense that writers of fiction – and for that matter, musicians, painters, and dancers, but also all those devoted journalists, researchers, curators, and craftsmen – can get by on passion alone, and hardly require remuneration. As it happens, this belief is already pervasive. It underlies the expectation of free content on the web – if bloggers did it for free out of sheer passion, why shouldn't newspaper columnists? – as well as the decades-long trend of unpaid internships in the 'industries of passion': publishing, fashion, arts, and humanitarian organisations.

Frost's thinking on the issue was indebted to the American transcendentalists, like Henry David Thoreau, whose lineage and legacy we traced in Chapter 1. Recall that Thoreau and Emerson were the American transplants of a Romantic tradition that harkened back to the nineteenth-century English Romantics, who were in turn vested in the thought of the German idealists. It is a branch of this same intellectual tradition that had such a marked influence over the young J. S. Mill.

In fact, that famous final verse from Frost's poem echoes almost as good a line from Thoreau's *Journal*, in which he concludes an 1841 entry with the aphoristic phrase: 'The whole duty of life is contained in the question of how to respire and aspire both at once.' Thoreau, of course, was very much taken up by the question of leisure, and by how work and play ought to relate to one another. The crispest statement of this idea is found not in the dreary and sanctimonious *Walden*, but in the more joyful *Life Without Principle*, written in 1863. In it, Thoreau proposes to consider 'the way in which we spend our lives'. He begins with a familiar complaint: 'There is no sabbath. It would be glorious to see mankind at leisure for once. It is nothing but work, work, work.' And in ways that speak even more directly to the current fashion for appearing perpetually busy: 'I wish to suggest that a man may be very industrious, and yet not spend his time well. There is no more fatal blunderer than he who consumes the greater part of his life getting his living.'[2]

Thoreau had an intuitive understanding of the recent crop of findings from behavioural science highlighted in Chapter 5. Intent matters for how a task is carried out: when individuals work from intrinsic rather than extrinsic motivation, they tend to devote more effort and show greater patience at the task. As Thoreau concludes, 'Do not hire a man who does your work for money, but him who does it for love of it.'[3]

But Thoreau also sees ahead to the socio-economic dilemma this posed. If the passionates work hardest, then the market has every incentive to hire them, but also little reason to pay them decently, passionate as they are.[4] He actually anticipates the issue and tackles it in an unexpected way. Rather than try and convince workers that their work belongs to the realm of disinterest – which risks being condemned as a self-serving ploy – he proposes the opposite. He argues that paying workers high wages allows them to perform their work out of intrinsic satisfaction once more. He even claims such high wages are cost-effective: the improvement in the quality of work done by labourers who conceive of it in intrinsically motivated terms more than makes up for the greater expense: 'even in a pecuniary sense, it would be economy for a town to pay its labourers so well that they would not feel that they were working for ... a livelihood merely, but for scientific, or even moral ends'.

On the face of it, this is an argument for paying workers decent wages. More intriguingly, it is a poet's proposal for transforming, through high wages (which remain, after all, a tool of the market) workers' perception of their work as non-work – all for the purpose of work.

A century later, Josef Pieper made a similar distinction when considering the remuneration of passion versus that of work. As Pieper observed, the distinction can be gleaned by contrasting honoraria and wages: 'The liberal arts are "honoured"; the servile arts are "paid in wages".'[5] So a lawyer speaking to her client is paid an hourly wage, but if that same lawyer then goes on to deliver an hour-long public lecture on a scholarly topic, she is paid an honorarium. As Pieper pointed out, 'The concept of the honorarium implies a certain lack of equivalence between achievement and reward, that the service itself "really" cannot be rewarded.' As all but the most famous public speakers can attest to, honoraria tend to be lower than their wage equivalents. But in a way that highlights the social expectations around remuneration for labours of love, the point is that the alternative to the honorarium is not a wage; it is volunteerism.

Leisure is *Useful*: Trouble Ensues

One reason why leisure is difficult to achieve is because our attention is constantly being solicited by entities that profit from capturing it. As Jenny Odell argues, 'doing nothing' therefore demands a countervailing effort of attention – because the current default behaviour, the path of least resistance, is to make the most of our time by checking our work email while on vacation.

But another reason is one we have already hinted at: leisure is under threat because it is *useful*. Pieper's very argument is that leisure is the 'basis of culture'. Bertrand Russell similarly asserts that 'it contributed nearly the whole of what we call civilisation. It cultivated the arts and discovered the sciences; it wrote the books, invented the philosophies, and refined social relations.' They're both right: the awkward truth is that the best of humanity has been achieved by people doing things for their own sake, rather than as means to other ends.

In part, it comes down to spare time, the common understanding of leisure. But beyond mere time, the bounty of leisure lies in something far harder to pin down, even as everyone keeps groping at it. Leisure is the source of human creativity and innovation; it is when we are at leisure that we are able to 'lose ourselves' in a task; it is in this state that inspiration seems to present itself unbidden.*

---

* Pieper goes so far as to attribute to leisure something of the sublime. To be at leisure is, in his words, 'at once a human and super-human condition'. This is

Is it any wonder that the market would seek to tap this outright mystical potential? If the state of leisure generated all of culture and science, imagine what it could do to the output of the firm...

The realm of 'total work' thus stands to gain not merely from capturing the *time* reserved for leisure – as happens when we spend our vacations carrying around devices that make us fully reachable – but even more so from taking the apostles at their word, recognising the potency of 'authentic leisure', and enlisting it for its own account. Picture employees working towards their deadlines with the devotion of the passionate entrepreneur toiling on a dream project. It is one thing to allow two days of leisure to get well-rested workers; it is another, altogether more profitable proposition to persuade workers that they ought to regard the rest of their week as leisure, too, and lose themselves in it accordingly.

This is not what the apostles of leisure anticipated. Given their view of work and leisure as warring camps, they expected instead that the market would be quick to muzzle any calls for greater, and purer, leisure. After all, aren't these a threat to any rational, purpose-driven system devoted to growth?

There is a distinctive sense of satisfaction that comes from holding subversive views. Like all dissidents, the apostles would rather regard their calls for greater leisure as threatening to established commercial interests. As Odell puts it, 'To capitalist logic, which thrives on myopia and dissatisfaction, there may indeed be something dangerous about something as pedestrian as doing nothing.'

---

drawing once again on Aristotle, who also saw in the state of being at leisure something transcendent: 'it is not in so far as he is man that he will live so, but in so far as something divine dwells in him'. We associate leisure with play and ease. But achieving such a state of ease does not come easily, especially when our default setting is aimed squarely at utility.

But what if the opposite is true? What if the suspicion and hostility the apostles feel towards the realm of interested commerce, the practical world of purposiveness and function, is not mutual? What if the call for leisure is not actually seen as a threat to the existing commercial order, but as an opportunity? To a developed market society, leisure represents a spring of untapped human potential in a setting where all other sources have been dutifully put to good use.

We know from prior chapters how valuable (and costly) it is for employers to replicate through extrinsic rewards the level of effort and engagement that one can get out of intrinsically motivated individuals. If only the neighbour can redirect the effort of Frost's happy logger to the blocks of beech in his own yard, how magnificent his gain is! And chopping wood is one thing, but the unique dividend of leisure is most apparent in creative intellectual pursuits. Haikus, plays, catchy melodies – or innovative apps, inventive algorithms. Now that 'knowledge workers' represent such a great portion of labour in advanced societies, the ability to tap this limitless creative potential has only further gained in value.

Yet unlocking that value runs up against a familiar contradiction. The unique 'life-giving forces' of leisure cannot be tapped at will. Creativity, inspiration, innovation: these are among the clearest examples we have of byproducts. They can only be achieved incidentally.

Pieper, who did foresee how a society ordered around work might capitalise on the semi-divine potential of leisure, hitches his hopes on this paradox. He seeks to assure us, and perhaps to reassure himself, that if the purpose of leisure is to leave us refreshed for more work, it becomes something less than leisure, and necessarily loses its superhuman potential. As he puts it, 'No one who wants leisure merely for the sake of "refreshment" will experience its authentic fruit, the deep refreshment that comes from a deep sleep.'

The mention of sleep, that primordial cousin of leisure, is apt. We might think that sleep would be immune to the encroachment of market forces – Pieper certainly seemed to think so. It would seem that unconsciousness does not readily lend itself to instrumental behaviour. But in this respect, the fate of sleep in a market economy has mirrored that of leisure. In both cases, the fact that it may be impossible to intentionally fake one's way into states that cannot be wilfully attained hasn't stopped anyone from trying.

The Wages of Sleep

In a recent book, *24/7: Late Capitalism and the Ends of Sleep*, the Columbia University social theory professor Jonathan Crary describes the dwindling number of sleeping hours of the average North American: from 10 hours a night in Veblen's time to 6.5 hours today. Crary, like the apostles of leisure, sees himself defending an inherently valuable good. He envisions sleep as the last bastion of resistance against the market system: 'one of the great human affronts to the voraciousness of contemporary capitalism'.

That much is familiar. The interesting part is what follows the firing of this first sally. Belying Crary's presumed 'affront' to capitalism, a funny thing happened: the smart money has embraced sleep. Far from seeing it as an affront, the market has been quick to appreciate its fruitfulness, and it has set about unlocking its full potential. Yes, by all means, we should sleep more – to be more creative, more functional, more *productive*. Just as hunters are the loudest voices among conservationists, so too have dyed-in-the-wool capitalists become the loudest voices in the defence of sleep.

A scant three years after Crary's eulogy to sleep under capitalism comes *The Sleep Revolution*, a book by Arianna Huffington, the founder of the Huffington Post media empire. Notice that it is Huffington, the businesswoman, calling for *revolution*; Crary, the critical art theorist, was not so bold. In a gushing blurb to the book, Sheryl Sandberg, the COO of Facebook, explained, 'Arianna shows that sleep is not just vital for our health, but also critical to helping us *achieve our goals*.'[6] Sleep has become a means to an end. One can hear Josef Pieper groaning.

The business world took the cue, and aesthetic codes were updated, as it were, overnight. Getting by on four hours of sleep is no longer cause for admiration; it is a sign that you're a small, stressed-out cog in the machine. No, the thinking person gets their full eight hours, and talks fluently of circadian rhythms. She tracks her REM minutes on a well-designed app. No self-respecting start-up is complete without sleep pods for employees who would like to take an energy nap and return, their best selves once more, back to work. An entire industrial sleep complex, peddling high-thread-count sheets and expensive pillows to help us be our best selves, has risen in response.

The little dialectic dance by which the social standing of sleep is transformed reflects the broader treatment of leisure. Those intent on reclaiming leisure from market incentives point to their quasi-divine character (left foot forward). But in the process, they also demonstrate its singular value to interested commerce (left foot back). As this potency comes into view, so does the incentive of market actors to enlist it for productive ends (step change and spin around). In doing so, they affect its very nature; they transform leisure into something with a definite objective, a means of reaching our personal goals: something better thought of as a factor of production (take your partner and dip them back). We get ping-pong tables, happy hours, and napping pods in carefully optimised offices. In the name of productivity, we see a corruption of sleep and leisure – at the cost of their full productive potential.

The Unholy Leisure Alliance

What harm is there in a market that relies on creative work by knowledge workers finally appreciating the benefits of sleep? In an earlier era, during the first half of the twentieth century, the embrace of leisure by interested commerce took a similarly benign form when leaders of industry came to recognise the diminishing returns to the exploitation of human labour. The industrial revolution's excesses became apparent even to those who initially benefited from them.

Henry Ford was the trendsetter in this respect. In 1926, Ford, who had already reduced the number of daily working hours in his factories to eight, then also reduced the number of working days in the week from six to five. What the utopian socialist Robert Owen had proposed in 1810 as a radical notion, the industrial magnate Henry Ford embraced a century later as good business. Ford's decision eventually led to the 1940 Fair Labour Standards Act, which turned the forty-hour working week into law in the United States.

We have rare insight into Henry Ford's thinking on the matter. In a 1926 interview following his factory reforms, he explained, 'It is high time to rid ourselves of the notion that leisure for workmen is either "lost time" or a class privilege.'[7] On the basis of such solemn words, one might almost mistake him for one of the apostles and make space for him at the banquet table alongside his contemporary Bertrand Russell. Ford was quick to rectify that impression. 'Of course,' he went on, 'there is a humanitarian side to the shorter day and the shorter week, but dwelling on that side is likely to get one into trouble, for then leisure may be put before work instead of after work – where it belongs.' There is no doubt on which side of the divide Ford stood: firmly entrenched in the realm of interested commerce, he was merely trying to reap the material benefits of disinterested commerce.

With an additional day of leisure, the reasoning went, workers would be more rested, and thus more productive. Ford explained, 'the 5-day week will open our way to a still greater prosperity'. And within Ford's factories, the move did pay off. As he rejoiced, 'We find that the men come back after a 2-day holiday so fresh and keen that they are able to put their minds as well as their hands into their work.'

What Ford discovered in 1926, today's Wall Street investment firms, which require expensively trained bankers to bank eighty-hour weeks, are bound to discover too. The realisation that they are operating with a mentally compromised, sleep-deprived workforce will eventually hit them. When it does, and when these firms hire three employees to perform the current work of two, they will likely find the productivity of their workforce increase, just as it did in Ford's time. The tech sector is leading the way, as firms notice that giving employees an extra day off a week seems to lead to overall productivity gains.[8]

Yet Pieper would have deplored Henry Ford's rationale as one more instance by which leisure was made subservient to what he called the 'total world of work'. Similarly, Hannah Arendt, who bemoaned how 'the spare time of the [working man] is never spent in anything but consumption, and the more time left to him, the greedier and more craving his appetites',[9] would have sighed at Ford's other rationale, which was just that: more consumption. As Ford explained, 'the people with a 5-day week will consume more goods than the people with a 6-day week'.[10] It need hardly be said that Ford did not value this increased consumption for its own sake, either, as Bertrand Russell did ('We think too much of production, and too little of consumption,' Russell once bemoaned).[11] No, Ford valued consumption as a source of aggregate demand that would further propel production, and lead to higher economic growth. In other words, a means to a means, to a means.

But what is so bad about seeing the utility in what thinkers from Aristotle to Odell have been pushing for disinterestedly? What's wrong with such a powerful alliance between Utopians and Utilitarians, even if the motivations differ – as long as they agree on the concrete policy of additional leisure time?

One reason is that it further cements the existing hierarchy between work and leisure. In practical terms, conceiving of leisure through its contribution to productivity is likely to determine what use individuals make of their newfound economic possibilities. The risk is that we end up with 768 million days of forgone vacation. Policy reform is one thing; a society-wide adjustment in what people perceive to be laudable is another. Yet the latter matters at least as much as the former in determining how much actual leisure individuals end up with, and the welfare that results.

The second risk that comes from such an alliance between Utopians and Utilitarians is that insofar as leisure, sleep, and disinterest are justified as effective means to achieving greater social ends – productivity, consumption, growth – they stand to lose any perceived worth as soon as they *do* come into actual conflict with the social goal of material utility. The pragmatic move is thus a double-edged sword. It ensures that any eventual clash between the two will always be settled in favour of one, rather than the other. The subservience of leisure to work means that the reasons of work always dominate in cases where the two are not perfectly aligned.

Yet as we have seen, the two *are* often aligned. Leisure does pay its unintended dividend, much as disinterested commerce generates value for interested commerce – so long as these remain unintended and disinterested. But as a result, justifying inactivity in terms of productivity can seem irresistible to those seeking to change minds and get results.[12]

Both Pieper and Odell are keenly aware of this risk. 'Now leisure is not there for the sake of work,' warns Pieper, 'no matter how much new strength the one who resumes working may gain from it.' Odell is alert to the modern-day instrumentalisation of leisure. She points to digital detox retreats, where participants pay, often handsomely, to be removed from their over-connected lives as they frolic in nature for a spell: Walden for rent, at weekly rates. The end goal of such retreats – often targeted at the very knowledge workers who create the tools that the retreats offer temporary release from – is silently understood. It is to allow a fresh return as improved versions of themselves, newly primed for creation. Like a cleansing of the liver to clear the way for benders to come. As Odell puts it, 'All too often, things like digital detox retreats are marketed as a kind of "life hack" for increasing productivity upon our return to work.'

Still, Aristotle aside, it is hard to deny the socially progressive aspect of Henry Ford's 1926 factory reforms. Ford was not dictating how workers should spend their newfound leisure; he simply wanted them more rested for Monday morning. That the intention behind Ford's decision was greater productivity may not have tainted the benefit that workers extracted from the additional day of leisure. This insight proves relevant to the final chapter: if the intent of the decision-maker and that of the affected parties are sufficiently distinct, then perhaps an intent born of commercial interest does not preclude the full benefits of disinterest. In other words, the ability of Ford's workers to disinterestedly enjoy the 'superhuman' aspect of leisure during that additional day may have survived Ford's interested intentions, simply because the workers need not have been aware of those intentions.

Seen in this way, Henry Ford appears harmless: he is a capitalist who presents exactly as such. Greater leisure was to him an innovation on par with his continuous-flow assembly line, and he was quite transparent about it. Yes, he was a hunter lobbying for conservationism, but he wore the kind of bright red hunting getup that ensured no one would mistake him for anything else.

Until that point, interested commerce was well behaved in this sense: it did not try to disguise itself. Today, few savvy capitalists would think of piously proclaiming, as Ford did, that we get into trouble by putting leisure 'before work instead of after work – where it belongs'.

'Authentic leisure' thus faces a more subtle threat, because the benefits of leisure are not limited to rendering workers refreshed for work. Henry Ford may have had little use for the transcendent side of leisure; all he required of his workers was that they be sufficiently awake to operate the assembly line. But today's knowledge economy is different. It prizes innovation, creativity; it runs on individual ingenuity. And once the regular returns from wage labour have been maximised, it is only to be expected that the knowledge economy would turn its sights on the boundless returns hidden in that 'something divine' which dwells in individuals who are at leisure. The greater peril comes not from the Henry Fords, but from those who have read their Aristotle, who have internalised the lessons of Pieper and Odell, and who now deploy these ideas for their own purposes.

Coopted: Tapping the Fruit of Leisure

The popular response that greeted Jenny Odell's *How To Do Nothing* should fill the apostles of leisure with a mix of hope and dread. Barack Obama was not the only one to take to Odell's call for resisting the productivity ethos and the encroachment of usefulness in our lives. The book struck a chord with many. But tellingly, the audience that was nodding along most avidly was in Silicon Valley.

How To Do Nothing features a blurb from *Wired* – the San Francisco-based glossy mouthpiece of the digital revolution – which turns out to come from an online feature titled, '9 Lazy-Ass Gifts for Your Favorite Couch Potato'. The article listed

Odell's book alongside a new robot vacuum, wool socks from L. L. Bean, and a high definition sixty-five-inch television. The *Wired* staff endorsed the book again on their Gadget Lab Podcast ('Everyone at *Wired* seems to like this book,' exclaimed one of the hosts), alongside the new keyboard from Apple.

The swiftness with which Odell has been absorbed into the productivity mindset, embraced by the techies at *Wired* and the readers of life-hacking forums, is all the more startling given how aware Odell was of the risk, and how unwilling she has been to let her ideas be captured and repurposed. *How To Do Nothing* is full of denials of its own functionality. It is upfront about its unwillingness to offer clear advice. It basks in ambiguity; it never quite provides the answer that we might expect from its 'how to' title. Pieper offered similar denials, lest one mistake his treatise on leisure for a 1946 guide to better living: in his conclusion, he cautioned, 'The intention of this essay was not to give advice or provide guidelines for action.'

But like the earnest superheroes in blockbuster movies, the apostles have a weakness. Given how they envision the realms of work and leisure as reliably hostile to one another, they view the boundary between the realms of interested and disinterested commerce as clearly defined. They imagine themselves safely on one side, and the Henry Fords of the world clearly on the other. As a result, they worry about Henry Ford and other self-professed capitalists, but they fail to see the incursion from their left flank, from voices far nearer to their own.

This misapprehension comes from a caricatured view of capitalism. To portray the market as hostile to the notion of leisure, as the apostles do, is to underestimate its ambitions, and its adaptability in attaining them. Yes, the market seeks to maximise utility – but it will bend into whatever shape proves best suited to attain it. It is interested in whatever works. And if what works cannot be fully explained, market actors will gamely go through the motions without asking to understand them.

Consider the masters of the universe who congregate in the Swiss town of Davos every year. In recent years, interspersed among the sessions on international monetary policy have been well-attended lectures on mindfulness led by the superstar Buddhist monk Matthieu Ricard, with titles like 'Secrets of Success'.[13] This strikes no one as incongruous, because capitalism, ultimately, is remarkably undogmatic: market actors will invest in whatever they think will deliver. Once the benefits of interested commerce have been maximised, we should expect the champions of interested commerce to start looking elsewhere for additional marginal value. The realm of disinterest beckons. Managers call on corporations to chase not only profit but 'purpose'.[14] This remarkable openness is lost on the apostles, who fail to see how the market is irresistibly drawn to outliers, mavericks, and nonconformists. They fail to see how the market swoons for dissidents like themselves.

We have seen the sources of this infatuation. Markets run on credibility. As far back as the eighteenth century, David Hume understood that people want to trust each other, but they are unable to do so because their interests are not aligned: they know the other party has an incentive to get the best of them. When trust is in short supply, those who are viewed as 'the real deal' rise above the rest. It is why Weber's Puritans prospered; it is also why the passionate entrepreneur has an advantage over his self-interested counterpart. Hence the market's celebration of the apostles, whose disinterest is palpable: all those denials of usefulness only serve to burnish their stock, and render them further irresistible to a market hungry for any scrap of 'authenticity'.

All their demurrals are in vain; the apostles can do little to resist the market's embrace. Soon, street vendors begin hawking little brass medallions of their likeness. Their words appear on well-designed tote bags. Before long, management consulting firms are handing out copies of *How To Do Nothing* to this year's new hires, in hopes that some of its disinterested passion may rub off, and buttress the firm's image as forward-thinking and dedicated to providing a work–life balance for its employees. Far from being shouted down, the apostles are brought into the market's fold.

We have seen such transitions in Chapter 5. But those earlier examples were different in one key respect. When the Puritans' descendants shifted their ideological allegiances to prosperity as the goal, rather than viewing it as a byproduct, or when the members of the nineteenth-century Oneida commune adopted a new mission centred around their commercial enterprise, they did so voluntarily. Not so in this case.

Call it cooptation, appropriation, or accommodation: it has a long history. The countercultural movements of the 1960s offer the prototypical example. The hippies did not have to cut their hair, put on business suits, and get corporate jobs (though many of them eventually did) for the symbols of the counter-cultural movements of the 1960s to be absorbed by the market and redeployed to interested ends. The sexual revolution may have started as an explicitly anti-consumerist movement, but eventually it provided the language of individual liberation and self-expression that continues to feed ad copy to this day. The revolution was not only 'contained' by the market, to use Herbert Marcuse's term;[15] it was repurposed to its ends. Neither was this an entirely cynical move, or a strategic means of buying off an opposition movement: as the historian and journalist Thomas Frank argues, the market's embrace of the symbols of the 1960s counterculture was in part a sincere attempt at reinvention: 'Business leaders were not concerned merely with simulating countercultural signifiers in order to sell the young demographic ... but because they approved of the new values and anti-establishment sensibility being developed by the youthful revolutionaries.'[16] The market was seduced.

We use the term 'commodification' to describe the transformation of previously non-traded goods into products that can be bought and sold. Sex becomes commodified with the emergence of a market for prostitution; data are commodified when advertisers are willing and able to buy people's personal information. But the term has a more specific meaning that proves especially revealing. *Commodity* comes from the Latin *commoditas*, which means convenience, or obligingness. The apostles' calls for reclaiming leisure from the market are not shouted down by the market, like they themselves might have hoped; instead, they are made obliging, convenient to market interests.

Of course, they were the ones to bring their ideas to market; no one coerced Jenny Odell into writing and promoting a book. But then as soon as those ideas were out, the market was, as it always is, free to repurpose them as it saw fit. In this case, that meant turning the apostles' insights – tricky notions of leisure as a state that cannot be willed; attention as a source of resistance – into more manageable shorthand ideas which find greater take-up: 'Less is more.' 'Embrace boredom.' 'Follow your whim.'

From the potency of 'pure leisure' emerges a whole new language, one that market actors soon learn to speak with as much eloquence as the apostles themselves. Hear their mellifluous tones as they sing of 'a new aspiration to live a life where the professional and personal don't compete with each other, but enrich one another'. That isn't the poet Robert Frost, but Vincent Montalescot, the head of marketing at Montblanc, the maker of luxury pens. Here's Montblanc's CEO speaking in the same voice, vaunting 'a different way of thinking ... [where]

it's no longer about status or reaching the top but it's about the meaningful, purposeful and enriching journey we take to get there, and the people we impact on our way'. The enriching journey in question is ad copy for a new campaign by Montblanc to sell $1,000 gilded ballpoint pens. The alchemy of marketing manages to enlist the force of disinterested ('meaningful, purposeful') behaviour to the service of interested commerce. It even affects open disdain for status-seeking ('it's no longer about status or reaching the top') in defence of an object that is the paragon of status-seeking – just what Adam Smith had in mind when he wrote of 'baubles and trinkets which are employed in the economy of greatness'.[17] We are so inured to the magic of this marketing alchemy that it no longer gives us pause, yet this is how the potent language of leisure is recognised and repurposed.

It was always thus. In the military, the *avant-garde*, or vanguard, used to designate the special units sent out immediately after the cavalry, and whose function was to engage the enemy in order to gain the main guard time and space for action.[18] The avant-garde has always had to contend with the uneasy fact that despite its best efforts at eschewing a social function – or precisely *because* of those efforts – it proved useful to the mainstream. The nonconformists have always been instrumental to the mainstream's self-renewal.

That self-renewal does come at a cost. Once they are rendered more obliging, the ideas of market dissidents lose much of their edge. And by the same token, they also lose some of what made them valuable to the market in the first place. Like the lumbering Lennie in John Steinbeck's *Of Mice and Men*, who unwittingly kills the pets he wants to caress, the market's love has a way of snuffing out the object of its affections. But it matters that the snuffing out is the result of holding dissidents a little too tightly, rather than aiming to silence them. The common view of an opposition between commerce and disinterestedness is not due to some market aversion to non-commercial activities; it's because of a Lennie-like need to stroke the soft fur of disinterest, and a tendency to stroke it too hard. As with music bands that are dismissed by their original fans just as they achieve mainstream success, the market appeal of market dissidents relies on their retaining their outsider status.

It is common to talk of the market as a unified, impersonal force. This correctly reflects one of its essential traits: the modern market is indeed based on impersonal exchanges. Market outcomes are the aggregation of countless individual decisions, though no individual market actor can singlehandedly affect those outcomes. But this level of abstraction obscures how markets are nothing but the aggregation of real individuals – individuals acting on market opportunities. Individuals like Cal Newport.

Leisure's Left Flank

A computer scientist and Georgetown University professor, Cal Newport is the author of multiple bestselling 'how to' books about various 'secrets of success'. *How to be a High School Superstar, How to Win at College, Deep Work Rules for Focused Success in a Distracted World.* Newport is a successful market actor, in more ways than one. He is a gifted programmer, pedagogue, and public speaker, as well as a prolific academic researcher – but more interestingly, his success is rooted in his success. That is, the main product he brings to market is the promise of greater productivity, based on his own example – how to unlock it, achieve it, maximise it.

In his books, Newport likes to draw on great minds, to try and replicate the secrets of their creative gifts. Take Michel de Montaigne, Carl Jung, Mark Twain, and J. K. Rowling: all of them, Newport maintains, shared a common ability for sustained 'deep work', which consists of creating 'new value' through long bouts of distraction-free concentration. We learn that Montaigne and Jung and Twain all retreated far away from daily distractions and achieved the products of their greatness in a state of deep solitary focus. Newport's recipe for success: be like Michel.

This mimetic approach is a common trope of the self-help literature. An author observes successful individuals, and divines the best practices that appear to correlate with their success. The appeal is easy to grasp. If we can just model ourselves closely on the people we admire, we too can achieve as much as they did. Like most, I am not immune to the charms of the 'habits of great minds' genre. I am as interested in Mark Twain's breakfast routine as I suspect all self-professed creatives are. I want to know whether J. K. Rowling writes longhand or on a keyboard, and what brand of coffee she drinks.

But mimesis as an approach begins to break down when the key to the success being emulated rests on an absence of intent. In such cases, to mimic Mark Twain is to adopt the position of the doomed faker from Chapter 4. It amounts to expending a great deal of effort mimicking effortlessness. We have seen the downfall that awaited von Kleist's ill-fated youth when he attempted the same. The behaviour may appear similar, but the difference in the underlying intent makes all the difference. Having read that Stephen King came upon the idea for his latest bestseller while waiting in a queue at his local grocery store, we may seek out the same store and wait in the queue with an empty shopping trolley and a pad of paper, ready for inspiration to strike us, but it is likely to be a long wait. Disinterest pays, but its self-interested emulation does not.

This point is not lost on the likes of Cal Newport. Those seeking to harness the potency of disinterest for interested ends do so by trying to blur the distinction between the two realms, trying to be at once at leisure and in pursuit of an objective. As a result, Cal Newport often sounds uncannily like Jenny Odell. Both warn against the same risk of distraction by the same devices and the same social networking tools. Both sing the praises of directed attention. 'A deep life is a good life,' Newport intones, sounding downright Aristotelian. 'Deep work' generates 'meaning', he notes.

In fact, writers like Newport can only go where credibly disinterested thinkers like Odell have gone before them. For there to be a language of disinterest that can be deployed for interested ends – for 'meaning' to be a desirable result of 'deep work' – other people must have used this same language in a disinterested fashion beforehand. The avant-garde must first provide the proof of concept. Whether they want to or not, that is their function: to forge a path so that others may pass. It is because Crary the social theorist writes his eulogy to sleep in the post-industrial age that Huffington the entrepreneur can then call for a sleep 'revolution' as a means of helping us achieve our productivity goals.

Writers like Newport are fluent in the language of disinterest, and they attempt to channel it to interested ends. Newport thus bemoans, in much the same way as Odell, the 'degradation' of leisure that is lost to 'a blur of distracted clicks'. Only he would channel this undistracted leisure to the achievement of greater productivity. Therein lies the difference between the Odells and the Newports of the world. One camp is concerned with reclaiming a space for leisure as leisure, while the other is interested in leisure as life hack. And it is here that the paradox presents itself anew: for the reasons we have seen from J. S. Mill onwards, the disinterested approach may ultimately bear more fruit than the calculating one, even as the sole interest of the calculating approach is reaping the same fruit.

As a result, authors like Newport find themselves perched at the confluence of interest and disinterest, attempting an uneasy dance between the two. Consider one of Newport's key ideas: 'productive meditation'. Newport describes it as focusing one's attention on 'a single well-defined professional problem' during a walk or a jog – or, yes, 'in the shower'. As Newport explains, productive meditation is 'like mindfulness meditation', only weaponised towards a specific goal. Never mind that the term 'productive meditation' is an oxymoron (though it is). Nor is the issue that meditation cannot boost productivity – meditation has in fact been shown in increasingly well-designed studies to boost concentration and creativity. Doesn't the cult filmmaker David Lynch swear by it?

No, the issue is that the reason why meditation is uniquely potent in generating productive spillovers is that it is performed as a non-productive activity. That, in fact, is what defines it: from its Buddhist origins, meditation has always been an attempt to empty oneself of intent. If there is one autotelic experience – an activity that is its own end – this is it. Once it becomes 'productive', it loses the quality of meditation, and by the same token, its productivity-enhancing potential. As soon as meditation is enlisted to external ends, it encounters the faker's paradox. In this respect, it is no different from the nouveaux riches trying their hardest to adopt the airs of the old money, which come down to not having to try hard at all.

Again, this is not to say that meditation techniques applied towards some 'well-defined professional problem' may not carry some outward benefit. Inhaling and slowly exhaling never hurt anyone. But if the fruits of leisure or meditation – the sudden bout of inspiration or insight – are byproducts of behaviour pursued for other ends, then planning for them is likely to be self-defeating. What's more, if these instrumentalised walks deployed towards 'well-defined professional problems' begin to crowd out walks for their own sake, strolling for the purpose of strolling, then the risk is that all the instrumentalisation may actually end up having a net negative effect on the creativity and innovation it is designed to foster.

Newport is unfazed. As he puts it, 'I think of productive meditation like pull-ups: It's really hard at first, but it gives you really big results.' The comparison to exercise is useful, in that it forces us to pose the question sharply: why wouldn't creativity and innovation be cultivated in the same way that one builds bigger biceps, or increases stamina? Much of the issue comes down to the difference between these two, and the question of whether this difference can be bridged.

If you want to become a better long-distance runner, you can work towards it by making yourself run long distances. There is nothing about the awareness that the goal of your running is to become a better long-distance runner that will take away from its effectiveness in attaining that goal. You do not need to accidentally 'fall into' running to get better at it. If you sprint unthinkingly through the airport to catch a late flight, it will not be any more effective at increasing your stamina by virtue of not being consciously directed at increasing your stamina.

This is not to say that exercise is easy; working up the will to make yourself run long distances is challenging. But working up willpower by reminding yourself of the goal of getting better at long-distance running is likely to help, not hinder, the reaching of the goal. Tricks like tracking incremental progress may spur you on. An exercise plan setting out various milestones may do the same. In other words, constant awareness of the aim is beneficial to its attainment.

Whereas the fruits of physical exercise are the product of strong will, the fruits of leisure come precisely from its opposite;

an absence of wilful intent. To go back to Pieper, pure leisure 'is not brought about through the application of extreme efforts, but rather with a kind of moving away', which is somehow 'less at one's disposal' than the effort involved even in strenuous work. By comparison, pull-ups are just that: strenuous work. For the same reason, if someone put a gun to your head, you could likely do ten pull-ups, but you probably could not muster a bolt of creative insight, no matter how hard you tried – precisely because of how hard you were trying. Yet the self-help literature, and authors like Cal Newport, treat the two alike. Both types of goal are reduced to tests of strong will, focus, conscious effort.

Still, why not try? What is wrong with wanting to be more creative and more productive? Why not wring as much as possible out of one's working hours, by whatever means necessary? Work hard so that you can play hard?

There is of course nothing wrong with the goal of wanting more per se. Rather, the issue lies in the mismatch between the nature of that goal and the means of attaining it. The risk is that even from a strictly Utilitarian standpoint, one might end up with less overall. Similarly, the Benthamite Utilitarian might ask, what is wrong with wanting to maximise happiness? And J. S. Mill's response would be: nothing at all. Happiness sounds perfectly desirable; it may even be a fine standard by which to judge our actions – but only after the fact. Because something unexpected happens when happiness is held up as the goal of those actions going in. The goal-oriented, instrumental approach makes it less likely that the very thing sought will be achieved. And this approach may actually make us less likely to pursue the things that, without our being entirely aware of when and how, sow the seeds of contentment.

Increasingly, we find ourselves living in a byproduct society: we value things that resemble the elusive character of leisure more than the readily attainable benefits of pull-ups. Yet we have not adjusted our approach accordingly. We go out for an aimless stroll, and we take a shortcut for the sake of efficiency.[19]

The deployment of intent to self-interested ends has elevated economic development and growth as the self-evident goals of our efforts, rather than as means to some higher end – what Keynes called 'the real values of life'. As societies grow more affluent, the contribution of economic growth to that higher end begins to decrease, while the comparative value of disinterest increases. Once the market has maximised all conventional investment opportunities – those based on the rational pursuit of self-interest – the remaining opportunities increasingly come from disinterested pursuits, from the tapping of individual passion, from a suspension of maximisation. This is when the paradox that interests us presents itself: leisure may make a great contribution to work through its impact on creativity and innovation, but only on the condition that it remain leisure, rather than a factor of production. And this condition, after a century of habituation to post-industrial life, is a difficult one to meet.*

So was Pieper correct? Is it harder to pick the fruits of leisure than those of hard work, and is leisure impervious to intentional action altogether? Is the notion of 'cultivating creativity' destined to remain an oxymoron? Does it amount to running to Tanizaki's open-air toilet so that haiku lines offer themselves up to us? This is analogous to the question in Chapter 4: can the faker ever succeed? William James didn't think so. Jon Elster, the Columbia University political scientist who has written more incisively about byproducts than anyone, does not think so, either. And, if anything, the challenge here seems even

---

* For this same reason, it may be that the wealthy are not after all, our 'advance guard' as Keynes put it, scouting out the prospects for full lives in the land of affluence. It may be instead that the wealthy are too bound up in the realm of interested commerce to be able to leave it. The means of attaining wealth may have

greater than in the case of fakers trying to persuade their audience: when it comes to reaping the fruits of leisure, it is not about persuading others, but about persuading ourselves. The trick is to somehow open the door to leisure without realising that we have done so. In this attempt, we are closer to the question posed by Fénelon, our seventeenth-century mystic archbishop, who wondered whether religious faith could ever be the product of instrumental behaviour (he, too, was doubtful). The question remains: are we who live in an instrumentally minded age doomed to being more or less successful fakers?

Having taken in the wisdom of the apostles of leisure, and having come to appreciate the value of such moments, can we do anything to increase our fair share, our hoped-for but unanticipated allotment? And might a society that has recognised the unique benefits of disinterest succeed in picking its fruits? Or is the attempt likely to backfire? These are the questions we have been converging towards all along.

locked them in. Their interests may be too deeply vested, and this may preclude the possibility of conversion. The New Testament may have been on to something with its talk of camels and needles.

8

Resisting the Intelligence Intelligently

Throughout the last seven chapters, I have drawn on the writings of generations of thinkers working in shifts, one atop another, across more than four centuries, all examining various forms of the same question. Given the work of all these political economists, theologians, ethicists, psychiatrists, and philosophers – what progress have we made in unpacking the paradox of intention? If disinterest pays, but only if it is seen to be genuine, where does this leave the self-interested? Those who seek to garner the esteem of their peers, to harness the fruits of creativity, to win the trust of their customers, their investors, and their constituents – can they transcend the limitations imposed by our instrumental age, our consumer society?

The Demurrers

Many of the thinkers who grappled with the paradox of intention also rejected the very notion of a solution. When Baldassare Castiglione, in the first half of the sixteenth century, laid out the benefits of that divine state of grace and studied nonchalance that determines the success of the courtier, his audience beckoned him to explain how such grace might be attained: 'Now since by praising this quality so highly you have, I believe, aroused in all of us a strong desire to obtain it … you are also obliged to satisfy us by teaching the way to do so.'

Nothing of the sort, Castiglione retorted. 'I am not obliged … to teach you how to acquire grace,' he answered before adding, 'it is almost proverbial that grace cannot be learned.'[1] We can hear his audience groaning in disappointment. That puts Castiglione with William James, the father of modern psychology, who thought it was impossible for an upstart to ever pass for a gentleman: one is either born into it, or doomed never to attain it. Which is hardly helpful to those who happen not to have come into Castiglione's natural grace or James's gentlemanly ways from birth.

Josef Pieper, who laid out the rewards of pure leisure, demurred in similar terms, though for quite different reasons: 'But now, what are we to do?' he asks. And his response: 'Now, the intention … was not to give advice or provide guidelines for action but only to encourage reflection … This essay, then, was not designed for an immediately practical purpose.'

Jenny Odell, of course, takes much the same line as Pieper. *How To Do Nothing* amounts to a thoughtful, book-length demurral. At its end, she writes, 'It's tempting to conclude this book with a single recommendation about how to live.' But, she vows, 'I refuse to do that.' That Odell would eschew offering any practical advice should not be much of a surprise: her very objective is to make her reader question the instrumental attitude that would make them seek such advice in the first place.

These writers stay true to the contradiction they have identified. There is unquestionable logical coherence in insisting that if byproduct states are defined as those that elude the will, then any advice offered to try and attain them will only backfire, ensuring they are never attained. Yet there is another motive here: writers like Pieper and Odell also have a vested interest in keeping the paradox intact. They both admit to the same fear, namely that the returns from disinterest may be captured to feed self-interested motives. Art, nature, sleep, leisure: these all risk becoming economic factors of production alongside capital and labour, all of them enlisted to external uses – increasing productivity, enhancing workers' efficiency. So these thinkers pre-emptively dig in their heels to avoid such cooptation: the fruits of art, nature, sleep, and leisure, they insist from the get-go, simply cannot be attained in an instrumental fashion. To try and do so is self-defeating, it erodes their potency. As Pieper warns, 'there are certain things which one cannot do "in order to..." do something else. One either does not do them at all or one does them because they are meaningful in themselves.'[2] To these thinkers, the paradox of intention is a safeguard, and it may be the only safeguard remaining.

We might safely stop here. Because all these thinkers are right, of course. The paradox of intention is a paradox for a reason. If the definition of disinterested behaviour is that it is not strategic, then it cannot be the outcome of strategic behaviour. Period.

But is there really no way forward? Is the path from interested commerce to disinterested commerce truly impassable? There is something deeply wanting in the notion that, as Castiglione and William James suggest, one is either born into grace, ease, spontaneity, and passion, or else for ever doomed to merely faking one's way in. It not only feels backwards, but it also does not quite match up with experience.

After all, the arc of history is bent against James' well-bred gentleman. The merchant classes *did* catch up. The upper classes shifted the parameters of competition as best they could, from material opulence to leisure and then away from it. Yet this did not stop the landed gentry from crumbling into a spectacle of pageantry. The kind of social capital that is associated with desirable byproduct states is amassed today on grounds that have little to do with the defining qualities of the upper class from William James's time. Insisting on the paradox's unassailability ultimately failed to preserve the distinction that the well-bred gentleman wanted preserved.

Similarly, the default mode of our instrumental age is not inescapable. Bertrand Russell bemoaned how modern people think that everything ought to be done 'for the sake of something else', yet this is not to say that some of those people do not sometimes shift to doing things entirely for their own sake. We all know accounts of mavericks who designed their own escape and pulled it off, fleeing spheres of interested commerce for worlds of disinterested action. We have heard of Wall Street types who left careers in finance to take up teaching positions. Lobbyists who walked away from well-paying positions in Washington think tanks to open up motorcycle repair shops far from the city. Or my hometown banker-turned-baker, written up in the local paper. We cherish these accounts precisely for how they testify to the possibility of successfully turning away from a purely instrumental mode. So much so, that the popular demand for stories of conversions of this sort is insatiable. In another instance of the market's hunger for credible shows of disinterest, books documenting the path from lobbying exec to motorcycle shop have a way of becoming the season's bestsellers.[3]

Nor are these isolated incidents. Shifts from interested to disinterested commerce appear increasingly common among millennials, especially. The trend through time is remarkable. A 2017 Deloitte survey found that 38 per cent of millennials planned to quit their job in the next two years. When the survey was rerun the following year, that number was up to 43 per cent. In 2019, it was 49 per cent. In trying to explain this emerging attitude, the same study found that 'Companies that are perceived to be fixated on profits ... do not engender loyalty [among their millennial employees].' This is one specific instance of the type of transition that the political scientist Ronald Inglehart describes seeing in worldwide values surveys over the past decades: in more secure societies, people place increasing weight on postmaterialist values like self-expression. A collective shift in attitudes is not only possible, it may already be discernible in the data, in these gradual changes in individual stances.

Similarly, some among those who seek religious faith do attain it. Even the most consummate insomniacs eventually fall asleep. And in seeming contradiction to Castiglione's assurance that it is proverbial that grace cannot be learned, we can trust that the graceful were all once graceless.

What's more, the figure with which this book began, J. S. Mill, stands as a personified rebuke to the naysayers. That is how he saw himself, too. Born into a hotbed of Utilitarian thinking, Mill succeeded in breaking away from it, both in his worldview and in his philosophy of life. Not for nothing did Mill draw on the language of religious conversion in describing this moment of self-realisation. He had identified a flaw in the Utilitarian conception of human behaviour. Happiness, the central aim of the Utilitarians, could only be had en passant. This insight never left him. It affected his own conception of human behaviour. As opposed to Bentham's view of pleasure-seeking, pain-avoiding automatons, Mill saw how passion might function both as hindrance and salvation in attaining individuals' goals.

The Crisis of Utility, and the Utility of Crisis

To the modern reader, J. S. Mill's *Autobiography* might call to mind the memoirs of individuals who escape the religious cults they are born into, and live to tell the tale. It is in its way one long indictment of his upbringing, his eccentric education, and the mental breakdown that resulted. And while that indictment stands, one also gets the impression that looking back on his life, Mill came to see his personal crisis, grim though it was, as having ultimately beneficial effects. It proved to be, alongside meeting Harriet Taylor, the formative experience of his intellectual coming of age.[4]

As a result, one gets the funny feeling that had J. S. Mill and Harriet Taylor had children of their own, he might have yet imposed a pedagogical regimen not so dissimilar from the one he had known himself: Greek and Latin for toddlers; political economy and logic through adolescence; and only then, Wordsworth's verse and music.

If we partake in a bit of counterfactual history, we can imagine what might have happened had it not been for J. S. Mill's breakdown. He would have remained one of Bentham's many followers. He would likely have become a great classicist, a thinker on a par with his father, James Mill; one of the many figures who moved the century along, rather than one who gave it a new direction. He would not have attempted the synthesis of two opposite streams of thought which he – as the peculiar political economist who was also up to plumbing the hazy depths of Carlyle's ruminations – was uniquely placed to accomplish. Without first drinking the Benthamite Kool-Aid, and then repudiating its ideas, Utilitarianism would not have had the complete rethink that Mill spent the rest of his life working towards. Were it not for J. S. Mill's particular outlook on the connection between social reforms and reforms of individual selves, our modern liberal system would be different in ways that are difficult to conceive of. To this day, indeed, liberalism could be usefully described as that system that aims to make space for individual conversions.

The model Utilitarian is of steady temperament, calculating every action's contribution to total social happiness. Yet Mill came to believe that it was precisely the lack of any inner turmoil that was to blame for Bentham's own limited view of human nature, and the philosophical shortcomings of Utilitarianism. Invoking the Romantics' misgivings over self-awareness, Mill faulted Bentham for having been blessedly devoid of any: 'Self-consciousness, that daemon of the men of genius of our time, from Wordsworth to Byron ... never was awakened in him.'

The portrait of Bentham that Mill paints is of a carefree, prelapsarian Adam. 'He had neither internal experience nor external; the quiet, even tenor of his life, and his healthiness of mind, conspired to exclude him from both ... He knew no dejection, no heaviness of heart ... He was a boy to the last.' But as a result of such innocence, Bentham's thought lacked an appreciation for the irrationality of the pleasure-seeking, pain-avoiding man. Having no internal spirit gnawing at him, Bentham could not understand how a social goal, once clearly identified – the greatest happiness for the greatest number – might be obstructed by the complexities of the human spirit, because he was charmedly lacking in them.[5]

In other words, what the happy go-lucky Bentham lacked was a reckoning of his own. The shortcomings of Utilitarianism was that it never grew a sufficient appreciation of man's passions, as malady *and* remedy both. As Mill saw it, the goal isn't to retain the innocence of the child. It is, rather, to gain a renewed sense of oneself, with all the inner wrangling that's entailed; to recognise the limitations of the self and to try and transcend them. J. S. Mill's conversion, his reprogramming of the self, was proof that such transcendence was achievable.

One of the more striking aspects of Mill's conversion is precisely its self-awareness. He deliberately sought a way to change his own mind, and he found it, in Wordsworth and Coleridge and the other English poets of his time. Romanticism's critique of modernity served as the wedge that dislodged the beliefs Mill had inherited from his father and Bentham. In the opening chapter, we saw how resonant this critique sounds in our own instrumental age. But we have yet to see what the Romantics suggested be done about it.

Indeed, even the nineteenth-century Romantics, who were most alert to the limitations of the instrumental, rational, and self-reflective mode of the Enlightenment, nonetheless sensed that there might be a way past it. They described this escape route in admittedly cryptic terms. They claimed that the recovery of naivety would happen once again via knowledge. They insisted that we must 'eat of the fruit of the tree of knowledge again to fall back into the state of innocence'.[6] That 'the hand that inflicts the wound is also the hand that heals it'.[7] That 'the mind ... is the only force that can defend us against itself'.[8] What sense can we make of this?

The Multiple Self as Curse and Remedy

The Romantics bemoaned the internal split that came with self-awareness, seeing in it a source of self-consciousness and inauthenticity; a sacrifice of intuition on the altar of analysis. They invoked the Fall from Eden as the symbolic representation of this inner division: for the first time, humans ceased behaving spontaneously, they saw themselves from the outside, and noticed they were naked. From that point on, they ceased being harmonious beings, and split into observer and observed. With knowledge came self-awareness, and with self-awareness came self-doubt. Two centuries later, we are pondering the best caption for our selfies: we find it harder than ever to act without fretting over how those actions might appear from the outside.

In this way, the Romantics were the first to put their finger on what turns out to be an essential component of byproduct states. Earlier, we made this point in passing, but it is now worth stating clearly. The hedonist's paradox, the paradox of teleology, Mill's 'theory of anti-self-consciousness', and the paradox of intention: these are all characterised by the presence of multiple selves. That is, they are all instances of one self thwarting another.

This appears plainly in cases where distinct individuals are interacting: the modern entrepreneur's self-interested attempt to come across as passionate fails if his intent is too obvious to his customers. When the up-and-coming nineteenth-century merchant attempts to mimic the manners of old money, the very intensity of his efforts betrays him to the members of the upper classes for whom those manners are effortless. When von Kleist's youth tries to repeat a gesture that had been performed spontaneously at first, for the sake of his friends, it is their stares that make him stumble. When humblebraggarts try to disguise their bragging as self-deprecation, their peers see through it, and punish their pretence. In each case, the attempt fails because there is an audience to detect the ploy.

The same split is also present, however, in instances that play out entirely within the individual. The novelist waiting on inspiration, the would-be believer questing after religious faith, the insomniac pining for deep sleep. In each case, we can imagine the individual as split into separate selves, with one self getting in the way of the other. The paradox emerges because of an overly keen awareness of one's own intention. Unless one can somehow conceal that intention from oneself, some of the things we most desire become impervious to wilful effort. Just as in the interpersonal cases above, one part of the individual may try to conceal its intention from another, but it is thwarted if that other part detects the ploy.

The multiple self is a powerful metaphor, and the Romantics were by no means the first thinkers to invoke it. It is an image that reappears regularly, from classical philosophy to contemporary cognitive science, to capture the idea that the self is not a unified being with well-integrated intentions, motivations, and beliefs, but an assembly of autonomous parts. In the *Phaedrus*, Plato thus compared the soul to a chariot pulled by two winged horses, one wild and unruly, the other noble and obedient. Nietzsche claimed that 'man conducts himself not as individuum but as *dividuum*'. Freud, of course, imagined a tripartite division of the self operating at different levels of consciousness.[9]

Modern neuroscience offers growing support for the notion of the multiple self. Today's cognitive scientists thus speak of psychological dualism, the mind's 'partitioning', 'compartmentalisation', or 'modularity', according to which our cognitive self is actually made up of a number of functionally specialised mechanisms that operate more or less independently. More evocatively, contemporary philosophers refer to the mind's three branches of government, each vying for power. Or they compare the self to a medieval city, with narrow tangled alleys and distinct neighbourhoods, some ancient and others more recent, each with their own functions and ways of operating.[10] All these conceptualisations share a common recognition: that the sense we have of a unified self is an illusion; we are in fact made up of subparts, and these interact and even bargain with one another just as distinct individuals might.

Tellingly, with the exception of the Romantics, attempts at charting the multiple self have most often been put in the service of elucidating problems of *weakness* of will. These are cases where we may intend to act purposefully and rationally, but we find ourselves unable to carry through on our resolve. That is, an intentional part of us is derailed by some more impulsive part of us. This is the predicament of Ulysses unable to resist the song of the sirens once he hears it; or that of my students who vow to finish an assignment over the weekend, but never quite get to it. The Greeks called this *akrasia*, or a lack of command. Today, people are more likely to refer to procrastination (literally, 'pushing forward to tomorrow'), or the instant gratification monkey. *Akrasia* underlies a whole host of modern complaints, from the inability to carry through on our projects to our failures to keep New Year's resolutions.

The problem we have been concerned with over the prior seven chapters is the exact opposite of *akrasia*: not weakness of will, but an *excess* of will. Across the different guises we have seen it in, the paradox of intention comes from holding on too strongly to a pre-defined intention. And while far more popular attention gets paid to problems of *akrasia*, we have seen why our modern malaise might result more often from that opposite, an excess of will – and that this becomes truer as a society grows more affluent. People increasingly will things that evade wilful effort.

Our very fixation on fighting akratic behaviour – behold the hundreds of apps and thousands of self-help tomes on beating procrastination once and for all – speaks to our biases. It's a testament to how much we privilege instrumental, goal-oriented behaviour. Steeling our resolve and strengthening our will seem like the remedy to every problem. Any failure is ascribed to not having wanted it enough. By contrast, as J. S. Mill and others have argued, our most meaningful failures may be due to our anticipation of the desired outcomes. If we could only lose sight of our objectives, we might be better able to reach them.

In spite of being opposite problems, the wealth of thinking on akratic behaviour proves useful. A great number of solutions have been proposed for dealing with *akrasia*. Most involve some way of strengthening one self against the other; empowering the intentional self and weakening the impulsive self. Ulysses told his shipmates to tie him to the mast and made them vow to only make his bindings stronger if he yelled to untie him. One can use similar pre-commitment strategies against smaller temptations, like making friends promise not to serve that chocolate-layered cheesecake, which they know we're defenceless against, at their next dinner party. People announce their resolutions in public to increase the costs of not meeting them. Well-designed websites allow you to put money in escrow, and automatically donate it to a hated political cause of your choice unless a work deadline is met. All such solutions involve a recognition of the notion of multiple selves, and either the arming of the intentional self, or the impairment of its counterpart, the impulsive, unreflexive self.*

Tackling the problem of excessive will is likely to pass through a similar recognition of the multiple self, with the difference that it is now the conscious, instrumental self that must be stifled. And herein lies the source of the Romantics' cryptic aphorisms. For it is no longer a question of a rational, far-seeing self tying the hands of an impulsive, short-sighted self. Rather than an open struggle, what is required is some sleight of hand.

---

* More sophisticated solutions will harness some passions against others, as when weight-loss programmes empower vanity in the service of health. But there, too, the design necessarily comes from the intention of many selves. Freud, of course, envisioned all of psychoanalysis largely as an exercise in buttressing the ego against the impulses of the id.

This brings to mind an old joke. A man walks into the city's most reputed jeweller with a huge raw diamond, to have it cut for an engagement ring. Given the value of the stone, the owner of the shop is called in. He considers the stone in awe, and finally calls out to his lowliest apprentice, as if ringing up an order for a pastrami sandwich: 'Avi, cut this stone for me.' And before the terrified customer's eyes, Avi goes to work on the stone, and soon wraps up his task. The stone is handed back, perfectly cut. Relieved but visibly rattled, the customer asks the owner, 'How could you give this priceless gem to a lowly apprentice to cut?' To which the owner replies, 'I know how much this stone is worth. If I tried to cut it myself, my hand would shake. Whereas Avi, he doesn't know any better, so his hand is steady.'

The takeaway, of course, is that when our self-awareness gets in our way, as when we realise how high the stakes are, we stand to gain from calling on an internal Avi, who goes ahead and simply does the job without second-guessing himself. Accessing the Avi within is how one attains Castiglione's state of grace. It is what von Kleist's ill-fated youth was unable to do, and what proved his downfall.

But the joke holds a further insight: Avi, essential though his role is whenever a priceless diamond needs to be cut, is not the one running the shop. He is called on when needed, but then he goes back to the menial tasks of his apprenticeship. The shopkeeper's limitation is that his hand shakes at the thought of the stone's value. But Avi's limitation is that he cannot be the one to call on himself. His aptness for tasks where self-awareness gets in the way is inseparable from the fact that he is unable to gauge which tasks these are. And that is why Avi is the apprentice, and the shopkeeper is the shopkeeper.

In other words, the intellect cannot be done away with in the name of passion, because only the intellect can perceive its own limitations and try to devise a solution. Only the intellect can delegate to another self, either internal or external, that is not plagued by the same limitations. As Hegel put it, 'The principle of restoration is found in thought, and thought only.' Suddenly, the Romantics' otherwise baffling insistence on how a return to Eden would require tasting once more of the forbidden fruit begins to make sense. At times, one must resist the intelligence, yes, but the intelligence can only be resisted intelligently.[11]

Resisting the Intelligence Intelligently

Tackling the question of sleep, a paradigmatic byproduct state, Jon Elster recalls a case where an insomniac is told by her therapist to carefully record in writing all her physiological symptoms at night, to better help diagnose her condition. She does so, and taken up by the note-taking, swiftly falls asleep. Elster was drawing on Viktor Frankl, the psychiatrist who first labelled those states that elude wilful effort as 'byproduct states'. Frankl instructed his own patients suffering from insomnia to try instead to stay awake as long as possible. Taking up opposite aims in this way, Frankl claimed, was a remedy for a range of instances of excessive will, from insomnia and sexual impotence to writer's cramp. Sometimes, the same ruse could even be arrived at by accident. Frankl recalls the story of a man with a severe speech impediment who tries to intentionally stutter to elicit compassion from a policeman, and finds that his stutter has suddenly left him.

According to Frankl, pursuing an opposite aim is a way 'to detach one from oneself', a way for people to become unstuck from their wanting, planning, instrumental self. Attempting to deliberately stay awake is designed to throw off that part within that is stubbornly trained on the objective of sleep. It is deliberately inefficient; once more, the roundabout way proves the shortest workable path.

Yet Elster, for one, remains characteristically pessimistic: the ploy can work once, he concedes, but as soon as it is seen for what it is, the patient becomes immune to it, and falls prone to insomnia once more. These folk remedies confirm how attempts to evade the paradox of intention are premised on some sleight of hand. In these cases, one person must know something the other does not. The trick for addressing insomnia only works if the patient remains unaware of its true intent. If the secretly intended result is anticipated, the familiar paradox rears its head anew, and all is lost – which hardly makes for a reliable remedy.

In discussing the French Moralists in Chapter 4, we stuck a pin in an idea that it is now helpful to return to. Of course, being helpful was never the Moralists' intent. As you will recall, these seventeenth-century salon wits were above all vandals, interested not in solutions, but in bringing down collective delusions. They rejoiced in the paradox's unassailability, and with each witty epigram, they buttressed it further: self-love was the one human motive underlying all others, so everyone was a faker, and any attempt to move past self-interest was just further calculation, one more means of self-advancement. Once the masks were torn off, there was no sense in putting them back on; the disillusionment was permanent.

But quite in spite of themselves, the Moralists left us a clue. Recall La Rochefoucauld's maxim from Chapter 4: 'We are so accustomed to pretending to others, that we end up pretending to ourselves.'[12] La Rochefoucauld certainly meant this as an indictment of the lengths to which some go in the pursuit of their self-interest. In the same way, he derided the show of affliction that follows the death of a friend, maintaining that by such mourning we mostly 'mourn for ourselves … So the dead are honoured with tears shed only for the living.'[13] And getting at the same notion of collective self-deception, here's my favourite of all of La Rochefoucauld's maxims: 'There are people who would never fall in love, had they not previously heard it mentioned.'[14]

And yet, fall they do. This, La Rochefoucauld doesn't deny; those he derides really are in love, with all that 'falling in' entails. He is merely poking fun at love's origins, and the need for outside assistance. So be it: read soppy love stories if you must. Doesn't everyone? In the personal notes of the philosopher Michael Oakeshott, one finds this observation: 'The stirrings of love can be felt, like those of ambition, before we have an object. This is true particularly of the young ... [who are] in love with love.'[15] The original authority on the matter, the Roman poet Ovid, said as much when he pleaded women to be forgiving of men's awkward feints: 'O ye fair, be kinder to those who pretend: / That passion will become real, which began as feigned.'[16]

We have seen how love is among the quintessential byproduct states: it cannot be willed; it must in fact be 'fallen into'. And it is accordingly defined by disinterest: love is only judged to be real insofar as it is unpremeditated, uncalculated, unreasoned. Yet La Rochefoucauld and Oakeshott both reveal all the stage-setting that goes into that eventual loss of reason. Stoking our own passions out of a design that we then conveniently forget: it's not only possible, it's what all teenagers do. Their first encounters with love are aspirational, a rehearsal for the later fall. This is the intelligence scheming against itself, with the help of books and movies and cheesy pop songs. Then, once the fall occurs, it ceases to matter entirely that the groundwork was set ahead of time.* Having seen the light, do the newly

---

* Elster refers to the 'self-eraser problem' in this context: 'The decision to believe, for instance, will hardly have any impact unless the person can bring himself to forget that his belief is the result of a decision to believe' (*Sour Grapes*, 1983, Cambridge University Press). This problem seems overwrought to me. Beliefs are self-absolving.

devout unsee it by being reminded of their motives in coming to see it in the first place? Unlikely. Once a conversion is complete, a belief is internalised, and all means used to attain it come to be seen as valid, precisely for having attained it.

So where La Rochefoucauld saw only reason for further cynicism, I instead see cause for hope. After all, what does it mean to believe in our passion enough to internalise its existence? To move ourselves into shedding tears and feeling sorrow? To coax ourselves into religious faith? Or to fall in love after hearing it sufficiently mentioned? How different are these states from true passion, sorrow, faith, and love? It sounds like a truism to claim that the most successful faker is the one who transforms himself into the genuine article. But in this case, it may offer a useful prescription for behaviour.

What La Rochefoucauld and the French Moralists denounced as hypocrisy looks quite different in light of the multiple self. We are not dealing so much with posturing, as with one inner self delegating to another. Both selves are in on the ploy. It's a peaceful transfer of power: an abdication rather than a usurpation.

The Multiple Self and the Market

In Chapter 2, we saw how much economic activity, especially in advanced societies, consists of market actors trying to persuade one another of their disinterested intentions. Yet for the very same reason that it pays to come across as disinterested, it also pays to detect attempts by others to pose as such. These two actions – posing and detecting – co-evolve. They are reared on the same process of learning. Observing their own incentives, individuals spot them in others. The result is a type of arms race between posers and their audience, where everyone takes turns being one and then the other, as sellers and buyers, workers and employers, rulers and subjects. The more disinterest pays for some, the more others will invest in detecting it. In this co-evolutionary game, there may be no more winning move than to actually convince oneself of one's own disinterested intentions.[17] It truly is the perfect crime: one that the perpetrator forgets having committed, and that the victim is unaware of having fallen prey to.

In the discussion of fakers in Chapter 4, we assumed that people are either strategic fakers, or true passionates. But recognising the notion of the multiple self complicates this easy distinction. Consider the art market. We have seen how the wages of passion are highest in industries like academia, science, public service, and the arts: settings where there is a strong premium put on disinterested behaviour. Any contemporary artist who would let slip that they were merely trying to maximise sales by catering to their audience's tastes would immediately see those sales dwindle. Art derives its market valuation from its proclaimed lack of interest in that valuation. Yet in spite of this setup, most working artists are neither instrumental fakers nor disinterested passionates.

Aware of the prevailing market expectation that art be made for its own sake rather than the market's, most artists may genuinely come to take this view as their own, even as part of them remains very much interested in the market's rewards. They succeed in channelling their instrumental impulses into non-instrumental directions, precisely because on some latent level, they know that such disinterest is also the way of appealing to the audience. There is a harmony between the passionate self and the instrumental self, and the latter lets itself be overtaken by the former, knowing that this also favours it. The suppression of one self results from collusion between the two. The intelligence defies itself because it pays to do so even by its own terms. Such artists would not think of themselves as posturing – which makes it more likely that posturing, insofar as it is taking place, bears fruit.

Take the British street artist Banksy, mentioned in the first pages of this book as the archetype of an artist whose market success is premised on an open show of disinterest, if not complete disdain, in market success. Consider a representative Banksy work, titled *Morons*: a screen print featuring a crowded auction house, with the painting up for sale inscribed with the words 'I can't believe you morons actually buy this sh*t'. The work is based on a photograph of an actual 1987 sale of Vincent van Gogh's *Sunflowers* at Christie's, which in its day broke auction records. A print of *Morons*, one of a series of 300 in sepia (other series having been produced in a gamut of colours), recently sold for over $75,000 at the same Christie's auction house depicted in the print. Christie's was so visibly delighted with this self-referential wink that they titled the entire sale 'Banksy: I can't believe you morons actually buy this sh*t'. The morons in question presumably ate it up, since the Banksy sale, which put up only minor works by the artist, and took place in the middle of the coronavirus pandemic in September 2020, brought it nearly $3 million.[18]

Faced with this dance between interested and disinterested commerce, art critics love to ponder the question of who is ultimately in the lead. Is the artist baiting the market, or being had by it? The question turns on discerning the artist's intent. It's on that basis that the call is made, either to indict the artist as a sellout, or to celebrate their whimsy in showing up the market.

The question arose in a pointed fashion following Banksy's most flamboyant ploy to date, the 2018 self-destruction of 'Girl with Ballooon' at Sotheby's, which I mention in the first chapter. There is no better, more credible means of signalling disinterest in material wealth than through its public destruction. And yet... some observers thought the coup at Sotheby's was just a tad too flamboyant, and the scheme a little too impeccably pulled off. Indeed, the destruction of the painting was only partial, a fact most media accounts glossed over. The shredding stopped midway, preserving just enough of the work for it to benefit from the spectacle. As it happens, the buyer of the piece, identified only as a female European collector, happily kept her winning lot. She was wise to do so: since that day, Banksy's market standing has risen spectacularly. A year later, a Banksy painting titled *Devolved Parliament* sold for a record $12 million, about five times its high estimate. There was little doubt as to why. As the head of the auction house cheerily explained, the shredding incident had 'really revived and refreshed the market'.[19]

In light of the market reaction, it becomes apparent that a purely instrumental Banksy and a wholly disinterested counterpart might have come up with the very same ploy. What's likely, indeed, is that both did. Whether or not there was collusion between the artist and the auction house is still in doubt, but the collusion between the artist's inner selves is not. Latent or overt, an instrumental self can still shape the form that artistic disdain takes. The art market thrives on the possibility of that collusion, and so do the artists themselves.[20]

It is unlikely that Banksy envisions himself as driven by market returns, but that is because the part of him that might actually be market-driven also knows better than to pipe up. To return to that favourite question of art critics, as to who is leading whom in the dance between interested and disinterested commerce, accounting for the multiple self now offers a third option. Namely that the intelligence need not lead if it knows the music: it can let itself be wholly led by passion, with some sense of where it will end up.

So it is with academics, too. Asked what motivates them to do their work, most university professors will boldly claim to be pursuing the advancement of science, or the satisfaction of their own undying curiosity. I suspect those feelings, moreover, would stand up to a polygraph test. But dig a little deeper, and it becomes clear that earning the admiration of their peers from a publication in a high-ranking journal is just as great a part of the drive. Were it not for the possibility of those small hits of glory, few scholars would put in the hours. In this way, the great triumph of the Western academic establishment is to have found ways of channelling ego into output, while maintaining the rhetoric associated with a selfless search for truth. Journal rankings, article citations, the ladder of prestige of universities and conferences: these are all means of keeping score, and most academics soon come to focus on these means rather than the noble end of the advancement of human knowledge. The proximate driver is another line on the résumé. Few academics own up to this, even to themselves – because it doesn't pay, and because they don't need to. As in the case of artists dealing with market expectations, the instrumental self and the passionate self have made arrangements.

The Romantics strived to achieve an authentic, harmonious, integrated self. They pined for that prelapsarian state devoid of self-awareness, a return to an Eden where one could just act, and be. In the face of increasing industrialisation, they sought a mode of purely disinterested commerce. But we might do better to heed the lessons of cognitive psychology instead. We might recognise that we are irrevocably composed of multiple subsystems. Rather than aiming at some elusive unity of the self, we might do well to exploit what we know of its multiplicity. When we pursue outcomes that lend themselves to efforts of will, we can buttress our rational self against shortsighted impulses that might derail it. And more cunningly, when we recognise that our instrumental selves have become their own greatest obstacle, we ought to seek ways of letting these instrumental selves recede into the background – ways of resisting the intelligence intelligently.

Going Through the Motions

The idea of enlisting the mind to defy itself comes up repeatedly from the thinkers mulling the paradox of intention in its various forms. They also converged on similar ways of actually accomplishing this. Once Blaise Pascal had demonstrated the 'reasons' for believing in God through the thought experiment of the wager, he also did his best to offer instructions to those whom he might have convinced by that reasoning. His solution was disarmingly simple. Those seeking religious faith, he suggested, should simply play along, and go through its physical motions:

> You want to find faith and you do not know the way? ... Learn from those who have been bound like you ... Follow the way by which they began: by behaving just as if they believed, taking holy water, having masses said, etc. That will make you believe quite naturally, and according to your animal reactions.[21]

There is much to hold on to in this famous passage. First is the presumption that those who found faith in the past did so through conscious effort.[22] Then we have Pascal's avowal that behaving 'as if' one believed is the way to believing in earnest. And thus, we get Pascal's praise of repetitive, unthinking rituals as ways of reaching a state that eludes direct effort. A purposeful benumbing, a delegation to our 'animal reactions', this is the way to illumination. The implication runs deep: to achieve the elusive belief in God, it may be sufficient merely to believe in Pascal. That is, to agree to follow him as he persuades us to go, unthinking, through the motions.

The last thing which may strike us in this passage is its tone, more reminiscent of late-night infomercials than ruminative seventeenth-century philosophers. We know this voice: 'You want to lose weight, but don't know how? Follow my easy twelve-step programme.' Trained as we are on the rhetoric of the market, such facile promises and demands for our trust put us immediately on guard, in ways that bring us back to the underlying problem of credibility. We detect the intent, and we grow mistrustful. The overeager peddling raises our suspicions, even as what is being peddled is precisely a disinterested state of being. The poet Paul Valéry put it best when he faulted Pascal in these terms: 'If you want to seduce or surprise me, take care that I not see your hand more distinctly than what it traces. I see Pascal's hand too clearly.'[23] As we will see, such suspicion may be warranted.

William James, writing more than two centuries later, also believed in Pascal. That is, he had similar faith in what might be achieved by going through the motions. What Pascal referred to as 'animal reactions', James called 'the nervous system'. Recall that it was James who claimed that the nouveaux riches were doomed never to pass for real gentlemen. They were kept in their orbit, James wrote, by 'an invisible law, as strong as gravitation'. The new rich tried through great effort to achieve what true gentlemen did effortlessly. The trick was not merely to know things and to own things, which anyone with money could do, but to know and to own them lightly. As James saw it, this progression from effortful to effortless was the very point of pedagogy: 'The great thing, then, in all education,' he wrote, 'is to make our nervous system our ally instead of our enemy.' In this, William James sounded every bit like the nineteenth-century Romantics:

There is no more miserable human being than one in whom nothing is habitual but indecision, and for whom the lighting of every cigar, the drinking of every cup ... are subjects of express volitional deliberation. Full half the time of such a man goes to the deciding, or regretting, of matters which ought to be so ingrained in him as practically not to exist for his consciousness at all.

We recognise the Romantics' association of the intellect with anxiety, indecision, and regret. James might as well have been talking about the doomed youth in von Kleist's play, and have added 'the lifting of every foot' to 'the drinking of every cup'. By relegating these concerns to the 'nervous system', they are removed from the ruminative deliberation of the intellect, and are placed instead into the 'effortless custody of automatism'. And in this way, the well-born take on the distinctive mannerisms of their class, whose effortlessness they will flaunt until their last breath, living off the interest of early investments made by their parents and tutors.

Trusting in the 'custody of automatism' also brings to mind the unexpected embrace of routine often observed in prolific innovators and creative types, those who manage to tap the superhuman aspect of a mind in a state of 'pure leisure'. A sedate external existence, in this view, is what allows for a fervent inner one. Haruki Murakami, who is among the most wildly inventive novelists writing today – and one of my favourites – holds to this kind of unvarying regimen when he's working on a book. He gets up every day at 4 a.m., writes, goes for a run and then a swim, writes some more, and is in bed by 9 p.m. As he explains, 'I keep to this routine every day without variation. The repetition itself becomes the important thing; it's a form of mesmerism. I mesmerize myself to reach a deeper state of mind.'[24] William James, who not only trusted in habit, but also shared the late nineteenth-century fascination with mesmerism, or hypnosis, would be pleased. To 'mesmerise oneself', of course, implies a multiple self: one self is the mesmerist and the other the mesmerised. As it happens, the word 'mesmerise' comes from a certain Franz Mesmer, a pseudo-scientist from the eighteenth century who postulated the existence of a universal vital fluid contained in all living beings that could be tapped for instrumental purposes. Mesmer was a quack, but Murakami's dozen novels are real.

Finally, Pascal and William James both draw our attention to the necessary role of time in the passage from the reflective to the reflexive. What begins as volitional and effortful can, if performed sufficiently frequently, and for sufficiently long, take on the form of habits, and be progressively removed from the dominion of the intellect. Over time, the dance steps that begin as self-conscious calculation are progressively delegated to the motor functions. They become free, in the double sense of the word: both unrestricted, and costing us no conscious effort. As with Castiglione's *sprezzatura*, however, attaining that double freedom may require considerable effort at the outset. The best dancers are those who have all but forgotten what their feet are doing; but for the intellect to be able to recede in this way, it must first be granted its hours of deliberate, effortful action.

When people are asked to shift modes, they tend to rely on the repetition of long-established, familiar rituals. Athletes thus run through the same set of gestures at crucial moments of play. Tennis players will bounce the ball a predetermined number of times before serving; basketball players go through a similar routine at the free-throw line. It is the intellect's way of summoning and giving way to muscle memory, the athlete's analogue to Pascal's 'animal reactions' and William James's 'nervous system'. It is one more way for an instrumental self to shut its own eyes.

Costly Signals of Disinterest

Given the arms race between those signalling disinterest on one side, and those detecting its misrepresentation on the other, convincing oneself may be the best means of convincing others. But such wholesale conversions may seem like a high bar to meet. Must the rational entrepreneur really go all in and turn herself into an obsessive passionate in order to seduce the market?

There may be something short of full conversion that can nevertheless yield some of these gains. One such possibility is offered by game theory, which as we saw in Chapter 2, has much to say about persuasion. One great lesson of game theory is that a signal becomes credible when it is costly. Claims must be backed up with some stake, otherwise, they will be dismissed as cheap talk. One means for market actors to convince others of their disinterested stance is thus to wilfully take a financial hit, or at least run the real risk of one.

In this way, it has become increasingly common for large corporations to engage in all manner of 'corporate social responsibility', a maligned buzzword that is commonly defined as encompassing all 'actions that appear to further some social good, beyond the interests of the firm'.[25] The second part of that definition is just as important as the first: corporate social responsibility cannot be too obviously reducible to the firm's interests, in which case it is just the company engaging in its day-to-day business. Firms may thus invest in their community by creating after-school programmes. They can reduce their carbon emissions, or lend out their employees to a local cause. The defining aspect of these initiatives is that they do not directly contribute to the bottom line: after-school programmes come out of company revenue; reducing carbon emissions may require installing costly new equipment; hours spent by employees working at the local food bank are hours not spent working on business spreadsheets.

Of course, a company will only engage in such small-scale corporate sacrifices if it can discern some downstream gain, however distant. It may be seen as a means of burnishing the brand image in a way that will appeal to customers, or a way of attracting those millennial employees who claim to value 'purpose' in their employer. A familiar conundrum results, which recalls that of the art market above: the company's well-meaning initiatives can contribute to self-interest, but only if they credibly go 'beyond the interests of the firm', as the very definition of corporate social responsibility requires. Similarly, artists must convincingly pursue a singular vision that disdains market tastes, in order to appeal to those art market tastes.

In both cases, the same arms race results: the makers aim at an appearance of disinterest, and the audience probes their credibility. Over time, each one gets progressively better at their task. As always, misrepresentation is swiftly punished. Artists who try too obviously to please are sellouts, and companies that proclaim their high-minded interests too eagerly are denounced according to a colour catalogue of corporate hypocrisy: greenwashing, bluewashing, purplewashing, or pinkwashing, all of which do far more harm than good to the company's fortunes.[26]

Put this way, the very notion of corporate social responsibility seems to defy logic: insofar as it is successful, it should also benefit the firm, which is a criterion by which to denounce it as hypocritical, which renders it a failure. But to view it in this way is to make the same mistake as conceiving of artists as either genuine passionates or strategic fakers. In the art market as in the corporate world, both selves can be in on the ploy – at least at the outset.

Consider a most unlikely candidate for drawing the wages of disinterest: Walmart. The same corporate behemoth that was once fined millions of dollars for flouting environmental regulations has recently set out on what it proclaims to be an ambitious green agenda. What is more surprising is that these moves have actually been well received by many environmentalists: the usually sceptical audience has judged the ploy to be credible. Walmart engaged in complex lifecycle analyses of its supply chains; it led efforts to create a global sustainability index; it founded the Sustainability Consortium, which now includes many of its largest competitors. The potency of these initiatives, and thus their utility to Walmart, comes precisely from how their utility is not immediately evident. Many of these moves are higher on substance than flash, and they have not been trumpeted too loudly. As outside observers have recognised, while these moves may contribute to a positive corporate reputation in the long run, the return on investment is difficult to quantify. If anything, the short-term costs are more apparent than the gains.[27] Which makes it more likely that those gains will eventually materialise.

One of my colleagues at McGill University, Hamish van der Ven, a young and earnest West Coast environmental science professor, is among those cautiously convinced by the ploy. In his view, the executives at Walmart have genuinely been 'socialised'. Whatever the initial impetus for their gesturing at environmental progress, that gesturing has had an independent effect of its own, part of which was likely unanticipated at the outset. And insofar as the gesturing has benefited Walmart, it has come precisely from that unanticipated part.

Walmart executives have thus joined the boards of organisations like Conservation International and the World Resources Institute. There, they find themselves in the same room as climate scientists and environmental activists. They hobnob with the likes of Al Gore. They drink the same coffee, talk about the weather, and discover it to be a fraught topic. It is plausible to think that the executives' view of themselves as market actors is affected by such contacts. In other words, consciously or not, they have found themselves going through the motions. Going to mass, lighting a candle, they meet other converts. My colleague Hamish points to a revealing quote from the CEO of Walmart, Lee Scott, who was at the origin of the firm's green initiative: 'I had an intellectual interest when we started. I have a passion today.' Do CEOs read the Romantic poets? I doubt it. But the language of nineteenth-century Romanticism, its elevation of passion above intellect, has in fact made its way into corporate boardrooms. Disinterest pays, and CEOs know it.

Whether Walmart execs believe in the initiative in their heart of hearts is impossible to know. But what we do know, from both real-life studies and laboratory experiments, is that it becomes easier to convince others of a belief when one believes in it one-self.[28] Walmart execs thus have *reason* to believe. The success of their green initiative may depend on buying into it them-selves. As the political scientist Jon Elster put it in reference to the opportunistic use of religion by rulers seeking to kindle pro-social behaviour in their subjects, 'for religious indoctrination to work, the indoctrinators have to believe in the religion them-selves'.[29] Once again, it's not so much that corporate executives suddenly lose themselves to blind passion; but that their instru-mental selves recognise that letting an emergent passionate self take over may serve them both.

If you are like me, you may still smell a rat. Hearing that Walmart has taken any steps beyond self-interest, you might scoff and dismiss it out of hand as another public-relations stunt by a large corporation. We weren't born yesterday; we've seen this before. Our shared scepticism is telling. It's indicative of just how much suspicion meets such attempts; it's a sign of how difficult it is for a market actor to draw the wages of passion. Disinterest pays, but those benefits are not easy to come by, precisely because of our vigilance as consumers, investors, and voters.

Josef Pieper and Jenny Odell ought to take comfort in this. They insist on the unassailability of the paradox of intention out of a desire to preserve the realm of disinterest. They fear that if the Walmarts of the world begin speaking the language of passion, passion will be emptied of its meaning. Their focus is on the passionates who hold out against market pressures. Odell, for instance, describes individuals who turn themselves into shapes that resist market cooptation: artists who make art that, owing to its form, cannot be bought and sold. But what the above discussion shows is that we can also trust in those on the other side of that equation: all the doubters, sceptics, and scoffers among consumers. A means of stemming market encroachment is to keep fine-tuning our ear as market participants. We can keep exercising doubt, gathering information, scrutinising true motives. In so doing, we act on the enduring incentive of all market actors: to assess one another's credibility. And in doing so, in recognising genuine passion and distinguishing it from strategic attempts at misrepresentation, we also inadvertently preserve the sanctity of disinterested commerce.[30]

The final insight from the story of Walmart, and the role that socialisation played in it, is that monetary cost is not the only way by which a signal can become credible. The costliness that makes signals credible can take another form. Gestures that represent no material stake can be persuasive if they raise the possibility that a small step might lead to a bigger one. To follow Blaise Pascal's line of reasoning, going to mass and lighting a candle is not especially costly in and of itself, but it becomes meaningful if it raises the probability of going to mass the next week, and the week after that, and then perhaps joining the church choir, taking unsuspected pleasure in the singing, and feeling some unanticipated awe at the possibility of harmony.

This insight draws on the work of the economist Thomas Schelling, who may be the most eloquent writer we have on the question of credibility. In a famous thought experiment, Schelling described a game where two players standing near a cliff edge are tied together at the ankle by a rope, and they will only be released if one of the two admits defeat, in which case the other player will get a large prize. How to convince the other to give in first? The most expeditious tactic might seem to threaten to throw the other player off the cliff unless they give in. But that threat isn't very credible, since it means a bad ending for both players. Schelling showed that there is a better solution, which is to start dancing close to the edge of the cliff. The point isn't to slip and fall, of course, but to increase the risk of slipping just enough to convince the other player to give in.

The symbolic gestures of the corporate world – the joining of boards by CEOs, the creation of corporate associations, the appointment of dedicated positions for corporate benevolence – are often rightly dismissed as cheap talk. But if they increase the risk of 'falling off the cliff' by just a bit, if they increase the odds of the initiative taking on a life of its own, then the gesture can become credible. Not because it attests definitively to a change of heart, but because it leads to a slight increase in the probability that such a change of heart might take place – that an 'intellectual interest' might turn into a passion.

Large corporations are the embodiment of interested commerce. That does not mean they are not tempted by the fruits of disinterested behaviour; quite the opposite. They understand better than anyone what there is to be gained. But by their nature they are ill suited for it. The odds of turning themselves into passion-driven entities are slim. Yet even corporations can court the gains of dis-interest by engaging in costly signalling. That cost can come from one of two sources: it can be a financial sacrifice, or it can consist of taking a first step that represents enough of a commitment that it raises the odds of taking the next step.

The discussion so far shows that there are indeed no easy solutions to the paradox of intention. Faking is always an option, but it is just a matter of time before it is found out. That's because the incentive to misrepresent is always matched by everyone else's incentive to detect that misrepresentation. The self-interested are left with the possibility of shaping their own intentions. Whether they are individuals or corporate behemoths, the solutions are similar. In one way or another, they must try to resist the intelligence intelligently.

The potential gains are significant. Insomniacs may finally fall asleep; shopkeepers avoid shaky hands when cutting priceless diamonds; religious seekers find faith; gentlemen-in-becoming reach states of effortless elegance. Novelists 'mesmerise them-selves' into bouts of creative flow. Athletes land the decisive free throw. CEOs convince their customers that their social concerns are genuine, and worth paying extra for. Different though these settings are, all of them rest on a strategic self agreeing to cede control to a non-strategic self. Such delegation, however, carries inevitable risks, and it would be unwise to omit these.

A Warning: The Perils of Disinterest

Imagine this section is written in tiny print. All remedies come with unintended consequences: pills against headaches warn us that they may cause nausea; those against nausea often cause headaches. And so it is with the nineteenth-century antidote to the Enlightenment's 'strong disease' of reason.[31] Side effects may result.

Insofar as our contemporary malaise is caused by willing what cannot be willed, our instrumental age may have much to gain from resisting the intelligence intelligently. But doing so also represents an unavoidable risk. When instrumental reason hands over the reins to passion, it can never be completely certain of the outcome. The same risk exists in any delegation of power: the uncertainty is an intrinsic part of the deal. For a demonstration of where this can lead, one need look no further than the originators of the remedy themselves.

The Romantics viewed passion as valuable in itself, a counterpoint to the instrumental rationality and the calculating coldness of commercial society. But they did not all obligingly confine their fervour to the contemplation of Constable's clouds and Wordsworth's golden daffodils. Instead, an entire stream of Romantic thought – especially, but not exclusively, among the German Romantics – fed the budding nationalist sentiments of the nineteenth century, which later turned into the institutionalized racism and anti-Semitism of the twentieth century. Here, indeed, was an end fit to be pursued for its own sake: the nation was an idea that passionate individuals could lose themselves in.

In truth, any sufficiently grand idea might have done the trick. But the Romantics were also predisposed to the aesthetic appeal of the nation. Their nostalgic longing for a mythical past naturally turned to national origins. In Germany, it manifested itself in a fondness for the Middle Ages. The devotion to nature turned into a predilection for shared bloodlines and the native soils of the motherland. Rousseau's merely patronising idealisation of the *bon sauvage* found a counterpart in the more dangerous *Volk*-veneration of the likes of Gottfried von Herder and Adam Müller.[32] By putting their trust in disinterest, in defiance of the Enlightenment's trust in self-interest, the Romantics proved bad at anticipating the direction their pent-up impulses took them in.

This is how we get a young Lord Byron, bored of Italy just as he had grown bored of England, eager to fight for symbols and ideas greater than himself, and moved to take on the cause of Greece under the Ottoman yoke. He died shortly after his thirty-sixth birthday. The impulse was aesthetic rather than principled. Byron understood little, and may have cared even less, about the underlying political dynamics of his foreign campaigns.[33] But the cause of national liberation quenched his yearning for an idea grand enough to pursue for its own sake. Byron had hoped to die in battle, but instead he succumbed to fever, far from the battlefield. Luckily, the wages of passion can be collected post-humously: Byron's ardour was nothing if not credible, and he continues to be held up as a paragon of spirit and nobility. The Greeks, who know of tragic heroes, have elevated him to their national pantheon. As the Byron scholar Peter Cochran puts it, 'Most of the world, Greece especially, has treated his self-delusive aspiration as heroic achievement.'[34]

A disinterested stance can prove profitable – it can impress and influence and compel others – but it necessarily entails a loss of critical capacity. Because critical capacity is precisely what is forsaken by credible passionates. This is also why fervent young Byronic men are often the willing tools of demagogues, whose business it is to stoke disinterested passion in the hearts of their followers. The same can be said of the passionate workers from Chapter 6. Their passion both increases their value to the market and makes them prone to exploitation by it.

J. S. Mill managed somehow to get the balance right. He found personal salvation in the Romantics' sensibility, but he retained a keen sense for the danger of what one might call Romantic spillovers. As it happens, Mill was always long Wordsworth, and short Byron. This is actually a matter of formal record: at the London Debating Society in 1829, Mill spoke for the position 'That Wordsworth was a greater poet than Byron'. Byron's passions, he explained in a two-hour address, led to self-sabotage. Wordsworth had a broader range of expression. Mill, needless to say, won the debate.

Fittingly, a shared contempt for blind Byronic zeal was part of what kindled J. S. Mill's own romance with the woman he would eventually marry, Harriet Taylor. Thus Mill discovered the full meaning of the English Romantics' passionate verse. He lost his head for a married woman, and weathered scandal and years-worth of gossip to be with her. That passion would prove the source of a great deal of reason: it was Harriet who inspired many of the key ideas in Mill's later work, including his work on women's emancipation. The latter insight proved decisive: it led Mill to work out his central argument about how an individual's freedom relies on the corresponding freedom of those around him.[35] As the next chapter lays out, this idea also bears on how best a society might allow its citizens to collect the fruits of disinterested behaviour.

But then Mill always had the unique ability, especially following the crisis of his youth, to move back and forth between the two realms. He was able to lose himself in mountain walks and Romantic verse, and then to re-emerge to read Ricardo's economic theory once more, this time in the light of Carlyle's polemics. He sensed that the value added consisted in oscillating between the two poles. In setting out, as his life's mission, to 'translate the mysticism of others into Argument', he had to be both the mystic and the political economist in turn.

So the shopkeeper needs Avi, his apprentice in the back of the shop. But Avi cannot be the one running the shop. So who should we most strive to be? Avi or the shopkeeper? At the societal level, the answer largely depends on the level of economic development. As we saw in Chapter 2, the more advanced a society, the higher the proportion of desirables that take the form of byproducts. Whereas consumption was once sufficient to gain the esteem of others, it becomes less so as the Veblen Treadmill keeps running. The less time and energy are spent securing basic goods like food and housing, the more gets devoted to a set of goals that do not yield to intentional effort. The more secure a society, the more time individuals can afford in the mode of disinterested commerce; the more affluent that society, the greater the market rewards for doing so.

Yet as the warning label on the Romantic remedy against the 'strong disease' of reason makes clear, there remains a risk to losing oneself in disinterested pursuits. The same analytical capacities that the Romantics chafed against are necessary to channel unbridled passions in fruitful directions. Otherwise, one risks dying of fever on foreign soil fighting for causes one doesn't fully grasp. Electing to do things for their own sake says little about what those things ought to be. It becomes increasingly apparent that the most favourable station is neither to permanently inhabit the realm of self-interest, nor that of disinterest, but to be a periodic visitor of both. Choose worthy ends, but then forget all about them. Set the stage, and then dance on it impetuously.

The ideal is easy to grasp, but it remains difficult to achieve. You may have come across people who have this uncanny ability. We talk about these lucky beings as having a talent for living. These are the people who devise their own boundaries, and then live freely within them. They do not elbow others to get ahead, and others in turn do not resent their good turns of fortune. When things go their way, they do not boast, and thus only grow in our esteem. They are the obsessives who manage to make ends meet, monetising their obsessions without forsaking them. Those capable of bouts of mad enthusiasm, but able to catch themselves in time, while others go astray.

J. S. Mill was one of those lucky beings. He managed both to defy the limited Utilitarian ideas he was born into, and to avoid the pitfalls of Romantic zeal. But if he is today the most famous British philosopher of the nineteenth century, it is not because he managed to successfully reshape himself, but because he successfully reshaped social thought and institutions in ways that remain visible to this day. Yet as we see in the closing chapter, these two transformations – that of the individual and that of society – are fundamentally connected.

9

Social Conditions for Individual Epiphanies

I began drafting this book at a winter artist residency, shortly before my first daughter was born. At least, that had been the plan. I had been offered a two-week stay at the Banff Center for the Arts and Creativity, a hallowed institution in the Canadian arts milieu, as part of a writing prize. I had never gone to a residency, nor did I know anyone who had. But I fully understood what a rare opportunity it was. Given the impending prospect of fatherhood, especially, I knew I needed to make the most of it. I wouldn't have another similar period of calm and contemplation for years to come.

The setting could not have been better suited to the purpose. Cal Newport, the computer scientist and self-help expert vaunting Montaigne and Mark Twain's 'deep-thinking' retreats in Chapter 7, would surely have approved. For two weeks, I would be put up in a beautiful airy room with a view of the mountains. I would have a separate writing cabin deeper in the forest, surrounded by signs warning against black bears. The cabin had a fully working kitchen, and a large reserve of coffee. There was a whiteboard, stacks of paper, drawerfuls of pens. There was a full-size piano. Forget Walden. Thoreau never had it so good.

For one, the food was better. The Center's participants came together every day at mealtimes. The dishes were inspired by local ingredients, which were listed on little labels; all dietary constraints were eagerly accommodated. Each artist-in-residence was also given a magnetic card that could be used to procure more coffee, kombucha, and snacks, if the buffet did not suffice.

And so, in ways I had not expected, I was offered a glimpse of what Keynes, writing in 1930, had envisioned for his 'grandchildren': as far as I was concerned, for those fourteen days, the economic problem had been resolved. Scarcity had been abolished. Any material need could be appeased with a wave of my magnetic card. I had been taken out of the menial obligations of daily life, the routine distractions of cooking, cleaning, commuting, doing laundry. I had only to walk a short way from my room to my writing cabin to reap the fruits of Pieper's 'pure leisure'. I was free at last to engage in the *vita contemplativa*, Aristotle and Aquinas's conception of the good life. For the time of my stay, I would live what I imagined the lives of the wealthy must be like, minus the nagging opportunity cost that comes with high hourly earnings. For a while, I would be Keynes's 'advance guard', scouting out the prospects of the promised land for the rest of us. And much as Keynes foretold, my early report is not entirely favourable.

I had come in with a plan. I would write before noon, and leave research and reading for the afternoons. I would keep to a single espresso at breakfast, and another after lunch. Knowing that many writers set themselves a daily writing quota of a given number of words, I resolved to do the same. If I could only steer clear of the black bears, I expected to pick the fruits of an unprecedented bounty of creativity. If not here, in these unworldly optimal conditions, then where?

On the first day, I marched to my assigned writing cabin and sat down at my desk, intent on making the most of my two weeks. I had my coffee, my whiteboard, stacks of paper, all those pens. Yet nothing much came of that morning. I sat as if waiting for a guest who never showed up. I blamed it on jetlag; but then the second day looked much the same. I struggled to reach my self-imposed word quota and reread the result with distaste.

Somehow, the knowledge of the place's purpose, its unworldly quality, its sheer optimality, all these proved stifling. Not that there was any formal accountability mechanism to worry about. There would be no report to hand in at the end of my stay explaining what I had achieved. Yet the mission was plain. It was right there in the name of the place: I'd come to a centre for 'creativity'. The command was clear enough. In the evenings, the participants would eye each other warily and ask how the day had gone. Everyone smiled and nodded. To admit that it hadn't been productive seemed a betrayal of the Center's generosity, an offence to the mountains themselves.

I looked out from my cabin window, pressed a D flat on the piano, and listened to its tone rise and die down into the woods. More than anything, I felt embarrassment: had I not just been granted all the conditions of optimal creative output? Were the Rockies on the horizon insufficiently majestic? Were the woods insufficiently dark and deep? I thought of overworked friends who would kill to have a day's respite from their daily chores. I thought of my partner, in her third trimester back in Montreal. I thought of my mother-in-law, who would ask me what I had achieved during my two weeks, having left her pregnant daughter to carry groceries up the stairs by herself.

By the end of the first week, I had little to show for all my freedom from scarcity. The thoughts I was trying to form, sensing they were being stalked, scurried before me. Efforts at simple sentences came up short. Nothing came of its own; it was all exertion. I felt like the insomniac, awake at night, brooding over the recent purchase of an inordinately expensive down pillow that promised to deliver deep and restful sleep. All that money for naught: it was enough to keep one up at night. I spent as much time thinking about what I was doing there as actually doing it. As J. S. Mill had written of the Utilitarians' aims, all that I sought was '[put] to flight by fatal self-questioning'. During my calls back home to my partner, I made sure not to reveal my petty struggles in the land of plenty; who was I to complain? I could spend my day sitting around in a cabin in the Rockies; she was bringing a baby to term while going to work every day.

The residency could remove all the material impediments to creative flourishing. But one thing it could not do was resolve the paradox of intention. It seemed only to make it more acute. It could not make participants forget what the sole purpose of all this facilitation was. And with every evident bit of optimisation – that perfectly designed writing cabin, the healthy food, all those pens and stacks of paper – the purpose grew clearer, and thus conspired to making itself less attainable.

We now have the terms to describe the ungrateful state I'd found myself in. I had gone to rural Japan to sit in Tanizaki's open-air toilet from Chapter 6, hearing that this was where lines of verse had come to Japanese poets for centuries. And I sat there with pen and paper, wondering why the trick wasn't working.

The problem lay once more in the anticipation of a desired out-come. Creative output is a paradigmatic byproduct state. As with social grace, commercial success, or political influence, fix-ating on the goal proves self-defeating.

Artist residencies are byproduct factories. They solve the problem of scarcity for creative individuals who are often beleaguered by it, with the express goal of maximising an out-come which has the property of eluding intent. The design is unquestionably well intentioned, but it runs into that recurrent issue: namely, that it is intentioned. It is a microcosm of Keynes's foretold age of abundance, and thus it also requires what he described as 'the readjustment of the habits and instincts of the ordinary man, bred into him for countless generations'. In short, an instrumentally oriented mind trained in a market society of aiming and striving does not shift over to the *vita contemplativa* on a dime. This is why Keynes, knowing the odds, admitted to contemplating that readjustment with 'dread'.[1]

On the twelfth day of my stay, having managed to write only platitudes and already thinking of my return home, I threw in the towel. That morning, I decided to skip the writing cabin entirely, leave the piano to itself, and go for a day-long hike. I was defeated, and figured I might as well cut my losses and enjoy the mountains. I bravely resolved to miss out on the lunch buffet, and I wrapped a hard-boiled egg from breakfast into a napkin to take as a picnic.

You will have seen it coming. Like the resigned insomniac who gives up on sleep, resolves to read until the morning comes, and then mercifully passes out, just as I gave up trying to grasp at ideas, these began arising on their own.

I had been working on a somewhat different book. I wanted to chart how views about market capitalism as a means versus an end had evolved over time. I knew that a change of heart had taken place among political economists sometime in the nineteenth century, and I wanted to put my finger on it. But as I set off on my day of resigned hiking, I found myself forgetting about my missed word quota, and wondering instead about how the bounty of the last twelve days had proved less than bountiful.

This is when the connection struck me: the parallel between my visit to the land of plenty and the puzzle of intellectual history I had been tracking down. In both settings, the resolution of the economic problem called for a fundamental 'readjustment of habits and instincts'. It required a similar conversion. And in both cases, the question arose as to whether it was possible to move away from an instrumental outlook for instrumental reasons.

The earliest political economists had viewed market capitalism principally as means to other social ends, though they also saw that for the means to be effective, market actors would have to be fully taken in by it. For the capitalist system to run at full power, the capitalist had to believe that material accumulation was the be-all and end-all, the one way 'to be observed, to be attended to, to be taken notice of with sympathy ... and approbation'.[2] This is the famous 'deception' that Adam Smith claimed 'rouses and keeps in continual motion the industry of mankind'. Smith both viewed it as a deception, and admitted to its necessity.[3] But then he also hinted at how, having reached some level of economic development, this confusion between means and ends would be recognised for what it was. Recall that Smith pointed out that 'the wages of the meanest labourer' were already sufficient to provide for the comforts of life.[4] He also suspected that natural and institutional constraints would eventually impose limits on economic growth. Nor was Smith the only one: as the economic historian Robert Skidelsky observes, 'All the classical economists had this end point in mind, at varying degrees of affluence.'[5]

It will come as no surprise that it was J. S. Mill who opened that breach wide, describing what he called the 'stationary state', when growth would slow to a standstill. Mill saw this stage of development in a downright favourable light. He believed it would leave 'as much scope as ever for all kinds of mental culture, and moral and social progress'. In fact, human improvement would only become more likely 'when minds ceased to be engrossed by the art of getting on'. Some have posited that Keynes had this very passage in mind in 1930, when writing his own essay predicting how once the economic problem was resolved, people 'shall once more value ends above means and prefer the good to the useful'.[6]

In this book, I have gone one step further. I have argued that come a certain level of affluence, shifting social energies away from the 'art of getting on' to progressively more disinterested pursuits may prove fruitful not only in terms of 'moral and social progress', but also in terms of economic productivity itself. We are back to the *Financial Times*'s koan-like assertion, from the first pages of this book, that the best way to build a global enterprise is not to try to build a global enterprise at all.

Over time, the anticipation of an eventual shift from further productivity improvements to higher social ends was set aside, and eventually forgotten, even among the scholars of capitalism. *Especially* among them, as it happens: the modern field of economics is sufficiently taken up by the task of understanding what leads to growth that it gives little thought to what subsequent purpose growth might serve, and how its contribution to that greater purpose may change at different levels of affluence.[7] The 'deception' has become a general one; the confusion between means and ends affects not only the actors operating the gears of the capitalist system, but its observers, too. Somewhere along the way, as the field of political economy – which Adam Smith and J. S. Mill contributed to morphed into that of economics, growth came to be seen as a self-evident good requiring no further explanation. It became the final aim in the chain of social means and social ends.

Walking in the mountains of Banff, these two problems presented themselves side by side: my own inability to make the most of a period of abundance and optimal tranquillity, and the anticipated challenge of shifting aims once in a post-scarcity society. The analogy kept striking me. I recalled J. S. Mill's mental breakdown, which had stayed with me since I'd read his account of it years earlier. There too there was a similar analogy between individual and social limitations. Mill saw his own dejection as proof of a defect in the Utilitarian view of the world he'd been born into. His own inability to wilfully bring about his own happiness meant that a society designed to maximise such happiness would confront a similar problem. As he wrote, 'I felt that the flaw in my life, must be a flaw in life itself.'[8] In the same way, an instrumental focus on outcomes would remain a barrier to reaching desirable byproduct states, for individuals and society both.

Writing retreats in the woods do not come with user manuals. But perhaps they should. Because confronting the paradox of intention, as we have seen, is no easy task. It demands a wholesale rethinking of the relation between means and ends. And as societies grow more affluent, a growing number of people, in a growing number of settings, will find themselves going through an analogous rethink in response to an analogous challenge.

I did not know it at the time, but I was not alone in my failure to make the most of a blessed period of freedom from worldly obligations. Considerably more experienced creative types have often spoken of the same. For instance, the recent Nobel Prize winner in literature, the poet Louise Glück, has described a similarly puzzling pass. Though in her case, it lasted not two weeks, but two years:

When I was young I led the life I thought writers were supposed to lead, in which you repudiate the world, ostentatiously consecrating all of your energies to the task of making art. I just sat in Provincetown at a desk and it was ghastly – the more I sat there not writing the more I thought that I just hadn't given up the world enough. After two years of that, I came to the conclusion that I wasn't going to be a writer. So I took a teaching job in Vermont, though I had spent my life till that point thinking that real poets don't teach. But I took this job, and the minute I started teaching – the minute I had obligations in the world – I started to write again.

And Glück concludes: 'you have to live your life if you're going to do original work', because 'your work will come out of an authentic life'. Being the poet that she is, we can trust Glück to choose her words carefully. The description of her period of single-minded creative toil as 'ostentatious' and its unexpectedly more fruitful opposite as 'an authentic life' are both revealing. What is ostentatious is a pretence, an affectation. States of privilege are desirable at face value, yet by their very nature they protrude out from reality. That protrusion triggers self-consciousness – as well it should. It's like donning an expensive new suit; one suddenly walks a little stiffly and sits too straight, careful not to crease the fabric. The result is the very opposite to what one intended. As the nineteenth-century Romantics had gleaned, excessive self-awareness is how the intellect does itself in.

The concern appears prevalent. The list of artists who insisted on keeping their day job even once they could have afforded to devote themselves single-mindedly to their art runs long. There's T. S. Eliot at Lloyd's bank, Walt Whitman and his real-estate dealings, Charles Bukowski at the Post Office. So much for Thoreauvian self-isolation. Or for aspiring to a life where one's vocation and avocation coincide perfectly. Instead, these writers designed lives for themselves where their vocation would get periodically suspended in favour of a more staid avocation, so as to better return to the writing later. This is of a piece with the discussion of the multiple self in the previous chapter. The compartmentalising of time might be a fitting response to the compartmentalising of the mind, a recognition of that dualism. There is something pleasingly consistent in how Whitman, the poet who claimed to 'contain multitudes', also made a point of keeping some of those multitudes tied up in negotiations over real estate.

Glück was set on a single objective: to write. Yet she found direct efforts of will singularly ineffective. The ostentation of that exclusive focus, the abstraction from an 'authentic life', turned out to be more stifling than freeing. Taking on conventional worldly obligations, instead, allowed the fruits of 'pure leisure' to be reaped. The roundabout way proved the straightest path.

Some artists' residencies have tried to grapple with the same conundrum. Residencies are by their very nature contrived environments; so how does a byproduct factory grapple with this problem? The Wapping Project Residency, which is situated in the trendy Kreusberg neighbourhood of Berlin, has tackled it head-on. Selected artists are invited to stay for free in Berlin, subject to one rule: 'It is a condition of the residency that NO work is produced during the eight-week period of the programme.' As a former Wapping Project participant admitted after her stay, 'The condition of the residency, that "NO work be produced" feels counter intuitive to an artist, however this limitation is definitely [the Wapping Project's] greatest strength.'[9] If it is counterintuitive to the artist, imagine how much odder still it must sound to the average instrumentally minded twenty-first-century knowledge worker.

The design of the Wapping Project, of course, recalls Viktor Frankl's instructions to his insomniac patients to try and stay awake as long as possible. The redirection is meant to throw off the instrumental self. Since there is no outcome to strive towards, the hope is that the instrumental self will recede, self-awareness will abate, and an otherwise unattainable state of creative flow can be attained. Constraints are often enabling, whether they are imposed by an artificial rule or by the obligations of daily life.

As I returned from the residency, I experienced something similar to what Glück described after taking her teaching job. Oddly enough, with a newborn at home and the return of the usual never-ending to-do list, I felt less stifled than I had in my optimal mountain surroundings. Somehow, I found that ideas flowed more freely in the early morning, before a day of house chores and campus duties, than they had in the uninterrupted weeks of the residency.

That experience affected the very conception I have of creative work. I began thinking of it as something that has to be surreptitiously pilfered from the day, rather than bought in the open. Obtained slightly dishonestly, under the covers rather than on schedule. I found it easier to write when I felt everyone else around me was still sleeping, unaware of my contrived efforts.

Yet this is not to say that my material circumstances were irrelevant – far from it. I was able to shift modes for a spell and steal time away during those mornings because I had benefited from a government-funded paternity leave from my university position, and because my partner was able to take a full year of maternity leave from her job, which was also publicly subsidised. When our daughter ran a fever, we had public healthcare to fall back on. Later, we were able to put her in a state-sponsored daycare nursery across the street from our house, a full day of which costs less than a movie ticket on cheap Tuesdays. All these conditions contributed to the maintenance of a protected province of mental space that could be devoted to non-instrumental thinking. I no longer had an isolated mountain cabin to sit in all day or a ready buffet waiting at dinner time. Yet all the same I relied on highly favourable circumstances.

Similarly, Glück found the worldly obligations that came with teaching oddly freeing. The daily constraints linked with living 'an authentic life' proved more enabling than not. But one can well imagine the effect would not have been so liberating if that authentic life consisted of working two limited-term teaching positions at two different places with long bus commutes to make ends meet. The demon of self-consciousness is one thing; the demon of economic precarity is quite another. The ideal environment, in this case, is one that manages to keep both at bay.

No one thinks of staid policy initiatives like parental leave and public daycare – not to mention rent controls, public healthcare, unemployment insurance – as designed to foster individual self-realisation. And that may be precisely why they prove so effective in doing so.

Self-Reform vs Social Reform

The nineteenth-century Romantics had little regard for the details of public policy. Insofar as they had any stance on the matter, they favoured reforming the self rather than reforming society. Development and betterment would not come by way of social institutions, they claimed, but through individual contemplation, reflection, and artistic epiphany. The Thoreau of Walden Pond and the Emerson of 'self-reliance' fame later advocated a similar view. There is an unquestionable logic to this: if the main problem is found within the individual, unmoored from his own self, then that is where the attention should go. It is an approach that is often associated with Eastern traditions, which operate from the premise that internally balanced individuals are the building blocks of an outwardly balanced society, and should thus be its starting point. The Indian sage Ramana Maharshi, one of the first Eastern gurus to attract Western followers in the 1930s, put it most explicitly: 'self-reform automatically brings about social reform'.

Drawn to the Romantics though he was, this was one idea that J. S. Mill never had patience for. Mill was ahead of his time in recognising that the opportunities for self-reform were not evenly distributed. Some had better conditions for contemplation and individual epiphanies than others. And Mill went further: even those who *did* have those opportunities would be harmed by the disparity.[10] His writings on the rights of women encapsulate this idea well: if women were not afforded the same rights and freedoms as men in both the household and the social sphere, Mill argued, this would not only hamper women's own chances for self-development, but those of men as well.[11] Here was the key insight that Harriet Taylor pushed him towards, and which would play a key role in Mill's view of liberal culture: a condition for the pursuit of one's own individual freedom is that others be able to pursue theirs.[12] In this sense, Mill proves far less of an individualist than he is sometimes made out to be.

Mill did agree that self-reform was what individuals should aspire to. Thinking for oneself, achieving an autonomous self, this was the very point of existence. But he saw that social reforms would be a necessary precondition for such self-development to stand a chance. Going by the example of his own life, Mill fervently believed people were able to defy their circumstances. To do so, they needed freedom from want, but also freedom from social strictures.[13] Individual conversions and personal epiphanies relied on sensible legislation and well-designed public institutions.

This is why Mill always viewed prosperity and economic efficiency not as goals in themselves, but merely as means of promoting individual autonomy.[14] In fact, Mill came to measure the success of social institutions by their ability to do just that. This led him to conclude that there would come a point when a sufficiently affluent society would make a greater contribution to the promotion of individual autonomy by stepping back from the maximisation of economic growth than by continuing to pursue it at all costs. Writing in 1848, he remarked dismissively that 'it is only in the backward countries of the world that increased production is still an important object: in those most advanced, what is economically needed is a better distribution'.[15] His concern was then to come up with a system of laws that might favour an equality of fortunes, while allowing individuals to claim the gains of their own industry. He viewed a high inheritance tax (the likes of which would be viewed as progressive even today), for instance, as a policy that accomplished both.

In the most famous passage of that famous essay on the stationary state, J. S. Mill made no bones about his annoyance with the elevation of material accumulation as the ubiquitous social goal:

> I confess I am not charmed with the ideal of life held out by those who think that the normal state of human beings is that of struggling to get on; that the trampling, crushing, elbowing, and treading on each other's heels, which form the existing type of social life, are the most desirable lot of human kind, or anything but the disagreeable symptoms of one of the phases of industrial progress.

So the elbowing phase is necessary, but it is only a phase. Past a certain level of industrial progress, a shift in social purpose becomes increasingly warranted. Keynes likely had this very passage in mind when he wrote his 1930 time-capsule essay to his 'grandchildren', envisioning a similar social conversion in the century ahead.[16] It isn't that either of them had some idealised notion of the simple life, *à la* Thoreau. And much as both Mill and Keynes admired and enjoyed the company of poets and philosophers, neither of them was under any sort of illusion: they were technocrats at heart, each spending the greater part of their lives chewing over minute details of policy with the intent of advancing a specific set of goals. Their bread and butter consisted of marginal policy improvements that might further well-being. Land-use reform and inheritance taxes and voting rights: these were, in their view, the technocrats' means of serving the poets.

And it was as enlightened technocrats that they recognised how the further pursuit of material accumulation would contribute gradually less to well-being, as economic development progressed. Both looked ahead with glee to a time when their kind might be progressively eclipsed; when, to use the phrase that Keynes liked so much he employed it more than once, economists would come to be regarded as 'humble, competent people on a level with dentists'. Mill and Keynes were both willing to give up some measure of productivity in exchange for more attention to higher human ends.

As I have argued, framing the matter in terms of such a trade-off misses an essential aspect of today's market society. That's because interested commerce and disinterested commerce are not, in fact, sealed off from one another. Similarly, governments need not choose to invest in either moral improvement or economic productivity, as if picking between guns and butter. To put it in economic terms, both Mill and Keynes premised their argument on the diminishing marginal utility of material consumption. While I agree with this first point, I have emphasised another: the increasing marginal utility of disinterest. As a society grows more affluent, it stands to gain relatively less from further expansion of consumption, and relatively more from an expansion of disinterested behaviour.

Throughout this book, I have argued that owing to the importance it attaches to credibility, in particular, commercial society runs in large measure on disinterest, rather than self-interest alone. The implication is that shifting away from a strictly instrumental outlook would contribute to economic and social flourishing at the margin, rather than take away from it. Such a shift becomes increasingly warranted as a society grows more affluent. Market actors have ever more to gain from appearing disinterested, even by their own self-interested criteria.

The Role of Government

In the previous chapter, we saw the different ways by which an individual might succeed in reaping the gains of disinterest, despite starting from a self-interested stance. A number of disparate thinkers across time have asked themselves a version of that question, and their proposed solutions have much in common. Many of these remedies rely on the notion of a multiple self. In one way or another, all of them describe ways in which the intelligence might resist itself intelligently.

That is all well and good: individuals can seek to withstand their instrumental impulses for instrumental reasons. They can go through the motions, until a stance that began as posturing grows genuinely disinterested. They can invest in habit, until what was conscious and effortful grows effortless. The Adam Smith baker can act on himself and persuade himself of his passion, so as to better persuade others. Failing that, he can hire a passionate Brooklyn baker and give him free run of the place.

Yet as J. S. Mill sensed, the very possibility of such self-reform is not equally distributed; it varies according to social circumstances. Most plainly, scarcity and need do not lend themselves to higher-order goals like self-expression and self-realisation. This is why, as the political scientist Ronald Inglehart shows, these become sought-after values in societies that have reached a threshold level of security. Otherwise, individuals devote their mental space to activities that have an immediate payoff.

Yet there are less self-evident conditions that can foster an attitude of disinterest. Among these, Mill saw access to solitude as essential 'to cultivat[ing] freely the graces of life'. As he put it, 'A world from which solitude is extirpated is a very poor ideal. Solitude, in the sense of being often alone, is essential to any depth of meditation or of character.' Proximity to nature, which by the 1840s was already being traded against productivity increases, was another means of facilitating the individual moral progress Mill had in mind: 'Nor is there much satisfaction in contemplating the world with nothing left to the spontaneous activity of nature; with every rood of land brought into cultivation, which is capable of growing food for human beings.'

As it happens, 175 years later, Jenny Odell points to the very same elements when she outlines means of 'resisting usefulness' in today's attention economy: the possibility of solitude, the possibility of communion with nature, and enough time for both. As she puts it, 'Thought and deliberation require not just incubation space (solitude and/or a defined context) but incubation time.' Of course, as Odell goes on to demonstrate, all these elements – solitude, nature, and time – are the very things that are in shortest supply in an attention economy which incentivises being permanently plugged in. As Chapter 6 argued, we are far indeed from Tanizaki's open-air outhouse. Technology is frequently denounced as the chief culprit. Odell is one of many contemporary writers who make the case that the way social media and handheld devices trigger our instrumental impulses – through dopamine-boosting notifications and the anticipation of strangers' likes – makes the shift to any sort of disinterested attitude all the more difficult. This implies a practical way in which the intelligence may need to resist itself intelligently, namely by keeping at bay the distractions that trigger our instrumental, reward-seeking self.

Beyond these general physical preconditions – the importance of sufficient security, access to solitude, time for deliberation, and engagement with nature – the discussion in the previous chapter points to the importance of another social precondition. Disinterest pays, yes; but it also demands that we wilfully give up some measure of control, with all that this implies. The wages of passion may be high, but they are also highly uncertain. By comparison, the path of instrumental behaviour may seem the safer bet.

Artists may thus have a keen sense of how the art market values a singular artistic vision that wholly disregards market tastes, but a genuine disregard for buyers' preferences may seem like a costly gamble. Similarly, disinterested passion may well seduce the baker's customers, but handing over the shop to a passionate Brooklyn baker might also spell financial ruin: passionates may not worry enough about keeping the books in order; or they may give away too many pastries for customers to sample. No matter how much students hear that the value of a liberal education rests precisely in how it is pursued for its own sake, these students (not to mention their parents) may find it more prudent to opt for an engineering degree over a BA in Byzantine history. My own experience at the Banff artist residency presented me with a similar choice. For as much as I wanted to believe in Pieper's grand idea of 'pure leisure', using my limited time for idle walks in the mountains struck me as frivolous. The more expeditious thing was to keep my nose to the grindstone with an eye on the number of words written that day.

That element of risk is not a side-effect of disinterest; it's an inherent part of shifting away from an instrumental stance. In resisting the intelligence, one necessarily forfeits the ability to track payoffs. Indeed, tracking payoffs is how the intelligence does itself in; it is precisely what is being resisted. The willingness to take that leap of faith is the very thing that distinguishes the genuinely passionate from the strategic faker, who makes no move unless it yields a discernible gain.

Bertrand Russell observed that for all its shortcomings, the leisure class of the past had nonetheless generated 'nearly the whole of what we call civilisation'. It did so inefficiently: for every Darwin, there were a thousand other gentlemen of means who spent their days foxhunting. And it did so unjustly; it relied on a hierarchical system of social exploitation – all those footmen and butlers and housekeepers. The result gave leisure a bad name; it associated it with the foxhunters more than the scientists, and bunched it all together with idleness.

Today, there are more people than at any point in history who can play at being Darwins. More people than ever who can devote a large portion of their lives to non-instrumental activities – whether it's starting a radio-play podcast, designing end-to-end encryption apps, devising the menu of a new restaurant, opening a motorcycle repair shop – or, yes, a microbrewery. Yet few can do so without running a risk. Successful devotion to passion implies a blindness to the payoffs. The question is, how might we maximise the number of Darwins, while avoiding the social disparity on which Darwins have historically been premised?

As we saw in Chapter 7, that question is all the more relevant in today's knowledge economy, which is particularly sensitive to the unique gains that come from individuals engaging in innovative activities for their own sake. Knowledge economies rely on modern-day Darwins for the innovation and creativity that drives progress at the margin. And while the picture presented by the media in this respect is often rosy, the numbers actually tell a different story. The number of start-ups in the United States has actually been falling since the 1990s. The amount spent on research and development, which can be thought of as companies betting on fruitful aimlessness, has been dropping since the Great Recession, and is only now picking up again, to reach its mid-1960s levels. The share of R&D that the US government funds is falling, as is the US's share of global R&D.[17] These trends are especially unfavourable to 'basic research', which is the curiosity-driven share of research, as opposed to 'applied research', which aims at specific industry objectives. The result is that the proportion of the US economy made up of older, larger, and more established firms is rising.[18] In other words, just as advanced economies have come to depend more than ever on individual Darwins 'working at leisure' on passion projects, it may be getting harder to find them. What can be done about it?

The element of risk that is an inescapable part of non-instrumental pursuits implies a concrete role for social institutions. We actually know a great deal about how to handle risk: the conventional means of addressing it is through some form of *insurance*. So if individuals are less likely to pursue activities in a disinterested fashion because of the risk involved, then social and economic policies can step in to cover the downside. There is a wide range of public policies that accomplish this. Whether through health insurance, wage insurance, or more targeted schemes like relocation allowances, these measures seek to assist citizens if they need it because of chance events.

The aspect of social insurance that is sometimes overlooked is that its benefits do not kick in only once that chance event occurs. People behave differently when they know that measures exist to catch them in the event of an unplanned shock. That awareness is what matters most; it's the greatest benefit of insurance of any kind. Without professional liability insurance, surgeons would never pick up their scalpel; house movers would not venture to pick up your piano. Without car insurance, getting behind the wheel would be an unthinkably risky move that only the very rich could afford. All insurance is designed to have this enabling aspect: it allows people to engage in behaviour that they would not otherwise engage in.

The tinkerer in their garage, the start-up founder in their dorm room, the writer at their kitchen table, or the musician in their attic studio: all of them engage in what T. S. Eliot called 'autotelic' activities – those that are performed for their own sake. Can social provisions that cover downside risk be one way of fostering such activity, and might they increase the returns of individual passion in so doing?

We are only now beginning to understand the relationship between social insurance and innovative activity. That's because until recently, economists were mostly concerned to see whether social insurance would have negative effects on individual behaviour. The idea was that by having less to lose, people might actually grow complacent, in ways that would inhibit productivity and growth. That concern has been convincingly put to rest.[19] Scholars are now turning their attention to how well-designed social insurance might make individuals *more* willing to engage in risky activities with high returns.

The ongoing findings from this research, which has focused especially on entrepreneurship, are promising. Social insurance provisions are associated with an increased number of start-ups in the economy, greater job mobility, and higher rates of self-employment. They make it more likely, in other words, that those millennials mentioned in the previous chapter, who planned to quit their jobs for more meaningful work, are actually able to do so. The passage from lobbying exec to motorcycle repair is made easier when one's health insurance is not on the line. The effect of health insurance, as it happens, has received particular attention. Greater access to health insurance has been associated with more job mobility, as well as greater rates of entrepreneurial activity. In the specific context of the US, we also know that the way health insurance is most often linked to employers tends to deter individuals from striking out on their own, leading to what economists call 'job lock-in'.[20] In sum, there is growing evidence that individuals become more willing to engage in activities that can lead to a temporary drop in earnings in settings that provide social insurance.[21]

Measuring the effect of social insurance on individual behaviour effects is not easy. The difficulty stems from how national policies tend to come as packages: countries that offer social insurance also tend to have more highly regulated labour markets, for example, which may actually have opposite effects on risk-taking behaviour.[22] We can point out that Sweden scores higher on innovation measures than the US, with more start-ups per capita, a greater portion of new firms in the market, and relatively more research and development spending.[23] But it is difficult to pinpoint which aspect of the Swedish package deserves credit for this.

For that reason, social scientists hunt for clues in subnational variation, where one part of a country sees a sudden change in social conditions, while the rest of the country does not. Such naturally occurring experiments are one means of isolating the effect of a policy measure. For instance, New Jersey implemented a set of reforms in 1993 that resulted in more people having access to individual health insurance. When compared against neighbouring Pennsylvania, New Jersey then saw a significant rise (of some 25 per cent) in entrepreneurship and self-employment in the years following its reforms, while Pennsylvania saw no change over the same period.[24] Alternatively, a country may suddenly implement a set of reforms that allows us to compare the before and after picture. A set of French reforms in 2002 which provided increased social insurance against failure was thus found to have led to a similar uptick in self-employment.[25]

With growing attention paid to universal basic income schemes, scholars have also been looking for natural policy experiments that would allow them to measure the effect of a guaranteed income. Alaska provides one such natural laboratory, since it pays out annual dividends to residents from its sovereign wealth fund. The available data suggest that the Alaska Permanent Fund Dividend programme has in fact led to more entrepreneurial activity.[26] Similar effects for guaranteed income schemes have been observed in other settings, from India to Namibia.[27]

Of course, not all entrepreneurs are engaging in passion projects. Many are driven to self-employment by necessity. And most of them are behaving highly instrumentally – if not aiming for a unicorn start-up hit, then hoping at least to make enough to live on without a boss telling them what to do. Yet a significant portion of these individuals are also engaging in a form of experimentation, an attempt to combine their day job with a passion. As a result, they work late nights and early mornings, in ways they would not dream of doing at a regular office job. They are living and breathing their fledgling enterprise, and the market knows it. Therein lie the wages of passion. But therein also lies the risk.

It is telling that even back in the 1840s, J. S. Mill saw entrepreneurial activity as a space in which individuals could cultivate their full potential – and not merely in monetary terms. He argued that this was especially true for women and for the working class.[28] There was a natural progression in the passage from hired labour to self-employment. The result was not only greater economic efficiency, as individuals chose the tasks they were best suited for, but *moral* progress. Very much under the influence of Harriet Taylor's ideas, Mill associated the shift to self-employment with self-emancipation, and with the cultivation of a space for autonomy, which he and Taylor envisioned as the highest good. As Mill sensed at the time, social institutions played a key role in allowing for this shift. And we are now getting a better sense for exactly how they can achieve this.

These humdrum policies – health insurance, wage guarantees, unemployment insurance – all fall under the label of the social safety net. It's an expression that is used so often that we no longer stop to consider it. When we hear it mentioned, we know to quickly place ourselves for or against, depending on our ideological priors. But this keeps us from appreciating the term's radical aspect. Actual safety nets, after all, are not designed for people who trip while walking down the street. Safety nets exist to catch circus aerialists who fall from thirty feet while doing somersaults. That is, the term itself hints at a social mechanism that allows people to leap. It takes on its full meaning when it drives people to take risks they would not otherwise be willing to take. And recent studies offer empirical support for this interpretation. As one economist put it, 'Social insurance, like private insurance, makes people more daring ... It makes people jump the dangerous chasms which otherwise would have put a halt to their economic endeavours.'[29]

These are not novel policy ideas; but the rationale I have laid out for them largely is. The reasons usually listed for social insurance are of a moral character. That's also the source of their divisiveness. Proponents of welfare schemes argue that a just society owes its citizens a degree of protection against incidents of fate. Opponents argue instead that it is up to responsible individuals to inform themselves about risks, and behave accordingly. But the reasoning offered here suggests a distinct argument, which is also less easy to place on the ideological spectrum. The ability to engage in activities for their own sake generates underestimated gains both for individuals and society. It helps individuals realise their full potential, which in turn generates beneficial social spillovers. Leisure becomes a rightful component of a productive society – not merely as a deserved measure of rest, but as a condition for further progress at the margin. Disinterest pays. And advanced economies gain from allowing individuals to take on the risk inherent in the pursuit of disinterested behaviour. What we have come to know about the effects of social insurance suggests that it is an effective means of doing so. It is, in other words, one way by which technocrats can quietly set the stage for those individual epiphanies.

The Technocrat's Unexpected Advantage

That policymakers can help foster any form of disinterested behaviour might come as a surprise. Are technocrats not defined by their instrumental, goal-oriented stance? And should such a stance not succumb to the paradox of intention? It turns out technocrats have an unexpected advantage in this respect. Societies may in fact have an easier time addressing the paradox of intention than individuals do. It is one more reason why social reform can be looked to as a precondition to self-reform.

To see why, it's worth revisiting Henry Ford's decision from Chapter 7 to shift his factories from a six-day to a five-day working week. Being the industrialist he was, Ford was acting entirely instrumentally: he found that with the extra day off, his workers were more productive, in ways that increased net output. He speculated that they might also spend their free Saturdays buying things, which would further spur the economy.

Such harnessing of leisure for the purpose of work would seem the very thing that the philosopher Josef Pieper feared modernity would bring. Recall Pieper's warning: yes, pure leisure may be a source of rest and superhuman creative capacities, and yes, these may be of great use to the world of work. But leisure only remains fruitful insofar as its purpose remains leisure, rather than work. Hence our familiar paradox: a byproduct state like leisure may be valuable to the capitalist, but this value is squandered as soon as the capitalist turns it into the goal. We sense Pieper wagging his finger at Henry Ford.

And yet, there's reason to think that finger-wagging would be uncalled for. After all, what was it to Ford's workers that their expansion of leisure was decided on instrumental grounds, as a means of furthering factory productivity and economic growth? They could allow themselves to overlook those reasons, or to know nothing of them in the first place. If, as a result, they also showed up well rested to work on Monday, this likely didn't take away from their picking the fruits of leisure on their free Saturdays. They could use the extra day to go for a stroll, to make love in the garden, or take the kids to a matinée. They could be weekend Darwins, poets, or brewers, taking up all the extra space provided to them, unhampered by the intent. In this way, it might just be possible both for the workers to pick the fruits of Pieper's 'pure leisure', and for Henry Ford to have his optimally rested labour force. If so, then Ford's policy change would have steered clear of the paradox that Pieper cautioned against.

The move to a five-day working week in Ford's factories highlights two distinctions between the self-reform that the nineteenth-century Romantics were set on, and the social reforms that Mill spent his life working towards. First, the notion of the multiple self is perplexing in the case of individuals, but it becomes unremarkable in the social setting. Delegating power to others is how the policy process works: the roles of those different selves can simply be played by different people. Secondly, and as a result of this ease of delegation, what requires a tricky sleight of hand in the case of the individual becomes readily achievable in the political setting. The intention of the reformer need not taint the behaviour of those affected by it, so long as the two are kept sufficiently separate. This is why parental leave and public daycare prove favourable to individual emancipations and artistic epiphanies: policymakers can act purposefully, so that individuals can live freely, without that purpose getting in the way. It's a stirring notion: the delegation between people that is inherent to social reform might enable individuals to resist the intelligence intelligently.

This hopeful thought comes with a necessary caveat. We have seen that the individual solution to the paradox of intention rests on a loss of control, as one self delegates to another. Social institutions can help, such as by providing a measure of insurance that allows individuals to take on additional risk. But delegating to policymakers to create the right social institutions in the first place generates a corresponding risk. It is because the factory workers could ignore Henry Ford's true intent that their free Saturdays remained free. In this respect, it is both true that ignorance is bliss and that knowledge is power. Turning a blind eye to policymakers' intentions in this way at once frees individuals, and makes them vulnerable to exploitation.

This double-edged aspect of delegation is built into the very design of democracy: we hand over policy control to political leaders so that we need not concern ourselves with the details of agricultural standards and aviation regulations, and so that we may live insouciantly within the results. If we had to constantly verify the soundness of our social arrangements, we would be paralysed, unable either to buy an apple or board an aeroplane. And yet, democratic delegation of this type represents a considerable loss of control – even in the lucky event that we have our pick of a leader.

Henry Ford's decision to shift to a five-day working week was benign enough. But the same instrumental reasoning could equally have led him to dream up less progressive measures. Not for nothing did Charlie Chaplin satirise Ford's assembly lines in *Modern Times*, as did Aldous Huxley, to less comic effect, in *Brave New World*, where the citizens of the World State take to exclaiming 'Thank Ford!'. Chaplin and Huxley both sensed that factory productivity and the well-being of workers are rarely in perfect accord. That is why we grow suspicious of motives that appear overly instrumental, and rightly so. Delegation to others underlies our modern political and economic existence, but citizens must remain sufficiently aware to know when to change modes, when to make their voices heard, and when to defend their interests and those of the people around them. The self-reforming individual cannot help but also be a political animal.

This need for vigilance arises in part because real-world policymakers are rarely as enlightened as we would hope. To wit, Henry Ford's move to a five-day working week is often said to have paved the way for the adoption of the same five-day working week into US law in 1940. It's a pleasing claim, and it does have truth to it: a famous industrialist rationalising the idea in terms of productivity undoubtedly normalised it in the eyes of other economic elites. Yet the eventual change in law might never have happened had it not been for the struggle of labour unions that had been agitating and pushing for reform from the start of the century.[30] The economic and political elites might not have got there by themselves. Policymakers must often be dragged towards enlightenment by those whom their policies affect.

This is the implication of this book. Policymakers must realise – or they must be dragged towards realising – that as societies grow more affluent, their citizens increasingly benefit from institutions and social conditions that promote the attainment of elusive byproduct states. Further expansion of people's purchasing power becomes relatively less valuable, because material consumption is increasingly ill-suited to attaining the esteem and consideration of their peers. By contrast, policies like parental leave, public healthcare and wage insurance become increasingly warranted – not only because affluent societies are better able to afford them, but also because the goals of the people living in those societies are increasingly served by such policies. Similarly, knowledge industries that run on innovation and individual inventiveness will find that maximising these is not achieved in the same way by which one maximises the production of widgets: the world of work will increasingly court what Pieper described as the 'superhuman' creative potential of pure leisure. In sum, the collective shift that Mill and Keynes envisioned becomes both more plausible and more valuable as societies grow in affluence. And as both thinkers claimed, humdrum public policies have a role to play in that collective shift towards disinterest. We are left with one last question: when?

A Schedule for Social Conversion

J. S. Mill and Keynes both looked forward to the time when, as Keynes put it, we could afford to 'once more ... prefer the good to the useful'. They both saw that such a change in preferences relied on attaining sufficient economic prosperity. But do we know how much prosperity is enough? When is the moment ripe for a social conversion?

Both Keynes and Mill were hazy when it came to predicting just when this collective shift in attitudes should, or would, take place. At times, Mill suggested that the British economy had already reached the required level of wealth to move away from a single-minded pursuit of prosperity, and the elbowing it relied on. But he also recognised that 'this ultimate goal is at all times near enough to be fully in view … we are always on the verge of it, and if we have not reached it long ago, it is because the goal itself flies before us'. As for Keynes, he placed this turning point conveniently far off into the future, a full century hence: 'Beware! The time for all this is not yet.' In the meantime, he reluctantly admitted, 'Avarice and usury and precaution must be our gods for a little longer still.'

So it is with conversions foretold. They are frequently delayed. The moment never seems quite right. As St Augustine bemoaned in his *Confessions*, in what remains the definitive standard of the genre, he could not keep himself from 'postponing from day to day the moment when I would despise worldly ambition'.[31] Augustine very much wanted to be rid of his lust, his vanity and his ambition – but not quite yet.

Perhaps that's for the better. Had Western countries ceased their 'trampling, crushing, elbowing, and treading on each other's heels' by Mill's time, most of us would not be around today.[32] Economic rates of growth, moreover, say little about its distribution. We have kept up with Keynes's prediction that 'the standard of life … will be between four and eight times as high' on average.[33] Yet even in the most affluent societies, let alone developing countries, too many are still dealing with economic necessity to be able to give much thought to the promises of 'pure leisure'. In recognition of this fact, perhaps everyone ought to avoid risky leaps of faith, keep their nose to the grindstone, and retain efficiency and productivity as our gods for a little longer still.[34] Yet as I have argued, it is increasingly unclear whether even now keeping our nose to the grindstone is the best means of promoting societal well-being. Whether the moment is already ripe for a shift, or whether we need to hold off a little longer still, it seems plain that the question is not if, but indeed when.

In this respect, Keynes's prophecy reminds me of another, made exactly 150 years earlier, in 1780. This one comes from

John Adams, one of the American founding fathers, who eventually became the country's second president. He, too, foresaw a conversion two generations hence — it seems that it is always our grandchildren who get saddled with the task of taking up 'the graces of life'. Though it is often referenced, Adams's imagined genealogy of occupations never fails to move me:

> I must study Politicks and War [so] that my sons may have liberty to study Mathematicks and Philosophy. My sons ought to study Mathematicks and Philosophy, Geography, natural History, Naval Architecture, navigation, Commerce and Agriculture, in order to give their Children a right to study Painting, Poetry, Musick, Architecture, Statuary, Tapestry and Porcelaine.*

Adams did not have an artistic bone in his body. He would have made a far better model for Max Weber's American Puritan than the bon vivant Ben Franklin. But here he was, conceiving a new country so that its grandchildren might have a 'right' to take up ceramics. Like J. S. Mill in the century after him, and Keynes in the century after that, Adams imagined a ladder of disinterestedness that generations would ascend by increasingly taking up occupations for their own sake. The reason for 'politicks and war' was to lay the ground for commerce and navigation, which were undertaken for the sake of painting, poetry and porcelain … which had no other reason but their own. The passage is often cited out of context, and you might picture Adams solemnly

---

* Upon looking at the manuscript of the letter, I discovered that Adams had initially planned for his children to get the right to study 'Painting and Poetry', but then he had a change of heart, crossed this out, and inserted another generational step: his children would first need to take up Naval Architecture, so that *their* children would have a right to Painting and Poetry.

reading these words out to a full house of Congress. But no, they are instead the final lines of a letter that Adams sent from Paris to his wife Abigail, who was back in Massachusetts. Reading the letter in full, it becomes obvious that Adams was not expressing hope for the future, so much as regret for the present.

John Adams was overcome by all that he saw around him in Paris. He wanted to convey it all to his wife, but ... there was no time. Here is the passage that precedes the more famous one cited above:

> I wish I had time to describe these objects to you ... but my Head is too full of Schemes and my Heart of Anxiety ... to observe these Objects with Taste and describe them so as to be understood, would require more time and thought than I can possibly spare ... I could fill Volumes with Descriptions of Temples and Palaces, Paintings, Sculptures, Tapestry, Porcelaine, &c. &c. &c. – if I could have time.

Few among Adams's grandchildren took up their right to study statuary, tapestry and porcelain, just as Keynes's grandchildren have grown ever more purposive, and recently increased their working hours rather than reducing them. There is some lesson to be gleaned from the recurrent pattern of thoughtful people working purposively towards an eventual desired state when they will finally have 'time and thought' to spare, but then bequeathing it always to the subsequent generation, who in turn roll that promise over to the next.

It might be that we still lack the time. Just now, as we are coping with a once-in-a-century global pandemic and its economic shortfall, as we grapple with political discord and the collective self-doubt it has generated, we once again find ourselves at an inflection point. The kind of critical juncture that occurs at the foundation of a new country, in the midst of a Great Depression, or in the wake of a World War. And this may also be the moment, as we question our most deeply held assumptions, to look beyond our immediate challenges, to remind ourselves of what our highest aims are, and ask ourselves whether our current means are best suited to achieving them.

This is a moment that calls for instrumental thinking, for sensible policy and practical solutions. Like Adams, Mill, and Keynes all did, we need to attend to immediate social and economic needs. It's a moment that calls for technocrats, but of the enlightened sort. The sort that grasps that the task of the technocrat is ultimately to serve the makers of poetry, musick and porcelaine – with the secret knowledge that the latter may, quite unwittingly, return the favour.

The potential for one day resolving the economic problem remains. From where we now sit, that day seems far off; but we have also never been so close to reaching it. In the meantime, more of the things we value will take on a form that does not yield to direct effort. The idols of our purposive, self-interested market society will continue to be those who spurn purpose and self-interest. The wages of passion will only continue to rise. Seeing this, the self-interested among us will have ever more reason to shift away from their self-interested stance – out of self-interest. Their ability to tackle this paradox and collect the fruits of disinterested behaviour rests on favourable social circumstances. Bringing these about should be our collective goal. 'Resisting the intelligence intelligently' is not a solitary exercise, but a political project.

NOTES

I CRISIS AND CONVERSION

1   John later recalled coming upon Samuel Coleridge's lines: 'A grief without a pang, void, dark and drear / A drowsy, stifled, unimpassioned grief.' The poem was titled 'Dejection'. That became the way John referred to his state from then on, calling it 'my dejection'.

2   The phrase 'dismal science' was coined precisely in J. S. Mill's time, and by none other than Thomas Carlyle, who plays an important role in Mill's life, and in this book's story.

3   A minimum age of thirteen for boys had been rejected as overly ambitious. See the Mines and Collieries Act of 1842. The Mines Act was among the generative legislative efforts of the Victorian administrative state. The motives of the reformists were not uncomplicated. The legislation was as much directed at alleviating suffering as it was at imposing social control and keeping the lower classes in their place through the inculcation of Christian moral values. See Heesom, Alan, 1981, 'The Coal Mines Act of 1842, Social Reform, and Social Control', *The Historical Journal*, 24(1), 69–88.

4   See Packe, Michael St John, 1954, *The Life of John Stuart Mill*, Secker & Warburg, p. 74. Similarly, Alexander Bain, a student of Mill's, and among his earliest biographers, thought 'beyond all reasonable

doubt' that overwork was at the origin of Mill's breakdown. Bain, Alexander, 1882, *John Stuart Mill: A Criticism: With Personal Recollections*, London: Longmans, Green & Co.

5   This period marked the passage from political economy to the more specialised discipline of economics, a shift in which Ricardo was a key figure. That shift, and the progressive abandonment of questions of ethics that characterised it, proves important to the story.

6   Senior, Nassau, 1828, *Three Lectures on the Transmission of the Precious Metals from Country to Country and the Mercantile Theory of Wealth*, London: J. Murray.

7   A double life is how Capaldi characterises Mill's relationship to his father during this time (Capaldi, Nicholas, 2004, *John Stuart Mill: A Biography*, Cambridge University Press, p. 55). Mill himself explained how he could keep up appearances in this way: 'I had been so drilled in a certain sort of mental exercise that I could carry it on when all the spirit had gone out of it.' But the spirit had in fact gone out of it.

8   Emphasis added. 'Offences Against One's Self' (1785), 1978, *Journal of Homosexuality*, 3(4), 389–405. <columbia.edu/cu/lweb/eresources/exhibitions/sw25/bentham/#32>

9   These efforts at reform by Bentham and his subsequent disciples eventually brought about legislation like the 1819 laws banning employment of children under the age of nine, 1833 laws limiting the working day to twelve hours in the textile industry, and the aforementioned Mines Act of 1842, banning labour by women and children under ten in underground mines. Florence, P. Sargant, 2013, *Industry and the State*, Routledge. See also: Kirby, Peter Thomas, 1995, 'Aspects of the employment of children in the British coal-mining industry 1800–1872', PhD Dissertation, Department of History, University of Sheffield.

10 From Mill's *Autobiography*: 'The "principle of utility", understood as Bentham understood it … fell exactly into its place as the keystone which held together the detached and fragmentary portions of my knowledge and beliefs. It gave unity to my conceptions of things.' (1981, *The Collected Works of John Stuart Mill, Volume I – Autobiography and Literary Essays*, University of Toronto Press.)

11 Such accommodations are seen as early as in Edgeworth, F. Y., 1881, *Mathematical psychics: An essay on the application of mathematics to the moral sciences* (No. 10), C. K. Paul. See Walsh, Vivian, 1996,

Rationality, Allocation and Reproduction, Oxford: Clarendon Press, pp. 164–73.

12 In Arendt, Hannah (1958), 2013, *The Human Condition*, University of Chicago Press.

13 See Capaldi: 'He holds onto his father's contention that our ultimate objective is happiness, but he adds to this the claim that it is only in the pursuit of the ideal that we achieve happiness.' Larsen, though focused on the religious and spiritual aspect of Mill's life, similarly gives the 'en passant' insight short shrift (Larsen, Timothy, 2018, *John Stuart Mill: A Secular Life*, Oxford University Press).

14 Not only did Mill dissolve the Utilitarian Society, but he stopped using the term 'Utilitarian' altogether. As he explained, he 'abandoned it from a growing dislike to anything resembling a badge or watchword of sectarian distinction' (Mill, John Stuart, *Utilitarianism and On Liberty* (1861), 2013, second edition, Blackwell Publishing, p. 186).

15 And further, 'This principle [happiness as a measure of action] contributes nothing to the establishment of morality, inasmuch as making a man happy is quite different from making him good and making him prudent and sharp sighted for his own advantage quite different from making him virtuous ... such incentives merely teach one to become better at calculation, while the specific difference between virtue and vice is entirely obliterated.'

16 Mill would thus go on to claim that happiness can subsume values like virtue: 'Does the Utilitarian doctrine deny that people desire virtue, or maintain that virtue is not a thing to be desired? The very reverse. It maintains not only that virtue is to be desired, but also that it is to be desired disinterestedly, for itself' (Mill, *Utilitarianism*, ch. 4). Virtue is thus not only a means to greater utility; there is room for it to be valued as 'a good in itself, without looking to any end beyond it'.

17 Mill's exact wording: 'having much in common with what at that time I certainly had never heard of, the anti-self-consciousness theory of Carlyle'.

18 So it was with Coleridge, who had first given words to Mill's 'dejection', and whom we think of primarily as a poet, the author of 'Kubla Khan' and 'The Rime of the Ancient Mariner': by the time Mill met him, Coleridge was mainly a social critic who leaned towards an Edmund Burke style of conservatism. He had left poetry largely

aside, and had dedicated himself to social thought, literary criticism, and philosophy, and wrote about everything from law to medicine. And though Coleridge was weak with lung disease and overcome by an opium habit, Mill considered this fallen poet 'the most systematic thinker of our time, without excepting even Bentham ... On the whole, there is more food for thought – and the best kind of thought – in Coleridge than in all other contemporary writers.'

19 Bentham's preference was for just the opposite: 'Wars and storms are best read of, but peace and calm are better to endure.'

20 Mill, *Autobiography*, p. 183.

21 Adam Smith was building on his two main intellectual influences, Francis Hutcheson and David Hume. Both had used the term 'spectator' to denote an external moral observer guiding the moral agent's behaviour (see, in particular, Hume's *Enquiries* from 1751), but Smith placed the spectator explicitly within the moral agent, highlighting the splitting of the self that resulted. (Hume, David, 1902, *Enquiries Concerning the Human Understanding and Concerning the Principles of Morals*, ed. L. A. Selby-Bigge, MA, second edition, Oxford: Clarendon Press.)

22 Smith, A., 2010, *The Theory of Moral Sentiments*, Penguin.

23 Von Kleist, Heinrich, On the Theater of Marionettes', in Wortsman, Peter, *Selected Prose of Heinrich Von Kleist*, Steerforth Press, 2010.

24 Tolentino, Jia, 2019, *Trick Mirror: Reflections on Self-Delusion*, Penguin Random House.

25 The different branches actually met. Emerson encountered Carlyle in 1831, on his first trip to Europe.

26 The inward turn of the modernists, and even the later embrace of a fragmented self, which we now commonly associate with postmodernity – these share a common point of departure. The debt is easily overlooked, but there is more affinity than commonly acknowledged between the Romantics and later thinkers and writers, from Baudelaire and Nietzsche to D. H. Lawrence and Musil, who all, at different times, explicitly defined themselves in contradistinction to Romanticism.

27 See, especially, Charles Taylor on the meandering path of the Romantics' intellectual legacy. Taylor, Charles, 1989, *Sources of the Self: Making of the Modern Identity*, Harvard University Press.

28 Ovid himself did express a similar sentiment in his *Metamorphoses*. About Pygmalion, the artist who created a sculpture so lifelike that he

fell in love with it, Ovid wrote, *ars adeo latet arte sua*: 'so completely did his art conceal his art'.

29 *'Dans ma conversation, me retenir ... ne pas chercher à briller ... pour être aimable, je n'ai qu'à vouloir ne pas le paraître.'* See Elster, Jon, 1983, *Sour Grapes*, Cambridge University Press, p. 45. For a fuller treatment of various attempts at overcoming the self in Stendhal, see 'Deception and Self-Deception in Stendhal', in *The Multiple Self*, 1988, ed. Elster, Cambridge: Cambridge University Press, pp. 93—113. Stendhal had not been born into a hotbed of Utilitarianism, but he too was sensitive to how planning could preclude the attainment of its objectives: 'Being natural, a lack of planning, seems to me the most rare, that which brings me most pleasure.' (*'Le naturel, l'absence de projets est ce qui me semble le plus rare, et ce qui me fait le plus de plaisir.'*) His novels are full of characters vying for the same effect, most often in vain, and to comedic effect. These were often provincial types who had made it big in the city, and suddenly finding themselves with money, tried in vain to give the impression of being in their element.

30 As he later wrote, 'the chief good they did me was not as philosophy to instruct but as poetry to animate'. (Mill, *Autobiography*.)

31 Thomas Carlyle's *Characteristics*, in which he comes closest to elaborating what Mill called his 'theory of anti-self-consciousness', falls somewhere between rambling essay and prose poem (1857, Chapman and Hall). But from its very first lines, it puts its finger on that paradox: 'The healthy know not of their health, but only the sick.' It's there from the start: health is granted to those who can ignore its meaning. But the remainder of *Characteristics* makes for laborious reading. In a letter to Carlyle, Mill delicately brought up the matter of his abstruse writing style: 'I do not say that it is not good: all modes of writing, in the hands of a sincere man, are good, provided they are intelligible. But are there many things, worth saying, and capable of being said in that manner which cannot be as well or better said in a more direct way? The same doubt has occasionally occurred to me respecting much of your phraseology, which fails to bring home your meaning to the comprehension of most readers so well as would perhaps be done by commoner and more familiar phrases.' (Letter 84, 5 September 1833, in *The Earlier Letters of John Stuart Mill 1812–1848*, 1963, University of Toronto Press.) In his reply, Carlyle, undeterred, responded that his writing

style was the only means of conveying the full 'bodily concrete coloured presence' of the things he was after.

32 The man was John Bowring, Bentham's executor. *Journals of Caroline Fox*, p. 113.

33 The product of that first attempt at reconciliation is the essay 'On Genius' (1832), in: *The Collected Works of John Stuart Mill, Volume I – Autobiography and Literary Essays*, 1981, ed. John M. Robson and Jack Stillinger, Toronto: University of Toronto Press, London: Routledge and Kegan Paul.

2 THE BYPRODUCT SOCIETY

1 Less surprisingly, J. S. Mill also bemoaned the social function of consumption, though with characteristically less humour. 'I know not why it should be a matter of congratulation that persons who are already richer than any one needs to be, should have doubled their means of consuming things which give little or no pleasure except as representative of wealth.' The word 'pleasure' is meaningful here, for that was the thing that the Utilitarians believed all men were busy maximising, while trying to minimise pain. Mill thought wealthy people seeking to double their wealth were fooling themselves, because that doubling offered them no pleasure other than what it allowed them to signal to others.

2 'To one who was to live alone in a desolate island it might be a matter of doubt, perhaps, whether a palace … would contribute most to his happiness and enjoyment.' Smith, *Theory of Moral Sentiments*.

3 Even by the end of the eighteenth century, the price of watches had fallen sufficiently for British artisans to be able to afford them as 'status symbols'. The turning point in the mass production of clocks came not from Britain, but from the United States: in 1816, the inventor Eli Terry received a patent for a low-priced wooden shelf-clock that, in the words of a contemporary observer, 'revolutionized the whole business', and became a major competitor for British clockmakers. See Church, R. A., 1975, 'Nineteenth-Century Clock Technology in Britain, the United States, and Switzerland', *The Economic History Review*, 28(4), 616–30.

4 Steinberg, Ted, 2006, *American Green: The Obsessive Quest for the Perfect Lawn*, W. W. Norton.

5 Veblen, Thorstein, (1900) 2007, *The Theory of the Leisure Class*, Oxford World's Classics. Veblen went so far as to claim the same pattern in the divine world, among the 'superhuman vicarious leisure

class of saints, angels', all arranged in a strict hierarchy where the lower orders of 'attendants or dependants ... perform a vicarious leisure' for the higher orders.

6   'The possession and maintenance of slaves employed in the production of goods argues wealth and prowess, but the maintenance of servants who produce nothing argues still higher wealth and position. Under this principle there arises a class of servants, the more numerous the better, whose sole office is fatuously to wait upon the person of their owner, and so to put in evidence his ability unproductively to consume a large amount of service.'

7   Mauss, Marcel, *The Gift*, note 142. Mauss, looking to Franz Boas, drew a consistent pattern between giving and destroying wealth in Haïda, Tsimshian, and Tlingit societies. (Mauss, Marcel (1925), 2016, *The Gift*, Hau Books.)

8   Graeber, David, 2001, *Toward an Anthropological Theory of Value*, Palgrave Macmillan.

9   Ibid., pp. 190–1.

10 Lutz, John, 1992, 'After the Fur Trade: The Aboriginal Labouring Class of British Columbia, 1849–1890', *Journal of the Canadian Historical Association*, 3(1), 69–93.

11 Ibid.

12 Veblen, p. 123.

13 Veblen does seem at least somewhat aware of the trap of functionalism: he concedes that the proximate cause of non-productive pursuits is not always the active signalling of one's status. Yet he insists that this function is what keeps such activities going. 'None the less, while manners have this intrinsic utility, in the apprehension of the performer and the beholder alike, this sense of the intrinsic rightness of decorum is only the proximate ground of the vogue of manners and breeding. Their ulterior, economic ground is to be sought in the honorific character of that leisure or non-productive employment of time and effort without which good manners are not acquired.' What Veblen does *not* allow for is the way that such awareness of the purpose of one's non-productive pursuits is not only unnecessary, but likely to directly counteract the intent.

14 It is the term Veblen himself also employed, as in, 'vulgarly useful occupations'.

15 See, e.g., Giridharadas, Anand, 2018, *Winners Take All: The Elite Charade of Changing the World*, Knopf.

16 Veyne, Paul, 1990, *Bread and Circuses*, London: Allen Lane, Penguin Press, p. 381.

17 Ibid., p. 131.

18 The phrase is from Thoreau, Henry David (1863), 2013, *Life Without Principle*, Yale University Press.

19 Currid-Halkett, Elizabeth, 2017, *The Sum of Small Things: A Theory of the Aspirational Class*, Princeton University Press.

20 Recall Mill: 'Self-consciousness, that daemon of the men of genius of our time…' (Bentham, in 1985, *The Collected Works of John Stuart Mill, Volume X - Essays on Ethics, Religion, and Society*, University of Toronto Press.)

21 Singer, Peter, 2019, 'Conspicuous consumption will be considered unthinkable 50 years from now', *Vox*, <vox.com/2019/3/27/18188801/conspicuous-consumption-luxury-items>

22 Cited in *Harvard Business Review*, September 2015, 'Luxury Branding Below the Radar', 26–7.

23 Deloitte, 2017, 'Bling it on: What makes a millennial spend more?' <deloitte.com/content/dam/Deloitte/uk/Documents/consumer-business/deloitte-uk-young-luxury-shopper-2017.pdf>

24 Douthat, R., 2020, *The Decadent Society: How We Became the Victims of Our Own Success*, Simon & Schuster.

25 Most recently, see Frank, Robert H., 2020, *Under the Influence*, Princeton University Press.

26 For an early, biting dismissal of minimalism as another form of conspicuous consumption, see e.g. Fagan, Chelsea, 'Minimalism: Another Boring Product Wealthy People Can Buy', *Guardian*, 4 March 2017.

27 'It is this deception which rouses and keeps in continual motion the industry of mankind. It is this which first prompted them to cultivate the ground, to build houses, to found cities and commonwealths, and to invent and improve all the sciences and arts, which ennoble and embellish human life.' (Smith, *Theory of Moral Sentiments*.)

28 *New York Times*, 5 Mar 2020, <nytimes.com/2020/03/05/health/stop-touching-your-face-coronavirus.html>

29 Farber, 'Thinking About Will', in Farber, Leslie H., 1966. *The Ways of the Will*, New York: Harper & Row.

30 Elster, Jon, 1983, *Sour Grapes*, Cambridge University Press, p. 46.

31 Frankl, Viktor, 1985, *Man's Search for Meaning*, Washington Square Press, p. 145.

32 Mill, *Autobiography*.

33 Railton, P., 1984, 'Alienation, consequentialism, and the demands of morality', *Philosophy & Public Affairs*, pp. 134–71, p. 140.

34 Scanlon comes up with the term *paradox of teleology*, 'following Henry Sidgwick, who gave the name "the paradox of hedonism" to the fact that one often cannot promote pleasure very effectively by aiming directly at it, but must have other aims which are not seen simply as means to pleasure'. (Scanlon, Thomas, 1998, *What We Owe to Each Other*, Harvard Belknap, p. 383.)

35 Graziani, Romain, 'Optimal states and self-defeating plans: The problem of intentionality in early Chinese self-cultivation', *Philosophy East and West*, 2009, 59(4), 440–66.

36 Ibid.

3 WHY DISINTEREST PAYS

1 Never mind that Smith was really only talking about exchange, and that he himself would have scoffed at the hoisting up of self-interest as the driving force of the economy.

2 The Fall from Eden thus falls squarely on the baker's brow, from whose sweat we must eat.

3 <columbian.com/news/2020/jan/11/donna-suomi-baker-and-co-owner-of-killa-bites/>

4 <timesofisrael.com/these-jewish-women-got-thousands-of-instagram-followers-selling-fresh-challah/>

5 <ottawa.ctvnews.ca/a-baker-s-bliss-in-an-old-chelsea-casse-croute-1.5451928>

6 <nytimes.com/2015/08/26/dining/start-up-food-business-changing-appetites.html>

7 <theatlantic.com/business/archive/2018/01/craft-beer-industry/550850/>

8 Ibid. Small size is a badge of credibility. The belief goes that as scale increases, so does the attention to the bottom line: 'In Ms. Rosenberg's case, for example, Cherryvale's growth meant moving away from all-organic ingredients … "As we grew, our margins were shrinking, and we decided that our customers cared more about other things," she said.'

9   I purposefully gloss over the key theological twist: how it was
     that the Calvinist belief in predestination – the belief that all souls
     were either saved or not *ex ante* – led Calvinists, and their Puritan
     descendants in New England, to seek to behave *as if* they were
     among the elect.

10   Contrary to popular wisdom, the Puritans did not abstain from drink.
     The first ship to come from England to Massachusetts allegedly carried
     more beer than water. Largely owing to a lack of clean drinking
     water, beer and whiskey were consumed daily, though drunkenness
     was condemned. See 'The Time When Americans Drank All Day
     Long', BBC News, <bbc.com/news/magazine-31741615>. See also
     the catalogue for the 2015 exhibition at the US National Archives,
     'Spirited Republic: Alcohol in American History', <archives.gov/
     publications/ebooks/spirited-republic.html>

11   Weber was explicit about the irony: 'The cultural effects of
     the Reformation [were] unforeseen and indeed unwished for
     consequences of the work of the Reformers, often far removed from,
     or even in virtual opposition to, everything that they themselves had
     in mind.'

12   Emphasis in the original.

13   Emphasis in the original.

14   Weber, Max, 1905, '"Churches" and "Sects" in North America. An
     ecclesiastical and sociopolitical sketch', in: *Max Weber: Essays in
     Sociology*, ed. Hans H. Gerth and C. Wright Mills, Routledge. The
     essay came out in German the year after *The Protestant Ethic*.

15   Or consider J. S. Mill's classic (and highly demanding) statement
     about Utilitarianism: 'between his own happiness and that of
     others, Utilitarianism requires him to be as strictly impartial as a
     disinterested and benevolent spectator' (Mill, *Utilitarianism*, ch. 2).

16   In market societies, the external end is most often financial gain, but
     this can be broadened to encompass all that Adam Smith describes as
     'bettering our condition': to be observed, to be attended to, to see our
     status elevated, and our vanities flattered.

17   Dalio, Ray, 2019, 'To Have Both the Money You Need And the
     Job You Want, You Have To Be Creative And Flexible',
     <linkedin.com/pulse/have-both-money-you-need-job-want-
     creative-flexible-ray-dalio>

18   Williamson, Oliver E., 1975, *Markets and Hierarchies: Analyses and
     Antitrust Implications*, New York: Free Press, p. 20.

19 In Adam Smith's words, once people get beyond self-sufficiency, providing not only for themselves but generating some surplus, they begin to divide their labour, and then 'every man thus lives by exchanging, or becomes in some measure a merchant, and the society itself grows to be what is properly a commercial society'. (Smith, Adam (1776), 2010, *The Wealth of Nations*, Harriman House Limited.)

20 In Hume's telling, 'Your corn is ripe to-day; mine will be so to-morrow. It is profitable for us both, that I should labour with you to-day, and that you should aid me to-morrow.' (Hume, David (1740), 1986, *A Treatise of Human Nature*, Penguin.)

21 Consider Hume's earlier usage in the same *Treatise of Human Nature*, where commerce denotes romantic dealings: 'When a person is once heartily in love, the little faults and caprices of his mistress, the jealousies and quarrels, to which that commerce is so subject; however unpleasant and related to anger and hatred; are yet found to give additional force to the prevailing passion.' (Book II, Section IV: *Of the Causes of the Violent Passions*.)

22 As Greif puts it, 'The collectivist system is more efficient in supporting intra-economy agency relations and requires less costly formal organizations (such as lawcourts), but it restricts efficient inter-economy agency relations. The individualistic system does not restrict inter-economy agency relations, but it is less efficient in supporting intra-economy relations and requires costly formal organizations.' (Greif, Avner, 2006, *Institutions and the Path to the Modern Economy: Lessons from Medieval Trade*, Cambridge University Press, pp. 300–1.)

23 See North, Douglass C. 1991, *Institutions, Institutional Change and Economic Performance*, New York: Cambridge University Press, p. 35.

24 A typical question on the General Social Survey reads 'Generally speaking, would you say that most people can be trusted or that you can't be too careful in dealing with people?' On social trust measures, see: <scholar.harvard.edu/files/laibson/files/measuring_trust.pdf>

25 Hicks, John, 1969, *A Theory of Economic History*, Oxford University Press, p. 78.

26 For the original formulation, see: Granovetter, Mark S., 1973, 'The Strength of Weak Ties', *American Journal of Sociology*, 78, 1,360–80.

27 Transaction costs also include activities like gathering information. But even this is often directed at resolving credibility issues, as when researching the reliability of firms based on user ratings, or their past clients.

28 Hume, *A Treatise of Human Nature*. Emphasis added.

29 See Weber, *Protestant Ethic*: 'the power of religious asceticism made available to [the Puritan employer] sober, conscientious, and unusually capable workers, who were devoted to work as the divinely willed purpose in life'.

30 <fastcompany.com/90426446/wefail-how-the-doomed-masa-son-adam-neumann-relationship-set-wework-on-the-road-to-disaster>

31 Ibid.

32 *Business Standard*, 2016, 'Focus On Passion, Purpose, Funding Will Follow: Adam Neumann', <business-standard.com/article/companies/focus-on-passion-purpose-funding-will-follow-adam-neumann-116011600457_1.html>

33 CNBC, 2017, 'Here's What Investors, VCs Look For When Investing In Startups', <cnbc.com/2017/05/05/venture-capitalists-and-investors-on-what-they-look-for-in-startups.html>

34 The study's purpose was to design an AI that would make investment decisions in an automated fashion. It found itself instructing an algorithm to look for signs of passion and mania among start-up founders. Brandt, Mathias and Stefánsson, Stefán 2018, 'The Personality Venture Capitalists Look for in an Entrepreneur: An Artificial Intelligence Approach to Personality Analysis', Thesis, KTH Royal Institute of Technology, School of Industrial Engineering and Management.

35 *Wine Spectator*, quoting a wine importer, 11 Sept 2012, 'New Order: Millennials Reach for Wine, But What Do They Want?', <winespectator.com/articles/new-order-millennials-reach-for-wine-but-what-do-they-want-47125>

36 Müller, J. W., 2016, *What is Populism?*, University of Pennsylvania Press.

37 In recent years, US presidential candidates from both sides of the aisle have been denounced on this basis. Mitt Romney and Hillary Clinton both raised suspicion because of what their critics denounced as insufficiently authentic, overly polished, poll-tested public personas. In reaction, the Hillary Clinton campaign announced that they would

soon roll out a 'spontaneity strategy'. The effort met with the expected derision. (Cilizza, Chris, 'The Reinvention of Hillary Clinton Almost Certainly Won't Work', *Washington Post*, 8 September 2015)

38   The line is from the conservative economist Thomas Sowell.

39   Riesman, David, 1950, *The Lonely Crowd*, New Haven & London: Yale University Press.

40   See Karl Popper for the most notable expression of such doubts: 'The old idea of a powerful philosopher-king who would put into practice some carefully thought out plans was a fairy-tale invented in the interest of a land-owning aristocracy.' (Popper, Karl (1957), 2013. *The Poverty of Historicism*, Routledge.)

41   Plato's *Republic*, 7, 521b1–11, 2004, Hackett.

42   Ibid., 520e4–521a2.

43   In later works, like the *Laws*, Plato himself seems to give up on the notion of a first-best, ideal city, and settles for the second-best setting that does not rely on the heroic assumptions required of the philosopher-king in the *Republic*. The shift from first- to second-best reflects the acquiescent path of political economy as a field over time. (Plato, 1970, *The Laws*, Penguin.)

44   Force, Pierre, 2003, *Self-interest Before Adam Smith: A Genealogy of Economic Science*, Cambridge University Press, p. 174.

45   Ibid. Emphasis original.

46   'When each individual perceives the same sense of interest in all his fellows, he immediately performs his part of any contract, as being assured, that they will not be wanting in theirs.' (Hume, *A Treatise of Human Nature*.)

4 ON FAKERS

1   Jones, E. E., and Pittman, T. S., 1982, 'Toward a general theory of strategic self-presentation'. In J. Suls (ed.), *Psychological Perspectives on the Self*, Hillsdale, NJ: Erlbaum, pp. 231–62.

2   '*L'intérêt parle toutes sortes de langues, et joue toutes sortes de personnages, même celui de désintéressé.*'

3   Esprit, Jacques. 1677, *The Falsehood of Human Virtues*, 1:17. In notes to V: 236, La Rochefoucauld, 2007, *Collected Maxims and Other Reflections*, Oxford University Press.

4   After Augustine's *amor sui*.

5   The book made its way across Europe and to Britain. As Roger Ascham, a secretary to both Queen Elizabeth I and Queen Mary,

commented on Castiglione's *Cortegiano*, 'Which book, advisedly read and diligently followed but one year at home in England, would do a young gentleman more good, I wis, than three years' travel abroad spent in Italy.' (Ascham, Roger, 1570 *The Scholemaster.*)

6   The original makes clearer that Castiglione is coining a new expression: '[*E*] *per dir forse una nuova parola* [and to perhaps employ a new term], *usar in ogni cosa una certa sprezzatura, che nasconda l'arte e dimostri ciò che si fa e dice venir fatto senza fatica e quasi senza pensarvi.*' (In Lovett, Frank 2012, 'The Path of the Courtier: Castiglione, Machiavelli, and the Loss of Republican Liberty', *The Review of Politics*, 74(4), 589–605.)

7   Force, 2003, *Self-interest Before Adam Smith.*

8   '*Nous sommes si accoutumés à nous déguiser aux autres, qu'enfin nous nous déguisons à nous-mêmes.*' The more literal, if lumbering translation might read: 'We are so accustomed to disguising ourselves for others that we end up disguising ourselves to ourselves.' (*Réflexions morales*, V: 119.)

9   Force, Pierre, 2003, *Self-Interest Before Adam Smith: A Genealogy of Economic Science*, Cambridge University Press.

10 Ibid.

11 Nietzsche, *History of the Moral Feelings*. In: Nietzsche, Friedrich (1886), 1996, *Human, All Too Human: A Book for Free Spirits*, second edition, Cambridge Texts in the History of Philosophy, Cambridge University Press.

12 Ibid., p.44, 'Perhaps belief in the good, in virtuous men and actions, in a plenitude of disinterested benevolence has been more productive of good in the world of men in so far as it has made men less distrustful.'

13 This point is made repeatedly through Jon Elster's work with regard to the strategic exploitation of social norms. Stated in its general form, for the strategic use of a norm to be profitable, it must be that others are following that norm non-strategically. See for instance, Elster, Jon, 1989, 'Social norms and economic theory', *Journal of Economic Perspectives*, 3(4), 99–117.

14 What are we to make, then, of the fact that these stories are themselves commodities? Means to a most definite end, created to sell movie tickets, merchandise, and T-shirts? (The snake takes another bite of its tail.)

15 Yet Pascal also spent much of his life arguing the opposite, namely that there was nothing one could do to achieve religious faith: it was

a gift that one had either received or not received. Attempting to reach for it would accomplish nothing.

16 This holy indifference, in Fénelon's telling, was at the heart of a 'disinterested love' of God. '*La sainte Indifférence si louée par Saint François de Sales n'est que le désintéressement de cet amour qui est toujours indifférent et sans volonté mercenaire intéressée pour soi-même.*' (Fénelon, François (1697), 1911, *Explication des Maximes des Saints sur la Vie intérieure*, Paris: Albert Chérel.)

17 Ibid. My own translation.

18 Ibid. My own translation: '*On voit une personne qui paraît toute aux autres et point à elle-même ... L'oubli de soi même est si grand que l'amour propre même veut l'imiter, et ne trouve point de gloire pareille à celle de ne paraître en rechercher aucune.*'

19 '*Ce n'est pas qu'il fasse toutes ces réflexions d'une manière développée: il ne dit pas: Je veux tromper tout le monde par mon désintéressement afin que tout le monde m'aime et m'admire; non, il n'oserait se dire à soi-même des choses si grossières et si indignes; mais il se trompe en trompant les autres; il se mire avec complaisance dans son désintéressement comme une belle femme dans son miroir; il s'attendrit sur soi-même en se voyant plus sincère et plus désintéressé que le reste des hommes; l'illusion qu'il répand sur les autres rejaillit sur lui; il ne se donne aux autres que pour ce qu'il croit être, c'est à dire pour désintéressé; et voilà ce qui le flatte le plus.*' Ibid.

20 Friedrich Schiller's *Die Philosophen (Gewissenskrupel)*: '*Gerne dient*' ich den Freunden, doch tu ich es leider mit Neigung / Und so wurmt es mir oft, dass ich nicht tugendhaft bin.' (In Josef Pieper's translation. Pieper, Josef (1948), 1998, *Leisure: The Basis of Culture*, St Augustine's Press.)

21 Elster, *Sour Grapes*.

5 ON SELLOUTS

1 Weber goes on, '... The "*beati possidentes*" [the blessed possessors] were often prepared to deny their old ideals.' (Weber, Max (1905), 2002, *The Protestant Ethic and the 'Spirit' of Capitalism*, Penguin.)

2 Ibid. Emphasis in the original.

3 There is a further twist to this love–hate dance between original fans and their self-compromising idols. The reason why music audiences are so merciless in evaluating the credibility of the artists they identify with is because their own credibility depends on it.

While musicians fight to defend their integrity as artists, their fans fight for their own credibility in turn, as members of an in-group united by a shared aesthetic canon. These two attempts at credibility are inextricably linked; the latter relies on the former. That this identification with musical idols happens to be especially common among young men, for whom perceived credibility is a dominant value, only raises the perceived stakes.

4   The Oxford English Dictionary lists a 1906 usage over trade protection: 'The Tariff Act ... was an ungodly and unblushing sell-out to the Sugar Trust ... [and to] the greedy manufacturing interests generally.'

5   Commenting on the pushback that Cannonball Adderley encountered after reaching mass success, the jazz historian Doug Ramsay quipped, 'Show me a solvent jazz band and I'll show you a band accused of selling out.' (Ramsey, D. K., 1989, *Jazz Matters: Reflections on the music & some of its makers*, University of Arkansas Press. Quoted in *Slate:* 'The Rise and Decline of the "Sellout"', <slate.com/culture/2017/07/the-history-of-calling-artists-sellouts.html>)

6   Clayton, J., Greif, M., Ross, K. and Tortorici, D., 2010, *What Was the Hipster? A Sociological Investigation*, N+1 Foundation.

7   Weber, *Protestant Ethic*.

8   Hans-Christoph Schröder also comes to the conclusion that Weber misinterpreted in a secular-economic sense the Puritans' high appreciation of the value of time, and that in fact time was precious to the Puritans above all for the purposes of prayer (Schröder, Hans-Christoph, 'Max Weber und der Puritanismus', *Geschichte und Gesellschaft*, 21, 1995, p. 464.)

9   Smith, *Theory of Moral Sentiments*.

10   Lemay, J. A. Leo, *The Life of Benjamin Franklin*, Vol. 2, p. 398.

11   Franklin, Benjamin, *The Autobiography*, p. 100 in 2004, *Franklin: The Autobiography and Other Writings on Politics, Economics, and Virtue*, Cambridge University Press.

12   Weber, *Protestant Ethic*: 'The Puritans wanted to be men of the calling – we, on the other hand, must be.'

13   Cited in Isaacson, Walter, 2003, *Benjamin Franklin: An American Life*, Simon & Schuster.

14   Klaw, Spencer, 1993, *Without Sin: The Life and Death of the Oneida Community*, New York: Allen Lane/Penguin Press.

15   Hinds, William Alfred, 1902, *American Communities*, Charles H. Kerr & Company, Chicago, p. 199.

16   Ibid.

17   Klaw, *Without Sin*, p. 7.

18   In the case of Oneida, Ellen Wayland-Smith (2019) writes, 'While the Oneida Community had dissolved as a social and religious entity in 1880, the bold "experiment in human relations" initiated by Noyes Sr. was carried forth in the economic sphere by Noyes's son Pierrepont and his fellow Community descendants, who took the "old principles of sharing and equality" inherited from his father and applied them to the industrial production of silverware.'

19   Hinds, *American Communities*, p. 211.

20   *Wired*, <wired.com/2002/04/free-love-and-selling-macs/>

21   Ibid.

22   Bowles, Nellie, 'Corporate Crucible', *San Francisco Chronicle*, 25 August 2013.

23   Deci, E. L., 'Effects of externally mediated rewards on intrinsic motivation', *Journal of Personality and Social Psychology*, 18(1), 1971, 105–115, <doi.org/10.1037/h0030644>

24   Ibid.

25   Kamenica, Emir, 'Behavioral economics and psychology of incentives', *Annual Review of Economics*, 4(1), 2012, 427–45.

26   Isaacson, Walter, 2011, *Steve Jobs*, Simon & Schuster.

27   In Ariely's experiment, the difference between the two groups is not statistically significant, but the point average remains higher for the non-paid group.

6 THE ANTI-INSTRUMENTALISTS

1   Tanizaki, Junichiro, 1977, *In Praise of Shadows*, New Haven, CT: Leete's Island Books.

2   Economists refer to knowledge workers as 'nonroutine cognitive jobs'. These represented about a third of all US jobs in the 1980s, while one recent estimate now places them at 48 per cent of the US labour force. See: Zumbrun, Josh, 'The rise of knowledge workers is accelerating despite the threat of automation', *Wall Street Journal*, 4 May 2016. See also: Daugherty, P. R. and Wilson, H. J., 'Using AI to Make Knowledge Workers More Effective', *Harvard Business Review*, 29 April 2019, <hbr.org/2019/04/using-ai-to-make-knowledge-workers-more-effective>

3   This is complicated by how the specific use of *a-skholia* was originally related to political activity, and life in the polis. See Arendt, *The*

Human Condition. Later, Christian philosophers like Thomas Aquinas modelled their own view of the contemplative life on the Greek concept of leisure: the *vita activa* drew not only its dignity but its very meaning from the *vita contemplativa*. See also Pieper, *Leisure*.

4   Hirschman gives his account a deliberate character: following centuries of bloody wars, he writes, 'the search was on for a behavioural equivalent for religious precept, for new rules of conduct and devices that would impose much-needed discipline and constraints on both rulers and ruled, and the expansion of commerce and industry was thought to hold much promise in this regard'. It is unclear who exactly would have been doing the searching; I am inclined to view this as more of a slow-moving structural shift, where norms that proved useful to stability and peace were then retained and elevated after the fact. (Hirschman, Albert, 1977, *The Passions and the Interests*, Princeton.)

5   Russell, Bertrand, 2004, *In Praise of Idleness and Other Essays*, Routledge.

6   Attanasio, O., Hurst, E. and Pistaferri, L., 2012, *The Evolution of Income, Consumption, and Leisure Inequality in the US, 1980–2010*, working paper 17982, National Bureau of Economic Research.

7   Gershuny, J., 'Veblen in Reverse: Evidence from the Multinational Time-Use Archive', *Social Indicators Research* 93(1), 2009, 37–45.

8   Ibid.

9   Frank, Robert H., 2012, 'Do the Wealthy Work Harder Than the Rest?', *Wall Street Journal*, Wealth Report, 27 April 2012, <blogs.wsj.com/wealth/2012/04/27/do-the-wealthy-work-harder-than-the-rest/>

10 Sevilla, A., Gimenez-Nadal, J. I. and Gershuny, J., 2012, 'Leisure inequality in the United States: 1965–2003', *Demography*, 49(3), 939–64.

11 Ipsos and Oxford Economics, 'Paid Time Off Trends In The U.S.', 2019, US Travel Association survey conducted 22 January–3 February 2019 with 1,025 American workers who had paid time off from their employer.

12 Pieper, Josef, 1948, *Leisure: The Basis of Culture*, St Augustine's Press.

13 Keynes, J. M., 'Economic Possibilities for our Grandchildren (1930)', in 1932, *Essays in Persuasion*, New York: Harcourt Brace, pp. 358–73.

14　These included Joseph Stiglitz, Robert Solow, Robert H. Frank, Gary S. Becker, and others. For the resulting collected volume, see Pecchi, L. & Piga, G., eds, 2008, *Revisiting Keynes: Economic Possibilities for our Grandchildren*, Cambridge, US: MIT Press. Tellingly, Skidelsky himself has since gone on to write a whole book about the essay in question. See Skidelsky, R., 2012, *How Much Is Enough?*, New York: Other Press.

15　Robert Gordon, 2016, *The Rise and Fall of American Growth*, Princeton Press.

16　Arendt, Hannah, *Human Condition*, Prologue, p. 5.

17　Notably, Arendt refused to address this problem directly, seeing it as primarily a policy problem that needed to be resolved through democratic deliberation. As she warned, 'To these preoccupations and perplexities, this book does not offer an answer.' Arendt thus filled in the contours of leisure by examining those of its opposites in work, labour, and action.

18　According to the theatre director George Rylands. Keynes, Milo, 1979, *Essays on John Maynard Keynes*, Cambridge Press, p. 48.

19　Barthes, Roland, 'Dare to Be Lazy', in *Le Monde-Dimanche*, 16 September 1979. Reprinted in Barthes, R., 2009, *The Grain of the Voice: Interviews 1962–1980*, Northwestern University Press.

20　The line is often translated as 'We work in order to be at leisure,' or 'Happiness is thought to depend on leisure; for we are busy that we may have leisure.' Here, I use Josef Pieper's 'more literal translation' of the phrase which underscores the construction of the Greek for 'work', *a-skholia*, as the negation of leisure, *skholia*. On the latter, see note 17 above.

7 THE PLACE OF LEISURE IN A MARKET ECONOMY

1　Monteiro, George, 1988, *Robert Frost and the New England Renaissance*, Lexington: The University Press of Kentucky.

2　Thoreau, H. D., 'Life Without Principle', *Atlantic Monthly*, October 1863.

3　Ibid.

4　In fact, the best means of recognising the passionate workers would consist of offering no recompense but the inherent reward of the task itself: only one group would show up. Working against this may be a social norm against exploitation by those who purport to disguise self-interest under the guise of disinterest: a norm against fakers.

5   Pieper, *On Leisure*, where liberal arts are 'ways of human action which have their justification in themselves'.

6   Cover blurb for Huffington, Arianna, 2016, *The Sleep Revolution*, Harmony Press. Emphasis my own.

7   Ford even held the belief, which Keynes would echo a few years later, that individuals would grow more proficient at leisure: 'We think that, given the chance, people will become more and more expert in the effective use of leisure. And we are giving the chance.'

8   Microsoft Japan has been among the tech firms experimenting with a four-day working week. It has reported significant productivity gains. <npr.org/2019/11/04/776163853/microsoft-japan-says-4-day-workweek-boosted-workers-productivity-by-40>

9   In the original, Arendt speaks of the *animal laborans*, the working animal.

10 Ford goes on, 'Instead of business being slowed up because the people are "off work," it will be speeded up, because the people consume more in their leisure than in their working time. This will lead to more work. And this to more profits.'

11 As Russell elaborated further: 'Whatever merit there may be in the production of goods must be entirely derivative from the advantage to be obtained by consuming them.'

12 A fitting illustration of this temptation is found in a short, acerbic pamphlet from 1883, titled *The Right to Be Lazy*, by Paul Lafargue. Lafargue was one of those principled individuals interested in results. A Cuban-born leader of the early socialist movement in France, he was a co-founder of the first modern socialist party in France, in 1882. He became Karl Marx's son-in-law when he married Marx's middle daughter Laura. He also happened to be something of a *bon vivant*; a staunch Marxist who nonetheless liked to enjoy life's small pleasures. The essay was a rebuke to the earlier socialist call for the 'right to work', which had culminated in the French labour laws following the Revolution of 1848. As Lafargue saw it, socialism had been complicit in letting the proletariat 'be perverted by the dogma of work'. Yet Lafargue nonetheless seized leisure by its relation to work. He was determined to reject the bourgeois work ethic, but could not avoid the temptation of doing so by demonstrating its productive virtues. After inveighing against capitalist France as a 'hairy-faced and bald-headed' creature, Lafargue then readily cites the claims of an industrialist of his day

to vindicate his own: 'We all work two good hours too much. I am convinced that if we worked only eleven hours instead of thirteen we should have the same product and we should consequently produce more economically.' Thus Lafargue, the socialist ideologue, found himself adopting not only the same position, but also the same reasoning, as Henry Ford would half a century later. Even for those desperately seeking to reclaim leisure from the realm of interested commerce, the temptation to do so by pointing to its utility runs deep. For more on Lafargue, see Derfler, Leslie, 1998, *Paul Lafargue and the Flowering of French Socialism, 1882–1911*, Harvard University Press.

13 'The Diary: Gideon Rachman', *Financial Times,* 25 January 2013, <ft.com/content/fade3od8-660a-11e2-bb67-00144feab49a>

14 See, for example, Larry Fink's letter to shareholders: 'Sustainability and Deeper Connections to Stakeholders Drives Better Returns', <blackrock.com/corporate/investor-relations/larry-fink-ceo-letter>

15 Marcuse, Herbert, 1964, *One-Dimensional Man*, Beacon Press.

16 Frank, Thomas, 1998, *The Conquest of Cool: Business Culture, Counterculture, and the Rise of Hip Consumerism*, University of Chicago Press, p. 26.

17 Smith, *Theory of Moral Sentiments*.

18 The current non-military meaning of the word first appears in English in 1910 to describe neo-impressionists like the 'pseudo-mystic Odilon Redon'. Weisgerber, Jean ed., *Les Avant-gardes littéraires au XXe siècle: Vol. I: Histoire*, John Benjamins.

19 This quip has disputed origins, but it is attributed among others to the economist Frank Knight. See, for instance, Stigler, George, 1984, 'Economics: The Imperial Science?' *The Scandinavian Journal of Economics*, 86(3), 301–13.

8 RESISTING THE INTELLIGENCE INTELLIGENTLY

1 The character Castiglione employs in this imagined dialogue is the Count, who teases his audience with the notion of *sprezzatura* and vaunts its merits, but withholds the means of obtaining it.

2 Pieper, *Leisure*.

3 Matthew B. Crawford's *Shop Class as Soulcraft: An Inquiry into the Value of Work* (Penguin) documents such a shift. When it came out

in 2010 on the heels of the Great Recession, it became 'the sleeper hit of the publishing season'. In it, sounding every bit like one of our apostles of leisure from Chapter 6, Crawford writes: 'Craftsmanship has been said to consist simply in the desire to do something well, for its own sake.' The mass market embraced another one of its self-described dissidents.

4   In a letter to Carlyle written in 1832, having dutifully lashed out against the narrowness and 'peculiar' nature of his upbringing, J. S. Mill nonetheless concluded, 'Fortunately however I was not crammed; my own thinking faculties were called into strong though but partial play; & by their means I have been enabled to remake all my opinions.' The thinking faculties, all that mental discipline, had doomed him, but they also proved his way out.

5   'Knowing so little of human feelings, he knew still less of the influences by which those feelings are formed: all the more subtle workings both of the mind upon itself, and of external things upon the mind, escaped him.'

6   Von Kleist, 'On the Theater of Marionettes' in von Kleist, Heinrich and Wortsman, Peter, 2010, *Selected Prose of Heinrich Von Kleist*, Steerforth Press.

7   Hegel, *Logic* in Hegel, Georg Wilhelm Friedrich, 1991, *The Encyclopaedia Logic, with the Zusätze: Part I of the Encyclopaedia of Philosophical Sciences with the Zusätze*, Hackett.

8   From the *Adagia* by Wallace Stevens, one of the modern heirs of the English Romantic tradition.

9   Not surprisingly, J. S. Mill also had a keen sense of the multiple self, and how it might account for internal personal conflicts. About the effort to resist some temptation, he wrote: 'But it is obvious that "I" am both parties in the contest; the conflict is between me and myself; between (for instance) me desiring a pleasure, and me dreading self-reproach. What causes Me, or, if you please, my Will, to be identified with one side rather than with the other, is that one of the Me's represents a more permanent state of my feelings than the other does. After the temptation has been yielded to, the desiring "I" will come to an end, but the conscience-stricken "I" may endure to the end of life.'

10 The evocative image of a medieval city map comes from Amélie Oksenberg Rorty. Theories of modularity are associated with scholars like Robert Kurzban and H. Clark Barrett. For a review, see

Barrett, H. C. and Kurzban, R., 'Modularity in cognition: Framing the debate', *Psychological Review*, 113, 2006, 628–47.

11 The phrase 'to resist the intelligence intelligently' is from a famous 1962 essay by Geoffrey Hartman, one of the foremost American scholars of Romanticism. As he put it, 'This idea of a return, via knowledge, to naivete – to a second naivete – is almost a commonplace among the German Romantics.' Hartman also pointed to how unique this insight was to the Romantic tradition: 'The remedy, however, which seems to me particularly Romantic … seeks to draw the antidote to self-consciousness from consciousness itself.' (Hartman, G. H., 1962, 'Romanticism and Anti-Self-Consciousness', *Centennial Review*, pp. 553–65.)

12 The more literal, if more awkward translation might go as follows: 'We are so accustomed to disguising ourselves for others, that we end up disguising ourselves to ourselves.'

13 La Rochefoucauld, 2007, *Collected Maxims and Other Reflections*, V:233, Oxford Classics.

14 Translation is my own. The original reads: '*Il y a des gens qui n'auraient jamais été amoureux, s'ils n'avaient jamais entendu parler de l'amour.*'

15 Oakeshott, Michael, 2014, *Michael Oakeshott: Notebooks, 1922–86*, Imprint Academic.

16 Ovid, *Ars Amatoria*, Book I (translation is my own): '*Quo magis, o, faciles imitantibus este, puellae: / Fiet amor verus, qui modo falsus erat.*'

17 Von Hippel, W. and Trivers, R., 'The evolution and psychology of self-deception', *Behavioral and Brain Sciences*, 34(1), 2011, 1–16.

18 Christie's, Sale 18952, 10–23 September 2020.

19 *New York Times*, <nytimes.com/2019/09/16/arts/banksy-brexit-painting-auction.html>

20 There is a collective aspect to this self-presentation that can come to play a large role. Artistic communities define themselves in part as groups united by their disdain for the market – even as this disdain is a condition for their success within it. The reasoning above implies that at least part of this self-construction may be strategic. Since it is not granted to all aspiring artists to have an innate disregard for how potential buyers perceive their work, they may seek to actively reshape their outlook by immersing themselves in such communities and, through such conditioning, acquire the 'correct'

non-instrumental outlook. As in all cases, and as Jon Elster argues throughout his writings, that some are able to strategically exploit a social norm requires that others follow it non-strategically. The further twist is that this may be true even *within* the individual: the fact that one self can seek to exploit a norm instrumentally is facilitated if another self is willing to follow that same norm for non-instrumental reasons.

21   Pascal, Blaise (1670) 1999, *Pensées*, Oxford World Classics, pp. 155–6.

22   Pascal would go on to contradict this idea in his other writings, where he emphasised the idea of religious faith as a gift from God, and one that could not be attained through any human effort.

23   Translation my own. The original reads: '*Si tu veux me séduire ou me surprendre, prends garde que je ne vois ta main plus distinctement que ce qu'elle trace. Je vois trop la main de Pascal.*' Valéry, Paul (1924), 2016, 'Variation sur une pensée' in *Oeuvres, Tome 1*, Le Livre de Poche.

24   *Paris Review*, Interview no. 182, Issue no. 170, Summer 2004.

25   McWilliams, A., Siegel, D. and Wright, P., 'Corporate social responsibility: strategic implications', *Journal of Management Studies*, 43, 2006, 1–18.

26   Greenwashing refers to insincere gestures at environmental concerns; bluewashing uses an association with the United Nations to make up for poor human rights records; purplewashing refers to self-interested campaigns proclaiming gender-equality ideals; pinkwashing refers to a strategic exploitation of the fight against breast cancer to corporate ends.

27   Van der Ven, H., 'Socializing the C-suite: why some big-box retailers are "greener" than others', *Business and Politics*, 16(1), 2014, 31–63.

28   That self-persuasion would be useful in persuading others has often been speculated about. Thomas Schelling, the Nobel Prize-winning economist, and one of the shrewdest thinkers on questions of persuasion and credibility, put forth this idea in 1960. He argued that the best way of deterring threats was to convince oneself that the threat would be ineffective; such self-persuasion was most likely to persuade the threatener that delivering on the threat would be futile. From *The Strategy of Conflict* (1960): 'if one can misrepresent himself as either unable to comprehend a threat, or too obstinate to heed it, he may deter the threat itself. Best of all may be *genuine* ignorance, obstinacy, or simple disbelief, since it may be more convincing to the prospective threatener' (emphasis in the original).

Schelling's hunch has since found support both in real-world studies and in laboratory settings. We now know that those who are able to persuade themselves are also best able to persuade others. This is even the case when dealing with verifiable misrepresentation. When students are asked to predict how well they will do on a test, and how well their peers will do, persuasion and self-persuasion turn out to be highly correlated. That is, those who rate themselves more highly than they should, given their subsequent performance, are also rated more highly by their peers. Those who successfully persuade themselves also succeed in (unknowingly) persuading others. See Lamba, S. and Nityananda V., 'Self-Deceived Individuals Are Better at Deceiving Others', *PLOS One*, 9/8, 2014, 1–6. As the authors of that study conclude, 'People may not always reward the more accomplished individual but rather the more self-deceived.'

29 Elster, Jon, 'More Than Enough', *The University of Chicago Law Review*, Spring 1997, 64(2), 749–64.

30 Walmart swayed part of its audience through its environmental initiatives. But when it tried to do the same on labour issues, it drew ire from critics for what was dismissed as a transparent attempt to limit reputational damage. The show of disinterest was plainly self-interested. Those failed efforts may have done the firm more reputational harm than good. They convinced activists that corporations speak only the language of interest, and that no progress would be made unless corporations were coerced. One would-be disinterested gesture succeeded, the other failed.

31 The phrase is from Wordsworth's *The Prelude*, in which the poet describes a depressive episode not unlike J. S. Mill's own:

> This was the crisis of that strong disease,
> This the soul's last and lowest ebb; I drooped,
> Deeming our blessed reason of least use
> Where wanted most ...

32 Herder elevated the notion of the *Volk*, but remained a cosmopolitan at heart. Müller proved more dangerous, and a century later, his writings were dusted off by the theorists of the Third Reich. See, for example, Kohn, Hans, 'Romanticism and the Rise of German Nationalism', *The Review of Politics*, 12(4), 1950, 443–72.

33 See Cochran, Peter, 2014, *The Burning of Byron's Memoirs: New and Unpublished Essays and Papers*, Cambridge Scholars Publisher.

34 Ibid.

35 See Capaldi, *John Stuart Mill*, who among J. S. Mill's biographers, gives the most complete account of Harriet Taylor's full influence on his ideas.

9 SOCIAL CONDITIONS FOR INDIVIDUAL EPIPHANIES

1 Keynes, *Economic Possibilities*.

2 Smith, Adam, *Theory of Moral Sentiments*.

3 A version of this apparent contradiction has kept scholars busy since the nineteenth century, when it became known as 'the Adam Smith problem'. Originally, the Adam Smith problem was the apparent contradiction between Smith's notion of sympathy in the *Theory of Moral Sentiments* and self-interest in the *Wealth of Nations*. It has since then come to refer more generally to the apparent clash between the views of commercial society in the two books, as examined most recently by Dennis Rasmussen (*The Infidel and the Professor*, Princeton, 2019). It largely turns on the 'deception' mentioned in *Theory of Moral Sentiments*, and the lingering question of who is actually being deceived.

4 'We see that they afford him food and clothing, the comfort of a house, and of a family.' (*Theory of Moral Sentiments*.)

5 Skidelsky, Robert and Skidelsky, Edward, 2013, *How Much is Enough? Money and the Good Life*, Penguin.

6 Pecchi and Piga, 2008, for instance, find it 'surprising that Keynes, while theorizing about the achievement of a state of consumption satiation where humans would devote themselves to nothing else but the art of living, did not give any tribute to John Stuart Mill who developed a similar doctrine almost a century earlier'. In Pecchi, Lorenzo and Piga, Gustavo (eds), 2010, *Revisiting Keynes: Economic Possibilities for Our Grandchildren*, MIT Press.

7 There is something pleasing in how economic theory may itself be used to explain this divergence within the field: once investments are made to address a given problem, there emerge vested interests that benefit from continuing to tackle the same problem, even once its urgency has passed. This is broadly referred to as 'path dependency', as described by Douglass North (1990). And since the skills required to understand growth are very different from the ones required to understand its purpose, it might then be expected that an academic field that arose in a period of real productivity growth and a high level

of interest in the drivers of growth would continue to be narrowly preoccupied with this question even past the point of affluence.

8   Mill, *Autobiography*.

9   The Wapping Project, <thewappingproject.org/berlin/>

10 This stance seems to have been spurred in large part by his discussions with Harriet Taylor, an intellectual debt Mill explicitly recognised. Mill was also drawing on the reasoning in Hegel's by then well-established master–slave dialectic.

11 See Mill's 1869 *The Subjection of Women*, London: Longmans, Green, Reader, and Dyer.

12 Mill made the analogous argument with respect to employers and hired labour: 'Capitalists are almost as much interested as labourers in placing the operations of industry on such a footing, that those who labour for them may feel the same interest in the work, which is felt by those who labour on their own account.' (*Principles of Political Economy*, Oxford University Press, 1998.)

13 Mill chafed against misguided social customs as much as against ill-designed social institutions. He decried 'wretched social arrangements' (*Utilitarianism*), but also the way that received opinion could result in a 'a social tyranny more formidable than many kinds of political oppression' (*On Liberty*).

14 I follow Capaldi in using the word 'autonomy', though Mill usually spoke of 'freedom' in this sense. Yet as Capaldi perhaps surmised, the term 'freedom' today is tainted by various ideological commitments, and its meaning has grown ambiguous as a result. Autonomy may thus better reflect the valence the concept would have had in Mill's time.

15 Mill, *Of the Stationary State* in *Principles of Political Economy*.

16 See Pecchi and Piga, *Revisiting Keynes*.

17 'U.S. Research and Development Funding and Performance: Fact Sheet Updated January 24, 2020', <fas.org/sgp/crs/misc/R44307. pdf> See also Mervis, Jeffrey, 2017, 'Data check: U.S. government share of basic research funding falls below 50%', <sciencemag.org/news/2017/03/data-check-us-government-share-basic-research-funding-falls-below-50>.

18 See Cowen, Tyler, 2017, *The Complacent Class: The Self-Defeating Quest for the American Dream*, St Martin's Publishing Group.

19 For an early, balanced treatment, see Atkinson, A. B., 1999, *The Economic Consequences of Rolling Back the Welfare State*, MIT

Press. There have been efforts at netting the negative moral hazard effect and the positive risk-taking effect on total output. See for instance, Acemoglu, D. and Shimer, R., 'Productivity gains from unemployment insurance', *European Economic Review*, 44(7), 1, 2000, 195–224, where the authors find that social insurance policies like unemployment insurance increase productivity by allowing workers to take on greater risk in seeking higher-productivity jobs, thus allowing firms to create those more productive jobs in the first place. On the impact of welfare systems on individual attitudes and commitment to work, see Esser, I., 2005, *Why Work? Comparative Studies on Welfare Regimes and Individuals' Work Orientations*, Doctoral dissertation, Swedish Institute for Social Research (SOFI). For a look at how different social insurance policies differ in their contributions to productivity, and for policy implications, see Midgley, J., 'Growth, redistribution, and welfare: Toward social investment', *Social Service Review*, 73(1), 1999, 3–21.

20 Gai, Yunwei and Minniti, Maria, 'Health Insurance, Job Lock, and the Supply of Self-Employment', *Journal of Small Business Management*, 53(2), 2015, 558–80; Madrian, B. C., 'Employment-based health insurance and job mobility: Is there evidence of job-lock?', *The Quarterly Journal of Economics*, 109(1), 1994, 27–54; Velamuri, M., 'Taxes, health insurance, and women's self-employment', *Contemporary Economic Policy*, 30(2), 2012, 162–77; Fairlie, R. W., Kapur, K. and Gates, S. M., 2008, 'Is employer-based health insurance a barrier to entrepreneurship?', RAND Working Paper, No. WR-637-EMKF.

21 See Bird, E., 'Does the Welfare State Induce Risk-Taking?', *Journal of Public Economics*, 80(3), 2001, 357–83. See also García-Peñalosa, C. and Wen, J. F., 'Redistribution and entrepreneurship with Schumpeterian growth', *Journal of Economic Growth*, 13(1), 2008, 57–80; Koo, J., Choi, Y. J. and Park, I., 'Innovation and welfare: the marriage of an unlikely couple', *Policy and Society*, 39(2), 2020, 189–207.

22 There is growing recognition that the policy combo most propitious to entrepreneurship, in particular, is the interaction of high social spending and low labour-market regulation. See for example Solomon, Shelby J., et al., 'Agency theory and entrepreneurship: A cross-country analysis', *Journal of Business Research*, 122, 2021, 466–76. Another limitation comes from measurement issues: the category of 'social

insurance' tends to contain a large portion of spending that has no real insurance function: public pension funds, for instance, are effectively an intergenerational transfer mechanism which plays little insurance function. Pension funds should thus have less of an effect on risk-taking behaviour, yet they make up a large portion of the social insurance measures in many studies in the European context, especially.

23 Research and development expenditure (% of GDP) – United States, Sweden. (UNESCO Institute for Statistics). See also World Economic Forum, 2017, 'Why does Sweden produce so many startups?', <weforum.org/agenda/2017/10/why-does-sweden-produce-so-many-startups/>

24 This effect was also highest for those individuals who were not covered by their spouse's health insurance, which offers further credence to the notion that health insurance had an effect on otherwise risky decisions to shift to self-employment. DeCicca, Philip, 2007, 'Health Insurance Availability and Entrepreneurship: Evidence from New Jersey', McMaster University.

25 Hombert, J., Schoar, A., Sraer, D. and Thesmar, D., 'Can unemployment insurance spur entrepreneurial activity? Evidence from France', *The Journal of Finance*, 75(3), 2020, 1,247–85.

26 Feinberg, R.M. and Kuehn, D., 'Does a Guaranteed Basic Income Encourage Entrepreneurship? Evidence from Alaska', *Review of Industrial Organization*, 2020, 1–20.

27 For a review of these findings, see Painter, A. and Thoung, C., 2015, 'Creative citizen, creative state: the principled and pragmatic case for a Universal Basic Income', London: RSA.

28 As Mill put it: 'that there should be no option, no other *carrière* possible [than that of wife and mother] for the great majority of women, except in the humbler departments of life, is a flagrant social injustice'. (*Principles of Political Economy*.)

29 Sinn, Hans-Werner, 1996, 'Social Insurance, Incentives and Risk Taking', in *Public Finance in a Changing World*, London: Palgrave Macmillan, pp. 73–100.

30 Ross, Steven J., 'Review: Living for the Weekend: The Shorter Hours Movement in International Perspective', *Labour / Le Travail*, 27, 1991, 267–82.

31 St Augustine, 1961, *Confessions*, Penguin.

32 Compounded growth was necessary to allow for the global population growth we have seen since Mill's time, a fact that Mill

himself was fully aware of: he explicitly made the 'stationary state' conditional on a stable population size. In part, this was driven by the fear that a densely populated country would offer limited opportunities for solitude, which Mill viewed as essential to the promotion of self-development, which was the point all along. Ecologists advance similar-sounding arguments about population growth today.

33 Keynes predicted that 'the standard of life ... will be between four and eight times as high', and so it has come to pass. For details of the comparison involved, see Fabrizio Zilibotti, 2008, 'Economic Possibilities for our Grandchildren 75 Years After: A Global Perspective', in *Revisiting Keynes*, Lorenzo Pecchi and Gustavo Piga, eds, MIT Press, 2018.

34 As Keynes himself recognised, 'it will remain reasonable to be economically purposive for others after it has ceased to be reasonable for oneself'. Keynes was also putting the matter optimistically; his implicit assumption was that growth would reach people at all levels of income, a hope that the study of economic inequality has recently been busy dispelling. We know that steady economic growth can be observed without necessarily seeing improvements in the standards of living of the bottom half of the population. Keynes was also focused on developed 'progressive countries' and implicitly discounted the economic possibilities of developing countries.

ACKNOWLEDGEMENTS

A book of this sort relies on a dense scaffolding of background reading that disappears as the work progresses, yet remains no less essential to the final outcome. In this way, the journals of the 19th century diarist Caroline Fox rendered the feeling of London in J. S. Mill's time better than any text I came across — from the intellectual hothouse atmosphere of the drawing rooms to the garden of John Milton's house, where Bentham and the Mills lived in turn, flourishing as much as the black London smoke would let it. Of the many biographies of J. S. Mill, Nicholas Capaldi's stood out by its ability to interweave the life and the work, in the way that both the life and the work demand. I owe a great intellectual debt to Jon Elster: he is a recurrent thread who runs through my own work, and that of countless others. Among them is Pierre Force, whom I rely on especially in Chapter 3, and who has beautifully demonstrated how literary ideas can spur advances in political thought. The writings of Edna Ullmann-Margalit and Laurie Ann Paul on rationality, and those of Geoffrey H. Hartman and Charles Taylor on the Romantics, were part and parcel of the scaffolding in ways that the references fail to convey.

I am indebted to the generosity and keen insights of early readers and conversation partners: Anna Berman, John A. Hall, Luis Felipe Mantilla, Arash Abizadeh, Frédéric Mérand. I am grateful to my wife, Laura – for your supreme wisdom – and our daughter, Elza, for making me type faster.

This is in part a book about the social institutions that allow individuals to pursue tasks for their own sake. Paid parental leave, universal healthcare, and public daycare are among them, and I benefited from all of these during the writing of this book. In particular, I am beholden to the staff of the Fleur de Macadam daycare in Montreal, for carrying on in the midst of a global pandemic.

INDEX

A NOTE ON THE AUTHOR

Krzysztof Pelc is Associate Professor of Political Science at McGill University, having held positions at Princeton, NYU and the University of Copenhagen. He is a contributor to publications including the *Washington Post* and the *Atlantic*, and regularly appears on television and radio to speak about current affairs. In 2021, he won the *Financial Times* essay prize, held on the bicentenary of the Political Economy Club. Born in Warsaw, Pelc grew up in Quebec and now lives in Montreal.

A NOTE ON THE TYPE

The text of this book is set in Fournier. Fournier is derived from the *romain du roi*, which was created towards the end of the seventeenth century from designs made by a committee of the Académie of Sciences for the exclusive use of the Imprimerie Royale. The original Fournier types were cut by the famous Paris founder Pierre Simon Fournier in about 1742. These types were some of the most influential designs of the eight and are counted among the earliest examples of the 'transitional' style of typeface. This Monotype version dates from 1924. Fournier is a light, clear face whose distinctive features are capital letters that are quite tall and bold in relation to the lower-case letters, and *decorative italics, which show the influence of the calligraphy of Fournier's time.*